# Wisdom of the Psy

MH01063793

"Emotionally personal, immediately useful, surprisingly original, beautifully deep, this page-turning read also turns the page into a new century of psychology. What an achievement." – James Hillman, former Director of Studies at the Jung Institute in Zurich

"Once again Ginette Paris demonstrates that she is quite simply the most original and eloquent of all writers on contemporary depth psychology. This book is a brilliant and beautiful account of how a serious accident, a near-fatal brain injury, became not just a trauma but a rare and wonderful opportunity. After the concussion and coma, Paris did not just regain consciousness. She experienced a life-altering transformation that led her to delve below all the gray matter of the current, trendy fascination with neuroscience to explore the "deep psyche." In this book Paris invents an entirely new genre of psychological writing, one that combines intimately personal autobiography, humanely inspirational stories from patients, and radically imaginative theoretical proposals for the future of depth psychology." – Michael Vannoy Adams, Jungian Psychoanalyst

"*Wisdom of the Psyche* is the bright book of the future for everyone involved with depth psychology and its creative transformation of the arts and sciences. Ginette Paris's stunning achievement is to combine autobiography, history of ideas, clinical originality, psychological theory and philosophical sophistication with the arts of a poet and novelist. Her book is at once lucid, erudite, a delightful companion. and a serious challenge to the academy and the consulting room. Paris gently and powerfully embeds depth psychology in the humanities, making *Wisdom of the Psyche* essential reading for the twenty-first century. We are all the richer for it." – Susan Rowland, Reader in English and Jungian Studies, University of Greenwich, UK

Ginette Paris uses cogent and passionate argument as well as stories from patients to teach us to accept that the human psyche seeks to destroy relationships and lives as well as to sustain them. This is very hard to accept which is why, so often, the body has the painful and dispiriting job of showing us what our psyche refuses to see.

In jargon-free language, the author describes her own story of taking a turn downwards and inwards in the search for a metaphorical personal "death". If this kind of mortality is not attended to, then more literal bodily ailments and actual death itself can result.

Paris engages with one of the main dilemmas of contemporary psychology and psychotherapy: how to integrate findings and insights from neuroscience and medicine into an approach to healing founded upon activation of the imagination. At present, she demonstrates, what is happening is damaging to both science and imagination.

**Ginette Paris** is a psychologist, therapist and writer. She teaches Archetypal and Depth Psychology at Pacifica Graduate Institute in Santa Barbara, California. Her books include *Pagan Meditations*, and *Pagan Grace*. She is a member of the Board of Directors of the *Foundation for Mythological Studies*.

# Wisdom of the Psyche

## Depth Psychology after Neuroscience

Ginette Paris

Routledge
Taylor & Francis Group

LONDON AND NEW YORK

First published 2007 by Routledge
27 Church Road, Hove, East Sussex BN3 2FA

Simultaneously published in the USA and Canada
by Routledge
270 Madison Avenue, New York NY 10016

Reprinted 2008 and 2009

*Routledge is an imprint of the Taylor & Francis Group, an Informa business*

© 2007 Ginette Paris

Typeset in Sabon by Garfield Morgan, Swansea, West Glamorgan
Printed and bound in Great Britain by TJ International Ltd, Padstow,
Cornwall
Paperback cover design by Lisa Dynan

This publication has been produced with paper manufactured to strict
environmental standards and with pulp derived from sustainable forests.

*British Library Cataloguing in Publication Data*
A catalogue record for this book is available from the British Library

*Library of Congress Cataloging in Publication Data*
Paris, Ginette, 1946-
  Wisdom of the psyche : depth psychology after neuroscience /
Ginette Paris.
       p. ; cm.
  Includes bibliographical references and index.
  ISBN 978-0-415-43776-9 (hardback) – ISBN 978-0-415-43777-6 (pbk.)
1. Psychoanalysis. 2. Unconscious (Psychology) 3. Jungian psychology.
4. Neurosciences. 5. Wisdom. 6. Psyche. I. Title.
  [DNLM: 1. Mind-Body Relations (Metaphysics) 2. Brain–physiology. 3.
Psychoanalytic Theory. 4. Unconscious (Psychology)
WL 103 P232w 2007]
  BF175.P275 2007
  150.19'5–dc22
                                                          2007007174

ISBN: 978-0-415-43776-9 (hbk)
ISBN: 978-0-415-43777-6 (pbk)

I dedicate this book to Lori Pye, Druscilla French and Denise Bilodeau, from whom I learned that friendship is as potent a medicine as love.

# Contents

# Preface

Only once are we born and once do we die. Psychologically, however, we die a thousand deaths and are reborn at least that many times. Moments of great suffering usually signal that the old self needs to die and because it is painful, we are tempted to look for quick solutions, buying into the common illusion that every psychological "problem" calls for a positive "solution." Yet, this well-intentioned approach increases the suffering because it ignores one of the great paradoxes of psychological wisdom: the activation of the death principle has more power than anything else in the psyche. The destructive impulse can be crucial if we are to get rid of what oppresses us. In other words, as far as our inner life is concerned, one could say that where there is death, there is hope! As the old self dies, one can take up the task of birthing a new self. But first, there has to be a letting go of all positive ego ideals.

Much has been written in psychology about interpersonal conflicts and how to resolve them. Many authors of popular psychology books and most therapy centers offer advice on how to save the marriage, improve communications, enhance self-esteem, and achieve love and success. I am investigating the opposite: the element in the psyche that wants to destroy relationships, to leave, to die, to go down and stay low for as long as it takes for the old identity to die. This turning inward and downward comes from an unconscious sense that if the exhausted old "me" does not die, my body will carry the death wish in a literal and terminal fashion. What the psyche refuses to acknowledge, the body always manifests. Whenever the body says "no more," it is sending a message that should get our attention; it may be inviting us to a voyage of descent. Even when intolerably painful, such a voyage can be an adventure all the same because it has the potential to reveal the natural wisdom of the psyche. Normally, what excites us about adventure is the aspect of surprise and great pain, be it physical or psychological. Dangerous voyages, internal or external, seem to open to us a treasure chest of endless surprises: the unconscious.

The word "unconscious" may sound too technical, too Freudian. It can be replaced by the term used at the time of the Renaissance: "imagination." In our moments of depression and anxiety, the imagination is paralyzed, cold, empty. Contrary to advice offered in most self-help books of popular psychology, the way out of such painful states does not start with an upward, positive, willful effort of the ego. It begins with an opening of the imagination, often producing dark, twisted, frightening images, symbolizing what needs to die.

I am a frequent traveler and have visited many countries. However, of all the trips I've taken in my life, the one that was the most fascinating was my descent to the dark recesses of my psyche, that place where we reside as if in a nightmare, a place that the ancient Greeks called the Underworld and that we call the unconscious. Watching the process of my own self-destruction was captivating, like watching a cobra poised to strike. When the unconscious opens, it disturbs every routine and life takes on a surprising quality. Madam Death insists that surrender be absolute.

I came to live in California 14 years ago, moving from the cold climate of the Atlantic coast. From my first day on the Pacific coast, I failed to notice how so much light and energy can be inflating. I gradually lost sight of what, in life, belongs to death – a sense of limitations, of exhaustion of old forms, of tiredness in walking the same path, of my minuscule significance in the universe. Santa Barbara's climate is close to perfection; the orientation of the bay creates a microclimate as pleasant as that of Provence, without the suffocating heat of a Provençal summer. The city has a feminine charm: small, chic, gentle, lovely, safe. More gardens than parking lots. Here is the ocean and here are the mountains; here is nature and here is culture. Living with this kind of beauty, I failed to notice that the darkness, silence and slowness of cold winter days used to provide a rhythm that was essential to me. I began working non-stop, tugging at life to yield what I had decided to extract from it, shamefully abusing the animal generosity of the unconscious, a good horse that will keep going until exhausted.

I failed to understand a sequence of dreams that suggested: You think you want a way out of the labyrinth? Wrong! Look for the entrance. A series of psychological disasters and a nearly fatal accident popped my shiny California bubble. Tumbling, literally, into an empty pool and sustaining a cerebral hemorrhage was just the right dose of death for equilibrium to return.

Psychology classifies fears according to their depths. Between the surface (for the sake of simplicity let's say "ego conscious-ness") and the abyss (or the "unconscious"), there is an abundance of fears, big or little fish that can be caught in the net of psycho-analysis. Prudence advises a slow descent with the guidance of an analyst, but if one is in a hurry, a tragedy may accelerate the process. At the bottom rests a single fear: death. Ah! Here you are, Madam, my Death. Pleased to meet you. During the days follow-ing my brain injury, my encounter with death taught me more about the psyche than had many years of analysis. For a psychol-ogist, this revelation is troubling, as it suggests that there is a very direct route to the core of one's being. Analysis is a fascinating zigzag path to consciousness, but there is also an expressway: a face-to-face encounter with one's death. Unpleasant, risky, pain-ful, but expedient. You don't choose this itinerary. It happens to you as an encounter with something like the Greek goddess Fate.

All fears are fundamentally the fear of death, but they vary in flavor. In the intensive care unit, I was first aware of my fear of losing the ability to walk, a primitive, animal fear. The next hour brought up the sentimental fear that I might die without telling my children, their father and all my friends, how much I love them. It was a fear of dying in exile, without saying my farewells to loved ones, a possibility that, in the Middle Ages, was dreaded as much as the fact of dying.

By the next day, experiencing how a damaged brain drastically diminishes mental capacities, I was haunted by the eventuality of the loss of my identity as teacher, therapist, and writer, a fear with the distinctive taste of ego. From there I realized that death also means the loss of an innumerable number of life's little delights – June cherries from the farmers' market, picnics on the beach, reading a good novel, cooking with somebody, for somebody, laughing and arguing with friends, swimming, dancing the tango. The sum of all those mini-epiphanies, I realized, is immeasurable.

Up to then, when faced with a difficult situation, I would shift into the heroic mode: don't tremble, thrust ahead. All-wheel drive, up the hill! Not this time. Mister Courage refused to appear on cue, leaving the stage instead to Madam Death. She stepped forward to remind me of my vulnerability, my brokenness. All I could do was quiver. It was a great lesson. Many times in my life it would have been much wiser for me to surrender, tremble and suffer rather than posture heroically. I entered the darkest period of my life and became as tormented as my most tormented patients. Suffering renewed my sense of the compelling relevance of depth psychology. I was in such darkness that there was no denying that the psyche has incredible depth, and I was falling into its abyss.

Paradoxically, as my commitment to my professional calling was renewed, I lost faith in almost all psychological theories. Thirty years of study turned to dust! Those brilliant theories, read, annotated, regurgitated in courses and articles – all now appeared useless. Depth psychology had been the great intellectual passion of my life. Now it felt like my hard drive had been erased, my intellect emptied of all its files. With no more confidence in psychological theories, it felt a bit contradictory to feel, more than at any other period of my life, the need for psychological insight. I began investigating what exactly had changed for me, theoretically as well as personally. I revisited everything I thought I knew about psychoanalysis and psychotherapy, about matters of the heart, about growing up and being an adult, about human nature, and human love.

This is why this book speaks with two voices. One is that of the therapist writing a critique of my field, observing the evolution of my trade from a theoretical point of view. After 30 years of teaching and practicing psychology from various approaches, I am taking a personal inventory: which ideas still feel useful and which feel dead? Given the takeover from neuroscience and pharmacology what is the future of depth psychology? What is coming in the next psychologies?

The other voice is not so detached. It is the much less assured voice of an ordinary person telling an ordinary experience of inferiority, brokenness, failure and pain. It comes from a need to test all the theories against my own experience of suffering – a very different posture than the lofty position of professor and therapist. It is a phenomenological stance and as such it excludes the clinical interpretive terminology, moving away from the medical model, away from psychodynamics, and towards literature.

Chapter 1 is an application of this phenomenological-literary-imaginal approach to my own account of a plunge in the dark river Styx. It is in writing in this imaginal – rather than clinical – style that I first felt the liberation that comes from abandoning the usual jargon of the bible of the profession: the *Diagnostic Statistical Manual of Mental Disorders.*[1] It was so liberating that I began questioning myself: what if, all through my career, I had written my patients' case histories with the same literary attention that I am now giving my own experience? What if I had given their cases the same kind of mythopoetic license? What about dropping the clinical taxonomy when writing case history, keeping only the story and dropping the case? Throughout the book, the vignettes show the result of my rewriting of some of my patient's insights (with their permission).

To sustain life, the psyche requires pleasure, joy, and a fascination with the world. This seems impossible in the face of acute pain. Yet, I believe the paradox can be sustained, if one is ready to go through the suffering bearing the curiosity and respect of a pilgrim traveling in the Underworld. I believe the next evolution of psychology will be concerned less with pathology – leaving it to neuroscience – and will become more like a philosophical training, capable of preparing the person for the voyage in the country of pain and joy – depth psychology as the art of not wasting the joy of life. The necessity of a descent into the Underworld is a core idea of depth psychology, one that I wish to explore anew in this book.

We all have a psychology because we all have an imagination. Inner imagery needs periodic updating because the virtual realities going on in the psyche need to change all the time. When the old script offers no more surprises, no more room to move, one needs a new identity. This is not something a trauma-focused clinical approach can do because the exploration of our psyche's depth definitely belongs to the humanities and the arts.

# Acknowledgments

I owe a great deal to Druscilla French, for her exacting attitude in the editing of my text as well as her generosity of assistance and expertise with the English language. This book would not exist without her help and support.

I feel a deep gratitude toward: Michael Vannoy Adams, Edie Barrett, Joe Coppin, William Doty, Christine Downing, Mark Kelly, Darcia Labrosse, Patrick Mahaffey, Gilles-Zenon Maheu, Lune Maheu, David Miller, Maureen Murdock, Marquita Riel, Murray Shugar, Dianne Skafte, Glen Slater, Dennis Slattery, Margo Steurer, Bill and Joanna Drake and their compassionate neighbours, Anne West. The generosity of their intellect, their emotional support, their physical presences, demonstrated for me how we are all part of all richly connected ecosystem of minds, psyches and bodies.

I thank all the patients, students and friends who gave me permission to use their stories to illustrate the theory.

I am grateful to my brother, Claude Paris, for the role he played in the shaping of my intellect, at a time when I was a "just a girl."

I thank Lori Pye for convincing me, by her exemplary commitment to the preservation of the natural world, that all depth psychology is ultimately, also, an ecopsychology.

Finally, I am deeply indebted to James Hillman, teacher and friend, whose thinking and writing inspired and guided me throughout my life. Those who know his work will see how much my perspective on depth psychology owes to his radical revisioning of the whole field.

# Chapter 1

# Denting my thick skull

My fall into an empty cement pool and the subsequent dance with death was not the only time I descended into a hole that year. Several months before the near-fatal accident, I had come to the end of a long marriage and was intensely depressed by that failure. This union had not been a placid one. My husband and I were often separated, living in different houses, cities, even countries. We had fashioned a life that accommodated two diametrically opposed natures, each willing to give the other freedom to follow their calling. Most of the time the tension had been creative, but it had become increasingly depleting, dangerous. With the end of the parenting phase, the escalating stress became exhausting. I lacked the courage to cut the knot. He had enough for both of us and slashed the Gordian knot in one stroke: he bought his plane ticket to go back East. Yes, I understood that with our children's maturity the marriage had lost its necessity. Yes, I understood that divorce or separation do not necessarily mean the end of love. Yes, I could see that marriage itself was damaging love more surely than separation. Yes, I understood that he had reached the stage of life where he felt entitled to follow his true nature, which required becoming a kind of recluse. Yes, I understood how badly he wanted to finally get his fill of reading, meditation, silence, solitude, peace. Yes, I understood all that. Yet, my whole being was saying NO! Intellectual understanding does very little to ease the impact of an emotional blow. No! No! No! Not you, not me, not yet.

Through my work as a psychotherapist, I have often observed one of the intriguing mysteries of human nature: the temptation to stay in a destructive yet familiar relationship, a willingness to grant others power over our lives, a denial of the possibility of freedom. Why are we so willing to ask husbands, wives, parents, friends, children, bosses, gurus, associates, subordinates, to carry the responsibility of our freedom? Experiencing abandonment, it was now my turn to feel this unbearable desire to be dependent. I tried suggesting that freedom might be okay, but not just yet. I tried begging: why not stay in our charming prison just a bit longer? He left as planned, taking only his books, leaving me with all the remains and the remains of all. He returned to the family home in the East and entered his longed for reclusion.

I thought I would find relief in blackening the character of the man who had left me. "After all the things I have done for him! What a monster!" I didn't realize, at that time, that love can have underground ramifications that run so deep that when I tried to pull these roots of love out of me, my heart came with it. I spent months in denial, uprooted in every possible way, until I fell into that cement hole and almost died.

This hole was no metaphorical hole, that great abyss of depression where abandoned women dwell. I'm talking about a literal hole, a small pool, actually, that served as the reservoir for a fountain that had been emptied in order to cement the tiles. One of the tiles on the very edge was unstable. I was one of the guests at this beautiful wedding reception, walking around the empty pool with my glass of champagne. My foot slipped (or desired to slip, I'll never know for sure), my arms windmilled the air, my body went tumbling backwards and my head shattered against the cement floor of the pool. Massive cerebral hemorrhage and a long dive into that frigid, metaphorical river called Styx.

After a brief coma, I awoke in the intensive care ward of a hospital in Santa Fe, where I was visiting at the time of the accident. I felt no emotion, in the sense that psychology has traditionally used the term. The physical pain was excruciating, but I experienced it with that strange detachment that animals seem to have, a patience under torture, the body busy doing its thing. There was no ego left to filter the impact of pain. I had returned to that point at which the dispersed particles of being either fuse again or disintegrate forever. In this primal state, I drifted like a mere collection of elements, fine drops of being floating between the infinite smallness of my person and the infinite vastness of the cosmos.

With a disintegrated ego, the experience of pain is direct, animalistic, but so is the perception of the beauty of existence.

Everything is immediately terrible and immediately magnificent. Emotions are extreme, impossible, strange. I felt an incomprehensible exaltation at the destruction of so much unnecessary clutter in me, physical pain acting as an instrument with which to scrape grievances, scratch out gripes, grind residues of resentment. This dangerous clean-up operation, done under the supervision of Madam Death herself, provoked unexpected surges of salty joy; the garbage truck is here, I am ready to fill it with all my existential junk, and my used up, tired, broken self. Death is deliverance. Welcome to you, Madam Death, come do your work.

## Cracked head

Like a wounded bull collapsing in the ring, I feel myself dying. It is just as well, for my heart is already dead. Soon there will be no body to suffer the failure of love. Pain, all modalities of pain, would all be over if I let this fragile bird or butterfly the Greeks called "soul" take flight. I shut my eyes and fall into a deep hypnagogic state where I seem to hallucinate a diaphanous butterfly hovering over my head like a minuscule parachute that might be able to carry away my soul. I am awake, yet this fantasy has the reality that images have in dreams, as if dreams are oozing through my injured brain. Whatever the brain pathology that creates that vision, I am grateful for this butterfly fluttering over my head, its wings dusted with gold. "Quick, butterfly. Hurry. Carry my soul; I'm open. This is a good time to leave. Let's fly off together." Like a bather poised on the edge of the water, anticipating the cool pleasure of deep water of forgetfulness, I am waiting, still and focused, ready for a plunge into death.

Instead, a procession of my mistakes and sins against love enters the room. I greet them. "Yes, I made all those mistakes." I let them go with a facility I have never experienced before. The color is drained out of my guilt; the passion departs from my suffering. I am consumed, dust on the butterfly's wings, feeling the sublime lightness of dying, heartbroken, sorry, regretful, but not guilty. I did my best, and it's over.

A male nurse in a white coat comes into my room pushing a gurney. He starts unhooking the crisscross of tubes and wires that cover my bed, explaining all the while that he is going to lift me onto his wheeled stretcher and take me to the MRI (magnetic resonance imaging) room. He disturbs us terribly, my butterfly and me, especially when he starts lifting the upper part of my body because I vomit, a volcanic eruption, shooting lava past the foot of my bed. The young man steps to the side, tells me not to worry, that projectile vomiting is a normal effect of a brain injury. Nevertheless, vomiting or not, he has to get me onto the gurney. This young man is handsome (at least I can still see that) but the explosion of vomit completely destroys the tranquility a butterfly needs to carry the soul. Too late! The moment is past for our escape.

It takes a long time for the young man to carry out his task, but he is skillful. He cleans and handles this heap of living flesh with gentleness. He brings me to my bed after the brain scan. I fall back into the trance. The butterfly is gone; instead there is a strong memory. At the age or 20, I saw El Cordobes fight a bull in Madrid. I believed at the time that I would never forget El Cordobes, his grace and elegance. In a pink silk toreador costume embroidered with gold threads, he was confronting a thousand-pound furious beast. But the image that now comes back most vividly is not that of the balletic toreador. It is that of the magnificent wounded bull. Hit by El Cordobes, the nape of his neck pierced by the sword, blood spurts out of him, in rhythm, just like my volcanic vomiting, yet the bleeding animal refuses to accept defeat. The memory is very precise: I see the bull's front legs buckle as he collapses, brought to his knees; he convulses, his muscles trembling under the black luminous shiny coat; the blood erupts from the wound, spurting with each heartbeat, turning the sand of the ring red; the crowd is silent for a long

time and then, as if angry at death herself, the bull struggles
desperately and gets to his feet. He charges once more, with
surprising energy. El Cordobes dances a ballet of avoidance.
Finally, the bull collapses, dead, and the crowd applauds this
last glorious fight as much as the toreador's victory.

There is within me such a beast, one obsessed with survival. I feel the same desperate energy, my body a heavy
beast weighed down with pain. The butterfly is not alone.
Instead of the lightness of sweet death, the bull that storms
out of my imagination commands me to get back in my
body, to charge once more, to accept pain and to fight
against death. The pain that grabs me is keeping me alive by
keeping me in my animal body. There is energy in pain; it is
the energy of that heavy, wounded black bull insisting on
life, while the butterfly prefers flight and light. Neither of
these images seems ready to give in. There is a battle of
internal images. A movie is playing in my psyche. I am
completely absorbed by the combat between bull and butterfly. The imaginal activity keeps me alert, interested.

Chaos can be freeing. The chaos of physical pain is breaking me open, like cracks in the wall that let the light in.
Strapped to my bed, there is nothing I can do. I can only be. I
feel a sublime surrender to the bruising, cleansing process of
destruction. The person that I was, and could not tolerate
being, is being killed. I find repose in this destruction.

At regular intervals, a nurse assaults me with a super-
bright light to see if my pupils' reflexes are still functioning.
The brain hemorrhage seems to have intensified, a worsening
of my condition since I was admitted to intensive care. Her
flashlight in my face feels like a scene out of an old detective
movie – a dazzling light directed at the suspect's face, endless
interrogation without respite. This nurse is a severe matron
with the doggedness of a cop. She repeats the same questions
every hour or so: what is your name, the city of your birth,
your age, the day of the week? After four of these sessions of
interrogation, I suggest that maybe the conversation would

be more lively if she would ask different questions and if I could ask her some too. That is impossible, she says. These are the questions she has been taught to ask to see whether the brain is still functioning correctly. Such platitudes discourage me. I feel utterly alone, an abandoned carcass, of no interest to anybody. I call on the butterfly. "Let's go. Spread your wings. Let me slip away. Farewell, one and all. I'm finally going to graduate and receive the supreme diploma that will prove my autonomy: I shall die alone! The queen of autonomy, dying without a fuss! Politely, I'll leave without imposing, so proud of my wings."

Every time I try to give the butterfly the victory, the bull rises in anger. "Stop your nonsense!" commands the bull. "I'll make you puke up the very water you're drinking." Bang! The volcano bursts into activity, splashing again, not only my pajamas and my sheets, but also the impeccable white uniform of the strict humorless nurse who is again checking my reflexes with her flashlight. She is offended by the vomit on her white uniform, her face frowning in disgust. I agree. I am a disgusting animal, and I apologize as best I can, shame inspiring a stupid excuse: that I have never vomited on anyone before and I am terribly sorry! She abruptly leaves, and I remain in my smelly mess for the next hour. I take it as punishment for my bad manners and feel strangely, profoundly hurt, sinking into an ocean of self-pity. This is so like my mother, impatient with me for being sick, for giving her extra work, impatient even with the expression of my clingy adoration for her. The professional persona of nurse seems to ask for busyness, coldness, remoteness. Mother was a nurse. All my complexes start having a party. I am a helpless abandoned baby again.

The nurse, having changed her uniform, finally returns in the company of an aide, a Mexican woman who does not speak English, and whose task is to clean up the bed and the body in it. This woman and I are left alone. She stares at me for a time that seems very long. That stare is something I

have never seen; she looks through me, not at me. Her silent
stare is a seeing and a speaking at the same time. I see that she
is seeing that I am someone between life and death, undecided.
Her eyes are saying that she has no intention of influencing
me, nor of scolding me; that there is no need for shame; that
she is not disgusted by bodies, dead or alive, or bodies in
between, like mine, spurting vomit and flirting with death.

She starts removing my soiled hospital gown; I let go of all
my rigidities. She holds my upper body in her arms, gentle
yet strong. I relax, cuddle, and she begins to hum a tune, in a
low, rich voice. It sounds like the Ave Maria, but not quite
that, although from what I understand of the words, they
seem to implore Mother Mary for my sake. I absorb every
note of the consoling song. Her voice penetrates me, as
profound a penetration as in lovemaking. A woman making
love to another woman with her voice? I snuggle up against
her heart, smell her skin, find refuge in her goodness. The
more I receive of her compassion the more her voice opens,
receiving the entirety of my being in her song. For an instant,
I love that woman I don't even know, immediately, totally,
absolutely. I love her body, I love her soul; it is a visitation of
the Great Mother. It opens up a silent stream of tears of
infinite gratitude that such human beings exist.

The strict nurse comes back and breaks the sweet spell. I
am saddened at the thought that the medical establishment
does not seem to understand the power of those rare and
precious individuals whose hands, voices, smiles, bodies,
eyes, smell, and heart have the power to give a transfusion of
life, from heart to heart. Their gift is immeasurable. The
strict nurse holds a form in her hand, a paper I am supposed
to sign, and she explains why. I can't understand her explanations. I feel very stupid for making her repeat herself. It
occurs to me that the blood that is increasingly invading my
brain is turning me into an idiot; my mind is slowing down
by the hour. I understand very little of her long sentences full
of complex causal links, scientific information, legal issues. I

can only "get it" if the sentence is short, followed by silence,
to give me time to process. I have been transformed overnight into a simpleton with an education. My mind feels
closer to that of a cat than to the intellectual person I used to
be.[1] Last night, when I was admitted to intensive care, I
could still remember my phone number. Not today. The
nurse explains a second time; she seems to get it that I am
somehow damaged goods. Finally, I get it. I am being asked
to sign a form giving the doctor permission to trepan me if
the internal hemorrhage doesn't stop before tomorrow
morning. Explanations. Explanations. Explanations. Finally,
the question: will you sign? The answer: okay! The feeling:
indifference. Do whatever you want with my body; I can't
stand it any more, it is garbage!

An hour after I have signed, the neurologist informs me
that trepanning might help me survive, but it is impossible to
foresee the damage that the ongoing hemorrhage might cause
between now and the decision to intervene. I call for the
nurse who'd brought me the form to tell her to tear it up.
The risk is too high, and I don't want to live like a green
cucumber strapped to a bed! This time there is agreement in
the menagerie. The bull and the butterfly form a consensus.
Let's get out of this mess by all means. Why have a body that
might not be able to walk, eat, swim, make love, ride a
bicycle, or dig in the garden? So, we agree; we tear up that
paper and take off, the butterfly on the bull's tail! I gesticu-
late, argue with the nurse, explain and beg her to tear up the
form I signed earlier, but I am confused, agitated, incoherent.
The words come out of my mouth unformed, like computer
garbage. The nurse doesn't understand. She thinks I am
agitated and delirious and boosts the dose of tranquilizer in
my IV. My inner screen grows fuzzy, and I return to the
night sky of half-consciousness for the rest of my second
night in intensive care.

The next day, I inspect the machines I am hooked up to
and the many screens by the bed that monitor them. From

what I can feel with my hands not finding any bandages on my head, there was no trepanation. A room in intensive care feels like being inside an airplane cockpit, a surrealist environment, a sci-fi set. I wonder which image will dominate today, black bull or white butterfly? A different nurse, sitting at her computer at the central station, which I see from the open door of my cell, hears an alarm and comes running into my room at top speed. She too seems to have scolding on her mind. "You're not breathing the way you're supposed to. This screen measures the amount of oxygen going to your brain. You have to maintain a level of 80 to 95 percent, and you're not getting over 55 percent!" For someone like me who has spent all her adult life in an academic environment, a grade of 55 percent means I am a failure. At least the capacity to speak with some coherence has returned. "Well, in that case, I guess I flunk. You'd better get one of those body bags. I'm ready to go." I happen to know the statistic: 80 percent of patients who are admitted to the intensive care unit and remain there past the first 24 hours of diagnosis come out as corpses. I have now been here more than 24 hours, so my chance of getting out of here alive is 20 percent. I can hear the sound of the long zipper on the plastic body bag and it doesn't frighten me at all.

The butterfly is winning when on the fourth day an unexpected event happens, a surprise of the kind that sometimes shows up when things reach their very worst. I would have called it a miracle if the literalists hadn't spoiled the word for the rest of us. Who wrote that the sense of the sacred is a step in the evolution of consciousness? I no longer agree. The sense of the sacred enters my room on that fourth day, as simply as could be, in the person of my 30-year-old daughter, a strong-minded young woman with an excellent sense of organization. She is a scientifically minded young person, just as the two registered nurses probably were before they burned out and filled with vinegar. Tall and straight, she appears in the doorway and lets me know, "Here I am!

Don't worry, Mom, I'm taking care of everything. I'll take you back to your bed in Santa Barbara." As her eyes take in the environment of the intensive care cell, I see her realize what kind of butterfly I am calling on, and I see her heart break. Her back, so straight an instant ago, begins to bend, and her lips begin to tremble like a little girl on the edge of tears. She moves forward, lies upon my bed, her head against my heart. She is my little girl again, a child who isn't at all ready to lose her mom. I can feel it. I hadn't considered that side of things until now.

The room slowly fills with golden light, absolute radiance. Her love for me, and mine for her, makes me aware of the blood moving through my veins, charging my cells with equal parts of oxygen and love. I literally feel my heart and my brain, even though we are not supposed to have the nervous apparatus to feel those parts of the body, but it feels as if I do. The strongest sentiment, the one that dominates, is the felt sense that all human beings are related, the ones we love and the ones we barely know, like the Mexican lady who sang to me; the living and the departed; the matronly strict nurse and my mom and my kid. All are part of the invisible rhizome that binds us to the same root, that sends the current from one pole to the other, that inverts pain and joy, love and death, presence and absence, pain and deliverance, the living and the dead, daughter and mother. I experience how the poles can switch. My daughter is mothering me as I surrender to my child's arms. I am her baby, and she the good breast. That's my sense of the sacred – that structure, that rhizome, that bond of love that decides if I am to live or die.

For one perfect hour, both of us lying still on the bed, I feel the physical warmth of that illumination. It is one of the sweetest and strongest experiences I have ever known, along with giving birth. I see my life scroll before me, like some kind of last-minute conscience examination. I ask my daughter to forgive me for my mistakes, which I now see so clearly. "I thought I was helping you, but now I see how it was a will to control. I'm sorry. I prevented you from finding your way by yourself." And more. Confessions! Some worded, others silent and private. Mostly failures of love. Blind spots that are suddenly revealed. All my defensive walls are silently crashing down to reveal my sins. These sins have nothing to do with the Christian God; they are all about human love in all its forms, including love of work well done. Sorry, God, you are not at the center of my attention, you never really were, and still are not at this ultimate hour. Frankly, I am glad my devotions were never really to you, because if they had been, it would now feel like an unbearable waste, bouquets of devotion sent to the wrong address. The regrets I do feel now have nothing to do with how I rejected you, transcendent Christian God, absolutely nothing to do with my lack of faith in your line of religiosity. My fallenness is not from your heaven. The examination of my conscience is not about sins against your kind of god. It is all about actual human beings to whom I might have been more generous, more receiving, more giving, more devoted; all about tasks I could have done better.

On my list of regrets, there is also one which is really simple but persistent: I wish I had spent less time getting things done, checking them off my to-do list, running toward the next item, and more time actually enjoying doing whatever it is I was doing. If I live, I vow to be somebody different, ideally somebody able to feel absolute bliss at the fact of having two good legs to walk with, eyes to read good books with, and a body to feel the sensuousness of every moment.

It is the very first time I am honestly willing to confront my shadow in its full dimension, wide and long. It comes again with the grace I felt the first day in intensive care: I see my faults but not through guilt. I am being led to understand that, try as we may to love well, we also do harm, even to, especially to, those we love; having a shadow is part of the world of the living. The grace is that the divinity of love seems ready to absolve me. I see my mistakes and I understand they are human. I am limited, a mix of light and opacity.

I have never seen anything as beautiful as the light that flows from the bed on which my daughter and I lay, never felt the bond of love with such simplicity, imperfection and all. It is a miracle happening, a very simple and common one: I have ceased to find fault with the world, even if it is delivering death to me. Tears flow again, tears of joy. I cannot tell if that hour of illumination is part of leaving the world of the living or if it signals my return. I really don't know, I am so completely joyfully exhausted. Am I coming or going?

The butterfly comes back to answer that question. It folds its wings into a cocoon, and takes refuge in my heart, as if to say: "We shall meet again, but not just now." The image of the bull also reappears. It has lost its ferocity; it is now a tired old bull, resting, breathing heavy, as quiet as a sleeping cat, calmed by infinite grace, not yet dead, just old and fatigued.

The next day, the neurologist pays me a visit. He is surprised, perplexed. According to this morning's brain scan, the hemorrhage has stopped and the blood is clearing out from what he calls the brain's cisterns (the folds of the brain). There is no sign of a clot forming. He has witnessed this kind of rapid healing before, but only among children. In the case of a woman my age, 55 years old, such an occurrence is highly improbable. He is smiling, talks about the sometimes random goodness of life's lottery, declares me a very lucky person. I would like to tell him that when I was sheltered in my daughter's arms, I was a child again. Through her arms, the Great Mother rocked me in a silence filled with the light shed by particles of love made visible. "That is how your patient was healed, Doctor." But the medical profession, in general, doesn't care for such leaps of mysticism. I simply thank him for his skill as a neurologist and demand that my legal rights be respected: I want a release from the hospital, now, today. I'll come in daily for routine checks but I want out this minute. Generous friends, the ones at whose house I was visiting when the accident occurred, have offered a place for me to stay with my daughter until I can travel. She and I remain alone in a truly magnificent house, I the baby, she the mother, for two perfect weeks. Then we fly home and try to resume our lives and our roles.

# Chapter 2

# A fable

## Mom, Dad, and me, me, me

### Wisdom can be learned

When I returned from my journey of pain, I found I had only one entry in my travel diary, one central idea scribbled on the envelope containing the release form from the hospital. It was a kind of memo to myself: wisdom can be learned. Life's ordeals offer an opportunity to penetrate the outer shell of our persona and to plunge deep into the core of our being, the place where our own psychological intelligence is waiting our arrival. One discovers a very simple truth: psychological *health* does not exist in the absolute. We all have the possibility of wisdom of which there are many forms: one of these is psychological *wisdom*. It does not show up as wisdom in full bloom, but as a seed, ready to germinate, that exists in every human being. Were our society attuned to the potential and value of this kernel, we would nurture the psyche's wisdom from a very early age. Wisdom is not a given, not some thing. It is more like an orientation. Just as the seed that is germinating grows toward the light, psychological wisdom is that compass within each of us, pointing in what seems like the most fruitful direction. Wisdom is a destination rather than a destiny, a goal rather than a state.

All forms of wisdom and all schools of spiritual discipline agree on one principle: we all start our journey as a needy, vulnerable, impotent child. If the needs of the child are not addressed properly the first time, the adult must eventually go back and finally address them. That is a basic task of psychotherapy: to go back and give the inner child what he or she needs to grow up. Nevertheless, the possibility of wisdom begins when one is finally able to leave the developmental model. There is a junction where Buddhism most obviously meets psychotherapy in proclaiming: yes, compassion allows this child to stop whimpering. Yes, paying attention to the inner child supports the life force that naturally grows toward maturity. Prophets, healers, and sages all show aspects of the Great Mother. They help us grow by feeding us the Great Mother's milk of compassion.

As an adult, I have drunk of this sweet milk; without this gift, I would now be dead. Nevertheless, the Great Mother also personifies the vigilance of the mother who expects the child to grow up – otherwise the inner child turns into a tyrant, the adult remains infantile, a puffed up, pompous tyrannical big baby in whom the seed of wisdom is lost. A wise psychotherapist addresses not only the unmet need for mothering, but also the unmet need for separation. Re-mothering consists of giving both the nurturing and the weaning.

Beginning with the basic cast of Mother–Father–Child, every school of psychology has offered theoretical variations, some bizarre and far-fetched, but all point at a core that is the same through thousands of years of philosophical and spiritual teachings. It is that core, that consensus, that basic archetypal story that will be my starting point. I am asking here, in this chapter, what is the basic plot, what is the nut in the shell? A consensus is often a truth that all can agree on because of its simplicity. Nevertheless, these "simple truths" are rare, and they are crucial because they are at the roots of our collective values. When a discipline develops as quickly and in as many directions as did psychology, there comes a point where we lose sight of the basics; we can't see the foundations of the huge theoretical building anymore; we forget to examine the solid anchors that are the places of agreement. It may be useful, from time to time, to remind ourselves that all humans (not just the wise psychologists) have some perennial values, archetypal principles, spiritual and theoretical cornerstones that sustain the whole edifice.

The following fable is my attempt at summarizing this consensus among philosophers, psychologists, gurus, sages and spiritual leaders of different periods and places. Instead of the genre of theory, I am presenting these ideas in the highly subjective genre of the fable, and as an invitation to compare my imagining with your own subjective version of the same story.

## Casting

The casting involves three characters: Archetypal Child; Great Mother; Archetypal Father.

### Archetypal Child

The Child represents the universal state of vulnerability and neediness of the newborn baby. The Jungians, who like the sophistication of Latin, refer to this archetype as the Puer (puer = child), or Puer Aeternus (Eternal Child). This archetypal Child remains active all our life and contains both the vulnerability and the vitality of youth. We regress back to its vulnerability each time life wounds us. We feel the joy of the Child each time we experience enthusiasm to learn, discover, experiment. The archetype is activated when the soldier can't sleep because of terrifying nightmares, when the worker is professionally burned out and starts crying on the job, when the lovesick person can't get out of bed to face the day's work. Archetypal Child screams: "Take care of me, I can't, I won't. Love me, give me joy, otherwise I'll die."

### Great Mother

She is compassion personified, a quality which is the essence of mothering. Mothering and compassion are synonymous and can be offered by a male or a female, a sister or an uncle, a friend, lover, cellmate, or, if one has luck, one's own biological mother. Sometimes, the biological father plays the role of Great Mother rather than that of Father and that is why we need an archetypal language to speak of it, not a literal designation. An archetypal role is distinct from the social or biological function; what counts is the experience of the archetype. One absolutely needs to have been touched by the caressing hand of a Great Mother, to have been held in a tender gaze that does not condemn us for our weakness. By "Great Mother" I mean that experience of unconditional love, without which nothing small, nothing vulnerable, nothing in its infancy can survive, not even the "baby" ideas, the tentative impotent style of the first sentences that were in the very first draft of this book. No writer in his or her right mind would risk showing a first draft to a critical mind, not until the text "grows up" to stand on its own and sustain some measure of criticism. Everything new, young, fragile – even the first shoot of what will become a mighty oak tree – first appears as a vulnerable sprout needing protection and nurturance; otherwise, it is crushed and dies.

Great Mother has many appellations: the maternal principle; the capacity for compassion; the tender-loving-care principle; or the chicken-soup-healing factor. I prefer not to call it the feminine principle, because that has led to many misunderstandings. To think that the female gender is more gifted with maternal qualities is a philosophical mistake filled with tragic consequences for both genders. Compassion is a human quality and "Mother" symbolizes it. If mothers were not motherly, humanity would never have survived because human babies are the most vulnerable creatures in the animal kingdom. Nevertheless, the archetypal quality exists in every one of us, with the same possibility of development or non-development.

The Great Mother's message is essentially one of compassion: "I love you, little one, simply because you exist. Don't cry. I'm here. I will take care of you, feed you, heal you, caress you, and give you a taste of the nectar of tenderness." When Great Mother refuses to give of herself (which means when the little mother is impatient and says: "Get out of my way and take care of yourself"), the archetypal Child experiences pure panic, the very essence and source of all panic.

### Archetypal Father

This powerful Father, or Cosmic Father, or Great Father, or God the Father, is the third and last character in our fable. This Father informs the Child that there is such a thing as conditional love, and that the principles of law and order, although they may vary in their applications, are universal. The archetypal Father is represented in mythology with that thundering voice and authoritatively raised eyebrows that the Romans represented as Jupiter, the Greeks as Zeus, and Christians as God the Father. These Father divinities personify authority and responsibility. The Child draws a sense of power and protection from a powerful father, expressed by all kids when they boast "My father is stronger than yours" (or richer, taller, braver, has a bigger car, bigger gun, bigger fist or the most powerful computer in the neighborhood). The projection is carried over to any person who holds authority (king, general, president, boss, chief, captain, sheriff). "My president is more powerful than yours and I follow as long as I feel I need the protection he offers."

The Father archetype is present in the teacher who flunks you at the exam but also can help you prepare for it; he (or she) may be the bank officer who informs you that you are overdrawn, but who will also help you start your business with a loan; he is the policeman who writes you a ticket, but also protects you from thieves and thugs; he is the Inland Revenue Service agent who disallows a tax deduction because he serves the principle of redistribution of wealth; he is the referee who sends you to the bench, thus keeping the game within the limits of fair play. The terrifying news for Archetypal Child is that this figure of authority will impose his rules and regulations, has strict codes of rewards and punishments, and holds on to principles of order. Archetypal Child rages: "What are you telling me? I, the Little King of the House, have to obey rules? If not, smack, whap? I really don't like it!"

Now that we have the cast of characters, let's look at the plot.

### First Trial: born needy

*Child:*              I am so small, Great Mother. I implore you to take care of me. I just came into this world. I don't even know how to distinguish between hunger and cold, between hurt and fear. My consciousness is undeveloped. I have no culture and no language. All I have is this body, this bundle of tyrannical needs. "It" feels pleasure or pain. It is not "I" because I don't have an "I" yet. To be honest, I don't have the slightest idea of who "I" is, or who "I" can be. I beg you to put sweet words in my ears to stir the desire to learn language. And once you have given me the words, I will want stories. I want them rich and complicated. I want the stories to make me feel the presence of a humanity that is dense, with many protective layers made of all the generations of wise humans. I need to feel a part of a large, knowledgeable, extended tribe, compassionate enough to contain my life and protect me from harm. Most of all, Great Mother, I want you to define me. Look at me with eyes of adoration. Become the mirror that reveals me as your Sun King, the source of all light, the center of all joy in your life.

*Great Mother:* Don't worry, little one. I'll give you all that. My task is to convince you to incarnate, to take pleasure in living in a body and for that you need pleasure and joy.

*Child:* Caresses, songs, cuddling, cooing and kisses, will you give me all those?

*Great Mother:* You need them as much as you need food, warmth, language and a clan. Without joy, you may not want to incarnate fully, you may fail to thrive. So, you shall get the whole package. But listen! You must begin right now to transform and start maturing to become a full human being.

*Child:* What if I don't?

*Great Mother:* I'll drop you, baby! And if I drop you, you die.

*Child:* Okay, I get it! What do I have to do?

*Great Mother:* There are many trials, each one interesting and difficult.

*Child:* If it's hard, I want you to do it for me.

*Great Mother:* If I do it for you, you will never be able to say "I". No ego, no competence; no ego, no freedom.

*Child:* I want an ego. I want freedom. I want the world and I want it now. What's the first trial? Bring it on then.

*Great Mother:* Here's the first trial: separate! Starting now, begin differentiating the discomfort of hunger from the discomfort of cold. Toilet train, because your shit stinks, even for Mommy. Discover that "you" and "I" equal two, not one. Understand that I am less and less at your beck and call. As you grow, you'll have to abdicate the throne.

*Child:* I don't want to.

*Great Mother:* Of course you don't. Your resistance is precisely the first step in your education. I'll be careful not to overwhelm you. I will administer the discomfort gradually. However, if you persist in your dependency, all the people around you will distance themselves from you. Here is your first

|  | choice: either you detach, or you'll remain forever without ego, without self, without a rudder, without a compass, without identity. |
|---|---|
| *Child:* | Well, in that case, I'll try. Is this ordeal as terrible as I imagine? |
| *Great Mother:* | It is. And many fail. It can also be exhilarating, since it is the beginning of your freedom. |
| *Child:* | I'm in. Test me. |
| *Great Mother:* | You see the apple on the table? If you are hungry, don't call for me. Grab it and bite into it with your new teeth. Devour the apple, not your mother. It's delicious. You'll feel free. |

### Second Trial: the matter of Matter

| *Child:* | I am ready for the second trial, Great Mother. |
|---|---|
| *Great Mother:* | It takes place in my realm, but I am not the guide. "Matter" will be your teacher. Discover the hardness of metal, the burn of fire, the freshness of morning dew, the softness of velvet, the beauty of water, and the danger of water. Matter sometimes resists and sometimes collaborates. Matter is demanding. If you show contempt for her, she extracts her revenge by polluting the very matter of which you are made. |
| *Child:* | Where, how will I meet Matter, Mother? |
| *Great Mother:* | Just play. For now, all you have to do is play with everything, to learn the multiple forms of matter. Productivity comes later, in the realm of the Father. |
| *Child:* | I can do that: play! |

### Third Trial: meet the Father

| *Father:* | Your third trial is with me, your Father. Discover that there are such things as war, competition, and strife. Enter a world of buying and selling, partnerships and takeovers, law and order, rules and regulations, rewards and punishments. |
|---|---|
| *Child:* | You mean I have to work? End of play? |

| | |
|---|---|
| *Father:* | It can still feel like play, but it has to be productive, to give something back. You can build, create, discover, invent, write, preach, teach, cook, carve, paint, produce wealth, administer it, pass it along, multiply it, distribute it. Work for yourself and work for others. Give your best, test your limits, give, get, go, go, go. |
| *Child:* | OK. Give me a job. |
| *Father:* | No. Find it yourself. |
| *Child:* | What if I screw up? |
| *Father:* | If you fail, you will be one of those weaklings who constantly complain that the system is rigged anyway and why work if I can't win and Father is asking too much of me and it's too hard and if I can't beat the system, I quit! |
| *Child:* | What if I fail at only one of the three trials? |
| *Father:* | To reduce the humiliation of failure, you will devalue everything that relates to the trial you just failed. For example, if you fail to honor the Mother principle, you will devalue desire. Why have desire if Mother won't satisfy it? If you fail to honor matter, you will be incapable of enjoying the sensuousness of the world because nature is matter. If you fail to honor my principle, you will end up homeless, incompetent, unreliable, useless. |
| *Child:* | And what if I fail all three? |
| *Father:* | You will never feel truly alive. You will never find meaning. Events will happen to you, good and bad. However, your focus will be on protection of your self-esteem and you will reduce all events to their concreteness, missing all the juice in life. No conversations, only monologues. No relationships, only manipulative tricks. No give and take, only steal, hit and run. |
| *Child:* | Wow! No glory, no money, no honey, lonely? I think I know what you mean because I met a little girl like that. I baked her a cake for her birthday, a recipe from the Great Mother, a really sweet-nutritional-bio-healthy-organic-wholesome-fabulous cake. She saw only a cake, only food, not the |

love that I was manifesting with it. I think she has failed all three trials.

*Father:*     Exactly! Imagine this little girl when she grows up: sex will be a token of exchange, marriage only a contract, work only money, success only a social obligation. If you fail all three initiations, you will think: "Is that all? Is that what life is supposed to be? It is not very much!" We have many names for those who fail: narcissists, egotists, egomaniacs, infantile adults who remain self-serving, self-centered, self-obsessed as only babies have a right to be. Selfishness is a curse, it takes you out of the rapport of exchange with the world. You live in penury because you can't see how life is a perpetual exchange of energy, a give and take, a lovemaking with the world. Selfishness is a state of damnation. What you want is love for your self, for others, for the world. Your Mother and I bless you Child. Alleluia.

# Chapter 3

# Therapy as cure
## The medical model

It is tempting to believe that the soul can be healed of its suffering, that analyzing one's emotions will fix the problematic psyche. "Please heal me doctor, I can't take it any more" is an attitude that characterizes the beginning of most psychotherapies. The pursuit of "cure" has kept the business going, everybody trying all kinds of fix-it approaches, some patients for the better part of their adult lives. The sad paradox is that real benefits of an expansion of consciousness cannot be obtained until one experiences the existential dead-end of believing in a cure. The pursuit of consciousness, of wisdom – even of happiness – is the opposite of a treatment. Human relations – and the suffering they generate – have been analyzed by all kinds of social scientists, and their findings fascinate, but the aspects of human relations that have depth and complexity cannot be revealed by explanatory models borrowed from science. Scientific modeling works beautifully for scientists, but fails miserably when trying to "explain" the psyche as one would explain the night sky with current findings in cosmology. Psychological constellations are unstable because they are based on one's personal myth, which is always replaceable by another myth. Here is an example of a situation where an approach focused on *healing* the symptom completely missed the deeper aspect of the problem. This young grandmother was my student and she was proud of having stopped the following attempt by the school psychologist to "heal" her grandson.

## Grandma, somebody killed my dog

My grandson's puppy dog was killed by a careless driver. The child – he is seven – was so distressed that he developed a nervous twitch in an eye. It worsened every day and at the end of the month the school psychologist called the mother (my daughter). The counselor insisted that the symptom was pathological,[1] that the child was not functioning, not inter- acting normally – withdrawn and sulky – and would the mother please suggest to the child to come to the office of the counselor on the next day for treatment. To this invitation, my grandson reacted by refusing to go back to school ever again. He felt he was being "summoned" to the counselor's office, an attack on his soul.

The school psychologist, I am convinced, would have done her best to help my grandchild, who was obviously in need of assistance, but I found the "summoning" very disturbing without quite being able to put my finger on the problem. I resented the idea of treating him as if it was "sick" to grieve a whole month for the loss of a puppy. So I got into my car, drove the 200 miles, stayed at my daughter's and kept my grandson out of school for a week. We talked about life and death, we discussed pressing philosophical questions: Do dogs have souls? Why is there death? Are we all mortals? Even Mom and Dad and you, Grandma? And why and how am I to live in view of such evil? On our last day, we performed a goodbye ceremony, burying – in lieu of a body – the pair of slippers the puppy had last chewed. We framed a picture. We discussed that spring might be a good time to get a new puppy because spring is the season of new life and that, just like his life continues the life I was given by generations of ancestors, a new puppy will continue a long history of humans loving the company of dogs. The twitch had disappeared on the third day, naturally, and never came back.

Of course, this boy's face exhibiting a "sudden, rapid, recurrent, non-rhythmic, stereotyped motor movement"[2] can rightly be

called a symptom, but a treatment approach to this kind of problem can also be deeply wrong. A symptom implies it should be
fixed. What exactly needs fixing? The boy's instinct told him that
his soul needed no fixing and he was right in resisting the
intrusion. The cure-it-fix-it model is absolutely fine with what
lends itself to fixing. A broken bone needs fixing, a rotten tooth
too. But this boy's symptom was covering a non-fixable issue: the
revelation of our mortality.

The attempt to "fix a soul" diminishes life, it harms the psyche,
it dries up the seed of wisdom. Children too are faced with deep
philosophical questions. The death of a puppy may bring up all the
big issues: mortality, the tragic sense of life, the suffering of the
innocents. At the age of seven, this huge discovery calls not for
treatment but for initiation, which is what the grandmother gave
him by having a week of talking philosophically with the child.
His initiation was the opposite of a fixing. It started with the
wisdom of his grandmother and ended with him a wiser little boy,
aware that we are mortals and that evil things can happen to nice
beings. As for the ritual, it prepared him concretely for a new
puppy in the spring.

The clinical competence of a school psychologist can be a
crucial element in the community. No one denies that medical
research has resulted in a more and more targeted medication for
the treatment of mental disorders based on neurohormonal or
chemical imbalances. The example of bipolar disorders was one of
the first obvious demonstrations of the value of a neurochemical
approach. No talking cure could ever pretend to compete with the
right medication for such physiologically driven problems. The
school clinician is asked to spot troubled kids and it is not an easy
task to differentiate between a psychiatric disorder that needs
clinical attention and a philosophical dilemma that calls for a
conversation with a wise adult. Nevertheless, that distinction is
crucial to the evolution or decadence of our culture.

For all its usefulness, the *DSM* remains organized around fuzzy
concepts such as "mood disorders," "anxiety disorders," and
"personality disorders" even though nobody in the field knows for
sure and with cultural and historical consistency what these basic
concepts really refer to. The introductory text of the *DSM* stipu-
lates: "the term 'mental disorder' unfortunately implies a distinction between mental disorders and physical disorders that is a
reductionistic anachronism of mind/body dualism. A compelling

literature documents that there is much physical in mental disorders and much mental in physical disorders. The problem raised by the term 'mental disorders' has been much clearer than its solution, and, unfortunately, the term persists in the title of *DSM-IV* because we have not found an appropriate substitute. Moreover, although this manual provides a classification of mental disorders, it must be admitted that no definition adequately specifies precise boundaries for the concept of 'mental disorder'."[3]

History is filled with examples of people who had alarming personality profiles, enough to justify hospitalization and heavy medication, yet were a gift to humanity: Virginia Woolf, Helen Keller, Albert Einstein, Leonardo da Vinci, Oscar Wilde, Amadeus Mozart, James Joyce, Henry Thoreau, Woody Allen. I personally know a few crackpots, marginal, fanciful, maladapted individuals, who score very poorly in terms of the categories of the *DSM*, yet who possess human qualities that make them precious beings to their friends and community. And a man like Adolph Eichmann seems to have been, according to psychiatric examination, absolutely normal.

The critique of psychology and psychiatry as a normalizing power in the service of dominant values has been written over and over again in the past 60 years. Jean-Paul Sartre, Michel Foucault, Thomas Szasz, Ronald Laing, Daniel Cooper and many others influenced a whole generation of intellectuals who took on the task of exposing the relativity of the norms by which mental health is judged. Their insights are still relevant and brilliant, yet their impact was primarily on university professors. Very little of their critique seems to have reached the practitioners, the American Psychological Association, the insurance companies, or the culture as a whole. To take but one example: many powerful organizations in the US, in Europe, and in Canada still use personality tests to screen applications and categorize their employees. Psychotechnicians administer the tests and the results are presented as objective. The calculations, for sure, are objective and the statistical analysis can help detect psychological deficiencies, or psychosocial pathology, which is a negative finding. Yet, for these tests to be able to do what they pretend to do (find the best person for the job), we would need a definition of the normal personality. We don't and can't have such a definition because as soon as we try to define mental health we enter a vast territory that cannot be put into neat categories, for the simple reason that this territory is never the same. Such testing confuses simple with simplistic, limpid with formulaic. Simplistic thinking is fallacious when dealing with psychological complexity.

If one had to choose one adjective that most qualifies the psyche, it would be "complex." This complexity is unavoidable in part because each psyche is a world unto itself. Complexity is unavoidable for another reason: the psyche won't lie still, it is not a fixed object. It dances with history, evolves or regresses according to the evolution of culture. For example, it would never have come to the mind of a gynecologist practicing in Victorian England to question sexual frigidity in a woman. Frigidity seemed perfectly normal to the good doctor. The personality profile for the well-bred woman of that time was described as naturally weak, naturally frigid, naturally dependent. The portrait of normality made her imminently vulnerable, with a weak libido, absolutely incapable of appreciating expert lovemaking. A proper husband was not to expect a strong sexual response from his wife. Unless a woman was ready to appear like a nymphomaniac, a prostitute, or a sexual degenerate, she had better not suggest that sexuality could be intensely pleasurable. Couples who discovered by themselves the possibility of reciprocal passion (there were plenty even in the Victorian era) remained discreet about the torrid nature of their discovery. They were content to escape between two sheets the dryness of a period ruled by a monarch obsessed with prudery. These ordinary people were "seeing through" the so-called personality profile for the normal woman, and in doing so augmented their freedom.

In itself, the fact that normal identity cannot be defined with any certainty is not a problem but a safeguard. The haziness of the definitions allows us to correct our mistakes and to avoid ideological corsets. The horrors of racism and sexism have at their core a rigidifying of identities. Whites are like this and Blacks are like that. Aryans are different from Jews. Men are from Mars and women are from Venus. Women are more attuned to nature, body and emotions and men to culture, spirit, and ideas. On and on, right out of the can of clichés. Rigid identities eventually burst at the seams – which is all the more convenient, since identity should be like a comfortable garment, sufficiently ample to allow for movement and growth.

Maybe the best historical demonstration of the impossibility of defining the normal personality is given by the history of the clinical judgment of homosexuality. Interpreting homosexuality as a sickness remains one of the most famous blunders in the history of psychology, one that was taken with a surprising lightness given that it is such an exemplary demonstration of the unscientific underpinning of the *DSM*. It is a fascinating story with a dramatic conclusion. Prior to the 1968 edition of the *DSM*, homosexuality (feminine and masculine) was considered to be a sickness. Psychologists published a great many theories about the possible causes for the "sickness" of homosexuality. A typical example was the often reprinted work of Frank S. Caprio,[4] which contained false evidence, invented case histories and much hysteria about the presumed danger of homosexuality for the morale of the community. The cause of homosexuality was often attributed to bad parenting (especially by the mother). In the case of male homosexuality, the mother was suspected of having been too seductive, provoking incestuous panic in the son; or she may have been too domineering, causing fear of castration. The mother of a lesbian was suspected of having been emotionally cold, causing the daughter to yearn for female affection, thus confusing the intimacy of mothering with that of mature sexuality. Psychologists made careers theorizing about the pathology of the homosexual personality: incapacity to grow up and meet the requirement of the traditional role of one's gender; unconscious fears of pregnancy and childbirth; envy of male (if female), envy of female (if male); wounded daughters of rejecting fathers; wounded sons of harsh fathers; wounded lovers whose heterosexual encounters had been traumatic; ugly ducklings desperate for affection; regressed narcissists who could only love an image of themselves through same-sex love.

The fact that homosexuality has always existed, in all cultures, through all epochs, demonstrates how a phenomenon can be a natural occurrence, even if not a statistical norm. Nature and culture are often at odds, and psychologists, as participants in a culture, have often taken their prejudices for granted. It took the rebellion of gays and lesbians to stir the controversy. Many of them were highly educated, professionally successful and tired of the stereotypes. They found allies among authors such as Thomas Szasz[5] who challenged the status quo by affirming that the fear of homosexuality had the same intensity and the same root as the fear of heresy. Szasz also suggested that the doctor, with his fabricated definition of "normality," had taken on the role of the priest forcing the rebellious elements in society to fit in with the herd.

It was only in preparing the 1973 edition of the *DSM* (the actual *DSM-IV*) that the so-called experts of the American Psychiatric Association (APA) decided to vote on the issue. Thirteen out of fifteen members were ready to rewrite the theory about homosexuality and present it somehow differently.[6] The following year, in 1974, the vote was put to the 10,000 members of the APA, and 58 percent confirmed the position of their leaders. Voting: what a curious way of ascertaining a scientific principle. How surprising that they did not drink of their own medicine, which should have been to diagnose themselves with a "thinking dis-order," i.e., an unconscious bias that makes psychologists medi-calize behaviors they do not approve of. The strangeness of their procedure (voting to define mental health) not only discredits the scientific pretensions of the *DSM*, but it brings back images of the pseudo-scientific posturing of the Dark Age doctors. They too, rather than following a rigorous experimental scheme, engaged in oratory contests and played games of social influence to determine if the king needed bloodletting, purging, cups, or all three. They talked, talked, talked, the large sleeves of their black robes agitating the air. When tired of fluffing their feathers, they would agree on a procedure. It was a safer strategy to agree than to risk dissension in front of the king, especially if the king's symptoms persisted.

Likewise, the members of the APA, prior to 1974, probably felt that it was safer to treat homosexuals as sick personalities, since they might otherwise risk being perceived by the ruling opinion as defending their own kind. But after 1974, the risk was that of being perceived as prejudiced against a powerful minority. The good doctors voted accordingly.

Organizational psychologists who blindly follow so-called "per-sonality profiles" to decide who gets a job offer and who doesn't, who is demoted and who promoted, work from a perspective similar to the pseudo-scientific logic of the *DSM*. It may not appear to be so because of the sophistication of the statistical presentation of their prejudices. The multifactorial analysis that allows the computer to correlate the 200 to 300 responses of a given subject with that of a few thousand other subjects randomly selected as being "the norm" is indeed a powerful, refined mathe-matical tool. This mathematical process of statistical validation is quite impeccable. What cannot be validated is the model behind the so-called "normal personality." It is that undisclosed model that allows for both the construction of the questionnaires and the interpretation of the statistical results. To replace the non-existing definition of a normal personality, these tests, like *the Diagnostic and Statistical Manual of Mental Disorders* (DSM), use a statistical median. In other words, the testers rely on an *average portrait* to decide who is desirable and undesirable for the position. To take the example of homosexuals again: they were, and still are, "eccentric" insofar as they, as a population, are not in the center of the statistical curve. But that is only a statistical position, like that of people who are color blind or those who have red hair. When the statistical eccentricity of homosexuality was translated into psychological abnormality, homosexuals were susceptible to exclusion. Similarly, an employee with a personality profile that does not quite fit the statistical portrait faces the same problem and may not be offered the position.

Insofar as we have a precise idea of what a test is trying to measure, and as precise a way of naming what we are trying to measure, testing is useful. If we know that the average secretary can type X words per minute, we can devise a test to see if the new applicant can do as well. We then know what we are measuring: speed at the keyboard. Many things can be measured as long as there is a standard of comparison on which we can agree: mathematical abilities, vocabulary, erudition in a specific field, competence with a software program, precision in manipulating a calibrated tool, capacity to follow a complex rhythm on a tam-tam, ability to retain a long chain of steps in a choreography, or the range and pitch of a voice, etc. Measuring can be as fair and useful as the invention of scales for merchants. It is extremely useful to know what constitutes one pound of potatoes, so that we can then discuss the price per pound. The problem with the "normal personality" is that it cannot be weighed. It is insubstantial, ethereal, and subject to change.

Clinicians do have a relatively reliable set of standards for judging an abnormal personality, because we have accepted standards of development for the human person. If, for example, a five-year-old child has less vocabulary than most two-year-olds, we can estimate that the level of verbal performance of the five-year-old is below standard because we do have a standard. Likewise, if an adult cannot understand a simple set of instructions, such as "green light means go" and "red light means stop," the common sense response is to refuse to give a driver's license to that person. Some psychological handicaps have the same clarity: if a person can't shake hands without going into a social panic, we can see the *abnormality* of such a behavior. Information about the abnormal is useful and relevant not only for potential employers but for the community as a whole.

It is another matter entirely when one considers the standards for the normal personality. The standards of normality have all been elaborated just as the *DSM* was elaborated. One evening, if you are a homosexual, you go to bed resigned to the fact that you are a sick person. The next day, when you wake up, a vote by the members of those who establish the *DSM*, following a change in social values, makes you normal! Oops! We are sorry for our big mistake, you may now get out of your closet. We apologize for the humiliation, the shunning and the suffering inflicted upon you. Who's next in the closet? To determine if homosexuality is normal (or if women are naturally frigid, or if this group, this race, or this gender is more likely to fit the desired profile) we would first need a working definition of a normal, psychologically healthy, human being. However, the definition of what constitutes a normal human being has been, and still is, consistently inconsistent. This inconsistency is a matter not for statisticians but for philosophers, as it involves the evolution of the whole planetary culture. It cannot, and should not, be answered by any one corporation, church, association, conglomeration, board, or committee of specialists. The range from acceptable to unacceptable for a "normal personality" is inextricably linked with history, belief, and cultural evolution. It has little to do with clinical categories or abnormal behaviors. Defining abnormalities belong to the medical profession and to neuroscience, whereas defining normality depends on the power of one myth over another. Freud believed religion was a cultural neurosis, a sickness that history might cure as humanity grows more mature. Believers obviously don't think so and the debate is still going on.

Practitioners of psychology are guilty of overstepping cultural boundaries each time they answer the question of what is "normal" from within the medical model of "abnormality." A lot of nonsense of self-appointed psychological experts does not appear like nonsense because of our belief that they possess a valid model of normality – and morality – although that model is never made explicit. Moralizing can then pass for sound psychological advice. When a talk show host declares on the radio: "If your fiancé doesn't suggest marriage within a few months, he may have a personality problem, he may be incapable of commitment, in which case you should drop him!" the moralizing, disguised as psychology, is made invisible. Some of these pseudo-experts of the soul have managed to convince the media that they are the legitimate voice of the profession because their use of the language of natural sciences seems able to explain inner life as one would explain the life of a cell. They profess to know what is "normal" and, with that assumption, pretend to have the means to heal the soul of most of life's suffering.

Some of them are simply well-intentioned, amiable impostors, unaware that their attitude expresses inflation and condescension rather than compassion. Their rhetoric is that of the Mother: "Come to me, I am the Good Breast." Others, more authoritarian in their approach, exhibit the rhetoric of the Father, clinging with tooth and nail to their pseudo-scientific theories: "You suffer *because*. . . ." Unlike politicians, who manipulate quite consciously, using the rhetoric of truth and compassion to build an image, most of our self-appointed experts of the soul are not really conscious of the pseudo-scientific nature of their theories. In politics, crooks are usually tolerated as long as they are successful. In psychology the quacks are tolerated as long as they can impress with their jargon which is also the language of insurance companies and social services. Although political parties all have their share of self-serving crooks, the average citizen has inherited, over many generations, a healthy suspicion toward political promises. We have a long experience in sorting out the political crooks from the political geniuses, some of whom changed humanity for the better. We are less alert in denouncing dictators of the psyche because they hide behind the language of the natural sciences, promising to "heal" souls.

## No family is ever normal

We learn relationships in a family, where conflicts are numerous, intense, and often frenzied. We are asked to choose sides, to make difficult, impossible, tragic choices. Should the money that this family has put aside to build an addition to the family house now go to offer grandma a better choice of hospices? This aging couple has dreamt for years of a vacation in Italy, and now is the time, but they also feel that they should stay home. Their pregnant daughter is expected to give birth during the time they had planned to be away. A rather soft-spoken wife finds herself suddenly furious at the fact that for years she has answered her mother-in-law's daily calls. This anger conflicts with her perception of herself as the epitome of family values. This father loves his son but finds that his parental responsibility seems never to end.

Despotism, tyranny, revolutions, fundamentalisms, heresies, triangles, alliances, and betrayals: all the causes of war have their parallel in family life where psychic combat is a daily occurrence. A normal family does not exist, if normal means a family without tension, truce, tears, without a little or a lot of drama, faults, cracks, and psychic abysses. In that context, what kind of nonsense is the psychological literature that brings our attention to an ever-growing list of family dysfunctions, as if an ideal family existed, a kind of aseptic paradise, no bugs, no shadow, no neurosis? The psychiatric model can only work when there is a standard of normality. We immediately know when a bone breaks in our leg because we have a standard of normality of how it feels to walk on a "good" leg. The sensation of having broken a bone can be confirmed by X-ray and it can be fixed by the proper medical procedure. To apply the medical model to the family "system," we would need a standard of normality for family life, which never existed.

The following account from one of my male patients illustrates how what we call "family" is in fact the only psychic place where we can feel that, as a Dolly Parton song goes, "It's all wrong, but it's all right!"

## My chaos theory of family life

I left the United States fifteen years ago, following a job offer in Paris. Each summer, I come back home to the US for a month. I visit my whole clan, family and friends, spending two or three days in each house, in five different states. Being the one who left, and missing them more than they miss me, I think I see more clearly than they do what family ties and old friendships have to offer. It is the realization that one is not the only one struggling, suffering and failing. My cousin Mary, forever on a diet, still has not lost weight. Neither have I. My brother-in-law invested all his retirement money in the farming of salmon only to discover that salmon require a silent environment to reproduce. The fish all died and he lost his shirt. I have made bad investments too. My sister is convinced that her son is addicted to marijuana but she herself can't stop smoking it. I had the same problem with my daughter. My brother's wife died three years ago in a car accident and my brother can't get "over it" because he feels guilty to be alive. He was the one driving. I too feel guilty and ashamed that I still can't figure out how to keep the love of a woman.

My annual visits fill a psychic need: to feel that I am no better, no worse than the rest of my friends and family. I need to feel our chaotic selves, our tragi-comic dramas, our successes that turn into failures and failures that are, after all, a shortcut to where we were heading with the fantasy of success. Our disordered life patterns find themselves relativized by a long, complex, intimate experience of each other through ups and downs. I define "family" as a chaotic place where one won't be prosecuted because of being imperfect, in other words, human. I include old friendships in that category; spirit can be as thick as blood.

No therapy in the world can "normalize" a family and at the same time keep it psychically alive. It is one place where the medical model that pervades much of the self-help popular psychology does more damage than good. The kind of attention that a troubled family is in need of is not psychiatric; it is more of an urgency to renew its myth about "family" to include the fact that the family is "naturally" the original place where conflicts are first experienced. Imagine a clinician who would look at a painting of a crucifixion and declare it pathological because it contains violence. We would think that person is a bit lacking in culture. For the same reason, one needs to turn to the humanities to understand the images that come out of the suffering of the soul. They are not to be looked at clinically. The failure to separate psychiatric approaches from a deeper psychological perspective contributes to the proliferation of incompetent therapists, who confuse trauma with trouble, pathology with human frailty. Psychologists and psychiatrists are schooled with less and less training in the humanities, and more and more courses in nosology (nosos in Greek means disease), pharmacology, legal and administrative issues.

There is very little information about the fact that drug companies fund research into the kind of medical diagnosis that later appears in the *DSM-IV*, so that their medications can be targeted accordingly. For example: Attention Deficit/Hyperactivity Disorder (ADHD) appears as a category in the *DSM* and – surprise – there is also a new medication for the new symptom. The vested interest of the pharmaceutical industry in the maintenance of certain diagnostic categories – and not others – and the money poured into research for these "mental disorders," shapes the *DSM* and blurs the line between a symptom that is due to brain pathology and the expression of the soul in distress.

The confusion between the territory of science and the territory of the humanities exists not only among inexperienced therapists; it exists as well in patients' mixed-up expectations. Almost all patients start the quest for self-knowledge with the medical model as their map. "Am I crazy? Can you fix me, doctor? I can't take the stress anymore, is there a cure, a drug, a healing for me?" Like most of my colleagues, my first reflex is to make sure I am not dealing with a pathology that is based on a medical condition. Then I try to be reassuring as any doctor can be, and suggest that help is on the way. I also agree to discuss or recommend medication for acute states of anxiety or depression, as a temporary support. However, to be true to a depth-psychological perspective, both patient and analyst must sooner or later abandon the medical model of the "cure" because the territory to be explored is one where the suffering part of every human being transcends clinical categories. The nosological sophistication of the *DSM*, and all the taxonomical refinements of psychiatry soon become steps in the wrong direction when dealing with the part of the psyche that is ineffable, deep, awesome, creative and of infinite complexity. No explanation can reveal the mystery of human consciousness, no theory can "explain" the relationship with oneself and with others as no theory ever could explain love. No living person can fully explain oneself to oneself, nor to another, any more than we can explain why music moves us. Still, we can all develop an appreciation of music and the arts. Similarly, an appreciation for the richness and depth of the psyche can be developed, an immense enrichment in the quality of life.

Because it follows a medical logic, the *DSM* has to define psychological symptoms in terms of their external characteristics, so that the clinician can make a diagnosis, a prognosis, a treatment plan. It is the only approach that insurance companies will pay for and for good reason, since they too belong to the clinical model. The logic of Medicare and *DSM* (reciprocally linked) excludes psychodynamic approaches because of the DSM's reliance on descriptive rather than etiologic (causal) criteria. The logic of the *DSM* is a binary one, and works like a diagnosis software; it tells the clinician how to code and branches out in a binary fashion (yes–no) until a diagnosis is made. It transforms psychotherapy into something that is increasingly technical: (a) the manual offers a precise description and statistical characteristic of a mental disorder (b) with a coding system that leads to (c) a diagnosis (d) for which the pharmaceutical industry offers a targeted medication (e) that Medicare allows on the billing form.

There is no problem with this medical logic, as long as we are in the presence of a medical problem. It must also be said that most competent clinicians don't function in that robotic mode, at least all those I know still use their "nose" to differentiate medical pathology from the ordinary manifestation of existential crises. Yet, the archetypal need to begin one's voyage into the unconscious is often mistaken and experienced, by the patient as well as by less experienced clinicians, as one form or another of "mental disorder," thus adding to the distress.

# Chapter 4

# Therapy as investment
## The economic model

The expensive education that I was offered at the Convent of the Sacred Heart was presented to me by the highly educated (and rather snobbish) Dames of the Sacred Heart as a means to maintain one's place in society; in other words, an investment to acquire or preserve one's wealth and social position. To be told that the purpose of education is to obtain wealth is to be told that the main assets in life are financial. What an error.

I am not denying the obvious financial benefits of a good education. Money is power. Who would say that he or she envies the biblical Job scratching his boils sitting on a heap of manure? The idea that poverty is a blessing sent by God to test our spiritual strength is one I don't buy into. Nevertheless, to consider education as primarily a means of social climbing reveals an inability to see the real heritage given by a rich country to its citizens: the possibility of educating oneself, a most magnificent gift. The worth of money is not in the object itself, but rather in the things and comfort one can buy with it, whereas education has value in and of itself, like life.

Considering the style of advertising campaigns they use to attract applicants, it seems that currently universities themselves "sell" their programs by putting forward their market value. This model, which makes money the supreme value, has permeated not only education but also the milieu of psychotherapy. New patients will often say they have decided to invest in a psychotherapy. They present problems that are felt as problems mainly because they are a hindrance to productivity. They want to get rid of the irrational emotions that distract the working mind, or the love affair that might break up the marriage and end up in a costly divorce. They imagine therapy as a problem-solving process, a removal of the obstacles for the homo economicus to function flawlessly, a coaching in transforming oneself into a high performance machine – a reliable, tough, all-wheel drive that would run on all-terrain without breaking down, until one reaches the end of life. Done! In this fantasy, death seems like the end of the "to-do" list. I have heard many formulations of the same utilitarian model: therapy as a kind of lubrication of the interpersonal mechanisms, as a means of improving comfort in human relations, as a method to maximize libidinal investments, or as a kind of diversification of one's spiritual portfolio. It is only later into the analysis – and sometimes never – that a patient is able to understand that awareness and psychological sophistication – just like education, art, elegance, gastronomy, philosophy, love, flowers, music – have intrinsic value.

A depth-psychological analysis is an occasion to discover that telling my "life's story" implies many degrees of refinement; it can be told with or without art, finesse, depth. The first beneficiary of an elaborate, stylish, rich version of my life's story is myself, just like the first beneficiary of a rich education is the person who is given that opportunity. The complex subtlety of life stories is not just the property of the well-read and highly educated. Anybody who cares about the quality of inner life can develop the necessary psychological talents. I resent the suggestion that developing self-awareness is reserved for the elite who can afford therapy. Exercises in self-awareness could very well be a part of the curriculum of every school. I have worked with children, with poor college students, with abused men and women, with patients who had received minimal education, and I have experienced first-hand how one needs only to take seriously the first gift that we all receive from our culture: a structured, complex, and very magical tool called language.

We can all learn some refinement of language to help us tell our stories more efficiently. This is where cognitive-behavioral approaches to psychotherapy (based on learning of conscious abilities) does overlap with a depth-psychological perspective (uncovering the unconscious psychodynamics). I find it annoying that cognitive-behavioral approaches still "sell" themselves by using the logic of the financial "bottom line" because there is much more to it. It is an obvious fact that, as short-term approaches, cognitive-behavioral therapies do cost less. Cognitive-behavioral therapies also do not look down on the need for "adaptability" in the workplace, whereas depth psychology has historically appealed more to those who were socially successful or competent but needed to make room for or peace with the rebellious core of their Self. Nevertheless, although arguments of profitability have helped sell the cognitive approach, I believe it is an error to put "cognitive" in opposition to "depth."

I have trained social workers who specialized in therapy for men convicted of domestic violence. The men were sent to me by court order; all, without exception, turned out to be suffering from a poverty of language, an incapacity to translate their frustration, anger, and disappointment into words. While there are plenty of categories in the *DSM* to label their violent behavior, the *DSM* does not have a category for "poverty of language."[1] Yet this basic cultural lack remains at the very core of violence: their cultural milieu has failed these men in the transmission of the most important legacy from one generation of humans to the other – language.[2] Along with the psychiatric diagnosis, I would suggest a cultural definition: a violent man is one whose repressed humanity, capable of so much more expressivity, is reduced to shouting, grunting, grumbling, and hitting. In most of these cases, a cognitive-behavioral approach does make sense, not only because of the time and budgetary limitations, but more essentially because the cognitive therapy implies an unlearning of the usual problematic response (i.e., hitting) followed by cognitive development of a new capacity to communicate: using words rather than blows. A cognitive-behavioral therapy is a form of *education* in human relations not at all incompatible with a desire to visit the Underworld.

The fact that the cognitive approach does not explicitly deal with the unconscious psychodynamics does not mean that they are not present. All stories that grip us like a myth, all ideologies, all cultural complexes hiding in the background, have extremely deep roots. Learning communication and cognitive skills is a worthy goal. Becoming aware of the immensity of the width and depth of our repressed humanity is a different end, and as worthy. Since life is a voyage, it is possible to visit both the place in us that honors the cognitive abilities, as well as places of great psychic depth. The following vignette reveals how the development of cognitive and communication skills is sometimes the necessary introduction to other more mysterious aspects of psychic life.

## My first lesson in communication

It's not as if I had a choice. The judge made it clear: either therapy or prison. At the first session the therapist asked me to replay word for word the scene that got me arrested. The other men in the group were all offenders like myself and they were clear about their intention of getting the story out of me. Here is how I told the story. I come home after a long day of work. I am tired, hungry and grumpy and my truck's transmission is showing signs of stress. My wife is on the phone, arguing with her mom, as usual. Dinner is not ready, dirty dishes from breakfast still on the table. There is nothing in the refrigerator, my wife doesn't even say hello. I shout, "Why can't you cook a decent meal? Because you're a slut, that's why!" She looks at me with contempt and blows her cigarette smoke in my face. I hit her on the cheek, and it dislocates her jawbone. She calls 911 and I end up in court.

The therapist went to the blackboard. With the help of the whole group, we analyzed my communications with my wife, breaking it down as if analyzing a movie. The therapist divided the huge blackboard into five columns. In the first column he wrote only what a camera would show at the beginning of a scene; in other words, the facts that establish an atmosphere in which the story begins: (a) it's 7:00 pm (I began my day at 7:00 am), and dinner is nowhere in sight; (b) dishes are piled up; (c) the refrigerator is empty; and (d) I just had transmission trouble with my truck.

To fill the second column, the therapist questioned me for a while to discover what a putative actor would want to know in order to play my part, which are the emotions, the sensations and the feelings of the protagonist (me). The therapist helped me discover the following: (a) I am hungry and angry that dinner is not ready; (b) I find the house unkempt and dirty and it makes me feel like I am a failure because I live in a dump; (c) I feel I am less important than the endless list of people my wife spends her time with on the phone; and (d) when she blows her cigarette smoke in my face, I feel my wife has contempt for me and it enrages me. I was really beginning to see the movie we were enacting.

The third column was for what, in a movie, would be the "ideas and values" communicated. This was much harder for me to fill in because I had no idea what these were for me. We began with a list of things I believed a wife "should" do and should be. I made some interesting discoveries, things that I didn't know I had believed; for example: (a) my wife should do all the housekeeping and cooking because she works only part time and I work full time – if she doesn't, she is a slut; (b) a wife should keep herself sexually attractive and available for her husband without foreplay; (c) a man should punish his wife, verbally if not physically, if she doesn't live up to his expectations or agreements. I had no idea that I had thought these thoughts.

The fourth column was easy. It was the list of actions of the protagonist that began to define the plot that had to unfold as a consequence of the first scene. My actions were: (a) to shout; (b) to insult; and (c) to hit.

The fifth column followed the plot in listing the consequences of the previous behavior: (a) the court order; (b) tension in the house; and (c) two therapy sessions a week. This is where I was in my own personal movie.

I never imagined I could talk as much as I did in this group. I learned to communicate. After three months of therapy, I had another fight with my wife. This time, I was a communication champion. Instead of hitting, I slowed down as the therapist had showed me to do. I breathed deeply and it slowed me down. I did my thinking before saying anything. I analyzed the whole situation in terms of the five columns. When I was clear about it, I said: "When I come home after a long day of work, I am very hungry" [sensation]. "If there is nothing ready for dinner" [fact] "and dirty dishes are piled up" [fact], "I feel as if I don't count" [feeling], "that I have no importance" [feeling]. "I don't feel very welcome in my home" [feeling]. "What I am going to do is go out to a restaurant to have a nice dinner" [action]. "I'll be back when I have eaten" [action].

And bing! I left and went to a nice restaurant. I have now used my new strategy a few times, and it is beginning to have a powerful effect on her (which is a consequence). My new behavior is shaking her, I can see, but in a way that does not send me to prison.

I have used cognitive approaches to teach basic communication skills, most of which are lacking in our educational system. The term "depth psychology" is also often presented in opposition to a behavioral-cognitive approach, which is mainly concerned with the possibilities of modifying conscious behavior, thus completely bypassing the notion of the unconscious. Cognitive-behavioral therapists will hold the prejudice that the depth perspective calls for too long an inner voyage, with the consequent danger of getting lost in too vast a territory. Depth psychologists will hold the reciprocal prejudice, depicting cognitive-behavioral therapies as a fix-it-quick-and-get-back-to-work approach dictated by managed care. Nonetheless, often these contrasting approaches are simply different tools, not necessarily in competition, and not theoretically incompatible, as in the example above. There is no incompatibility between a behavioral-cognitive approach, focused on learning some better adjusted behaviors, and an imaginal approach focused on the inner voyage. Like the choice between two areas of study, choosing between a behavioral-cognitive approach or an arche-typal-imaginal approach depends on whether one wants to accomplish the long pilgrimage that is the search for a new self or to take a course in communication to improve relationships.

Both the cognitive-behavioral approach as well as the depth-psychological approach involve the learning of a sophisticated, even sumptuous language. These two approaches coincide precisely at the point of learning new linguistic patterns. They differ in the choice of what needs to be accomplished. The cognitive-behavioral approach is symptom oriented and presents itself as "profitable" in terms of behavior modification, which is why it is so appealing to the prevalent economic model of managed care as well as to the judicial model. Yet it is not the whole story because the meaning that develops with the learning of new words is one of the deepest, most complex aspects of any culture. Any ideology that tries to reduce words to their utilitarian or technical meaning turns out to be a totalitarian one. Words have deep, deep roots. The man who can learn about his sexist values and his limited grasp of language can initiate a process of transformation that will last a lifetime. The cognitive therapy that helps him learn a new behavior may be over, but the opening of the psyche is just beginning.

One can learn a second or third language for utilitarian, professional reasons, but many persons learn a new language for less rational reasons: to discover another country or its literature, as an intellectual exercise, or because it appeals to the soul. I have a friend who is a judge in a criminal court, which means he spends most of his days hearing stories of deception, meanness, and perversity. At the age of 40 he felt an urge to learn Italian, to be able to sing along with the operas that he loves on his CDs, in the language in which they were written. It is perfectly useless; he has no plan to travel to Italy, and he will never be a professional singer. His pleasure is enough of a justification. He is a different person when he sings in Italian: his usual reserve disappears and his whole being is infused with Mediterranean passion. His Italian fantasy balances his life in a way that is very similar to the benefits of an in-depth analysis. His singing is an expression of his soul. It is an unproductive, frivolous waste of time if one follows the economic model, yet it contributes to the quality of his life.

There are many metaphors that can move psychoanalysis away from the economic model; one can imagine it as singing a duet with one's soul, or as a dance between one's body and soul. In many traditional societies, laborers, even when they do back-breaking chores all week, are eager to go to the village dance on weekends. Why? Dance is useless; it is a spending of precious energy. The energetic waste of dance was one of the arguments used by the Puritans to forbid dancing, along with the frivolity of flowers, lace, the indulgence of pastry, and lovemaking without the goal of procreation, an unacceptable waste of sperm.

If one considers dance from an economic perspective, it is indeed an expenditure of energy without compensation. Nevertheless, humans in all cultures throughout history seem to have enjoyed dancing. Why? They also enjoy endlessly complicating the intricate steps of the dance, a proof that complexity can be pleasurable. Consider the complexity of flamenco, the intricate rhythms of tap dancing, the sensual intermingling of the tango, the extra subtle grace of the minuet, the jovial tricky intermixing of square dancing, the exhausting heat of rock and roll, the impetus of the polka. All these styles reflect one form or other of the complexity of the modalities of human relations. Yet, their complexity is there to be enjoyed for itself; it serves no other purpose. It is play, not work, a being, not a doing.

Human relations can be experienced as pleasurably complex, filled by the psyche's infinite capacity to dance with life. That we now do our "workouts" alone at the gym, with expensive mechanical apparatus, instead of dancing with a partner or a group, says something about the predominance of the economic model. A workout seems less frivolous, more efficient, and more easily accommodated to our work schedules. It is a basically puritanical attitude. A workout may be fine if the objective is to build muscle mass or a persona that sells well on the personality market, but when applied to relationships the let's-work-on-our-relationship attitude is just the kind of workout that destroys the very thing it is trying to save: pleasure. How important it is indeed to remember that relationships are a dance, not a set of problems to figure out and work through.

The glory of money in our culture is such that we are constantly led to believe that if only we had enough of it, everything would work out fine. Many things are in fact made easier with money, but it is interesting to examine what happens psychologically when one suddenly receives a lot of money, either by inheritance or sudden financial success. The magical feeling is felt in the first few months but it evaporates quickly. The intense jubilation of the newly rich is not renewable; it is a once only experience, like losing one's virginity, or seeing one's name in print in one's first published book. Why? Feelings of comfort, security, appreciation for nice things may last, but not the magic. The psyche that bought into the economic model is surprised to find itself still hungry, and frustrated to discover that the magic is not working as potently as expected. As one client noted:

> When I was poor and frustrated I knew what I desired –
> money, more money, encore money! Now that I have

reached this overrated peak I feel like I did after spending a
month climbing Kilimanjaro, only to discover that after a
few hours of looking at the absolutely gorgeous panorama, I
was bored, and wondered, "What am I doing here?"

The prevailing financial model of our culture suggests that money
is the only bottom line, the one magical power, the solid foundation upon which rest work and love. There is, no doubt, a financial
aspect to all relationships, even the most romantic. Early feminists
were absolutely right when they insisted that women become
financially independent because money is a basis that supports the
bullish reality of the market, an essential material foundation
indeed. Nevertheless, on top of that rock-solid foundation there is
another level, this one fragile, elusive, crystalline, made of dreams,
a house where the butterfly dares challenge the god Money. "OK!
Thou art a foundation. What shall I build on top of you?" The
acquisition of wealth only feels like a mirage when one confuses
the hunger of *having* more with the hunger for *being* more. An
economical model can satisfy a strictly economic craving. It
cannot, however, satisfy an ontological craving.

   Rich and healthy societies function at their best when they can
reconcile two opposite systems of values. On the one hand the
economic model is a system of pure competition, a war without
frontiers, a worldwide global competition that stimulates production. It creates winners as well as losers, an inevitable outcome of
any kind of war and of progress. Yet, a truly affluent society also
considers the ecological system or model of limited growth, protection, preservation, conservation and, contrary to the economic
model, is attached to a sense of place and local communities.
The ecological model implies a refusal to benefit financially if
the exploitation of a collective resource represents a risk for its
preservation. Depth psychology definitely belongs to the ecological
model, and as such balances the cognitive-behavioral necessity for
short-term efficiency and economy of means.

   The adventure of self-discovery never did, and never will, fit
within the financial model of managed care programs that allow 9
or 12 sessions to repair a psyche and fit the person back into the
workplace or the family system. To be sure, we do need the best
possible repair shops for broken souls, more of them indeed, with

the best theoretical fix-it kits that even a beginning psychotherapist can apply with confidence and competence. Public funds used for those programs is money well invested. Here, the economic model is relevant. Yet, brief therapies and strictly cognitive-behavioral approaches cannot replace and cannot compete with the winding paths that call to inner adventure for no other immediate purpose than to satisfy one's soul, much as a neophyte in antiquity went to Eleusis, in order to be initiated into the mysteries. Depth psychology offers an education in lucidity, a personalized program in the humanities, an esthetic experience of dancing and singing through the complexities of life. It may or may not "fix" one for the workplace, but it does bring something immensely valuable to those wounded by the grayness of their lives, to those lacking inner adventure, deprived of sensual perception, concerned by the absence of pathos in their drama. Some lives suffer from a tragic poverty of imagination. When the imagination loses its vitality, one loses the sense of meaning, the point of living. A flat, tired, worn out, unimaginative myth kills one faster than work-related stress.

The following young "dot.com" millionaire was shocked to discover that retiring at 25 years old had unsuspected psychological drawbacks for which there was no "fix."

## Having and being, and figuring out the difference

I worked very hard for a year and a half and was quite lucky. I made a fortune and retired at 25. Then I created a website, thinking that all my friends, all those whom I had made rich, would be interested in the progress of the building of my mansion and its ecological garden filled with exotic, rare plants. In three months, I had 20 hits. In my business I usually had 100,000 or more a month. Those 20 hits were from my mom, dad, brother and sister – each a couple of times, commenting on the photos from the family album that were posted on my website. Then I understood. I understood that I didn't understand a thing about money, that money is only that – money. Once you have it, even lots of it, you still have to *be*. How am I supposed to do that? What should I *do* to *be*? Where to begin with beingness? I only know how to do. Doing is how I captured wealth and now I feel I have become its captive. Naively, I married a woman who is the consummate "trophy wife." My lovely expensive doll expects me to do the same trick again and again, to earn fresh money, to leave the house every morning and be defined by the addition of millions to our portfolio. This is who I am to her – a genius at making money, her pension plan. When I try to find other values, she says she doesn't know me anymore. She doesn't understand why I am looking elsewhere because I am so talented at doing what I do best, and by that she means making money. I want to be a master, but I am a servant. I need guidelines on how to *be*.

This young successful adult did not know that a financial portfolio can grow by addition, but this is not so for the psyche. He did not understand how the psyche expands, lightens, darkens, unfolds, dances, and falls; how it sings, shouts, moans, and laughs; how it deepens through repeated experiences of joy and tears, pleasure and pain, birth and death, connection and loss, abandonment and mating. He had bought into the myth of "psychological growth," one which reveals its association with an economic model.

# Chapter 5

# Therapy as plea

## The legal model

The hostile adolescent who steals money from his or her father's wallet, who refuses to apologize when he or she wrecks the grandfather's car, or who has learned neither the art of love nor the art of war, is not yet civilized. The Greeks would have said he belonged to Artemis, not yet ripe for the life of a citizen, still wild, unbroken to the bridle of adulthood. This adolescent is someone who has not yet fully grasped the fact that there is no avoiding the paternal principle. The adolescent mind has no comprehension of how the multitudinous authorities of civilization can impact his life once he leaves home. An adolescent has yet to learn to confide intimate feelings, knowing only how to growl, grunt, or furiously pluck the strings of his or her electric guitar to express the cacophony within himself or herself. To be able to communicate deep confidences, one needs not only words but also a culture that is not cynical toward the need for sincerity, a sympathetic heart to relate to, and a certain kind of psychological intimacy. Such capacity for intimacy is not fostered by a trend in family therapy that borrows the style of legal mediation. Many family therapists talk about their work as being that of mediator, borrowing this term from the judicial model. Members of the family speaking to the "mediator-therapist" also adopt a style that resembles a legal defense.

The basic technique of such psychological mediators seems fair enough. Each member of the family is respectfully invited to give his or her side of the story. What is less discussed is the therapist's role as the judge of the authenticity of these disclosures and as judge of who is hurting who. The therapist's judgments are not handed down in any forthright manner but communicated through the body language of the therapist. The problem with this approach arises when the participants leave the therapy room and start playing the same game but without the presence of the therapist. Soon, the expression of an emotion, "I hurt," appears as an accusation: "You are hurting me." The next step is even more problematic: "You hurt me, therefore you owe me." Family members have learned a transactional game of victims and perpetrators (the legal model) with no mediator in sight and the game can become quite nasty.

A family's need for therapy usually indicates a lack of psychological intimacy but it is a mistake to think that any sort of communication about emotions necessarily leads to familial closeness. If the verbal exchanges have the slightest hint of a game of victims and perpetrators, the therapy will never lead to intimacy. Ordinary experiences of intimacy are frequently non-verbal and happen in sharing the space in which our bodies interact. Intimacy can be created in silent exchanges, while doing all the things a family does together under one roof. The belief that therapy happens mostly in verbal exchanges about what hurts (modeling the legal offense) can deprive a family of much of its natural psychological wisdom. Being "psychological" and "intimate" does not necessarily imply the mediation of the therapist. Here is an example of intimacy between friends which is at the very opposite of the genre of the therapeutic disclosure, yet it is intimacy of the kind that is often missing in a family in trouble.

## Redefining intimacy

I visit a long-time colleague at his home to work on a text we co-authored and that needs editing. At dinnertime, we are still not finished. He invites me to stay and have a bite, so that we can continue our work. I go into the kitchen to help him fix dinner. We have been colleagues for many years, most of the time allies, sometimes enemies in a few departmental wars. Perhaps we should call ourselves friends, although, somehow, we never share any intimate details about our private lives. It is the first time I have seen his house. Helping fix dinner reveals to me his culinary style and preferences. We are the same kind of cooks – fast and messy – using tongue and finger more often than recipes or measuring cup. We whip up a very good dinner in no time! Now I understand why collaborating with him on this project seems so easy; our minds work in the same way.

With our dish cooking in the oven, he leaves the kitchen to listen to his voicemail. I go back to the living room and browse through his bookshelves. Given the importance of books in both of our lives, this perusal represents quite a high degree of intimacy. In actuality, I am not being indiscreet since his books are openly displayed on the shelves. I choose at random one of Jung's books and see that we have highlighted some of the same passages. Next, I browse through his CD collection, also on display. We have many of the same oldies and many of the same classics. More surprising is the CD on his player, an old recording of Nina Simone with the song "Consummation." I believe her voice most perfectly expresses that love is joy. He is not in the room, yet I have an immediate sense of connection.

Mostly, we exchange ideas and information. No confidences or talking about ourselves. Yet, the world of his books, of his CDs, the decor of his house, a certain sadness that I read on his face, the absence of pictures of his ex-wife, all this is as revealing as an exchange of secrets. In this moment I feel closer to him than ever before in our years of being colleagues. We are having "physical contact" – not through our bodies but within the body of the house; not through telling secrets, but by reading the secrets of the mind revealed through the books. The secrets of our souls are revealed through the voice of the singer he savors as much as me. Those secrets are there; one has only to have the desire to read them.

Many sorts of intimate contact are wordless and without an arbitrator who might determine their psychological validity. A therapeutic context influenced by the model of mediation has popularized an approach that is like holding court in the family living room, talking about *you and me and us*, each defending their actions and reactions. All the *talk* about feelings can unfortunately also take the place of having them. I am not denying that the validating of everyone's feelings is important, but there are other forms of communication between souls, equally expressive, valid, and profound, even if less verbose and even if no one takes on the role of mediator. Some elements of communication have no intermediary; they cannot be interpreted by means of a theoretical grid, and won't manifest if someone takes on the role of judge.

The creation of a story belongs to each person. In a family, we each have our version of the same, yet different stories. The temptation to use the tools of the therapist to rewrite the other's story is often irresistible. Here is a typical case where a woman has to fight against her husband in the battle of stories. His training in psychology works against his desire for intimacy, because he takes the position of judge. He has given himself the gavel and regularly declares his wife guilty of perpetrating neurotic behaviors.

## My husband, the psychologist: the battle of stories

I am a cabinetmaker, an artist working with wood. I sculpt the furniture I make with my own flowery designs. My husband is a psychologist. Our marriage is at the breaking point. I can no longer take his interpretations of me. We make each other crazy – he by pursuing me with his brilliant insights, and I by erecting a wall of platitudes to avoid hearing him. He feels I am cynical because I tell him his insights are brilliant and then completely ignore them. I am not making fun of him; I really think he is the most astute psychologist I have ever known. He is right on target each time he interprets my complexes.

What I cannot tolerate is the fact that he listens to me through a theoretical filter. I feel as if I were talking into a mike hooked into translating software. For example, he tries to convince me to stop seeing my family, that they are not good for me. He is absolutely right about that. My family fabricates trauma as others make music together. My husband's theories are valid, but they seem to imply that my family has victimized me. That is the part that I reject, and why I go on seeing them. It is my form of resistance. As a defense against my husband's brilliant interpretations, I wrote him the following letter:

If the goal of therapy is to really help me evolve beyond my earlier context, does it not also suggest that I have the power to refuse the interpretations in which you wish to imprison me? I don't want to be defined by my abusive childhood. When you give all that importance to the faults of my parents and siblings, you define me by my traumas, as if the traumas had the power to create the person I am now. Why do you systematically downplay the psychological influence of the teacher who taught me woodworking? He lived next to my parents, and he was an admirable being, someone upon whom I have tried to model myself. Your theory also does not account for my horse. Yes, my horse. At the craziest period of my adolescence I loved that animal more than I have ever loved any person. He may have been only an animal; yet, he was the living presence who really accompanied me through my teens. My horse heard my troubles, felt my sadness, carried my body and my psyche. In summer I spent entire days on his back. He had the power to calm me. He reassured me about the goodness of life. Since I loved this horse more than I loved my father, why does your psychology not allow me to say that I was parented by a horse? When I visit home, I like the smell of the barn, that particular barn, where my old saddle still hangs on a hook. Why do you keep on analyzing the relationship between you and me as if you-and-I-and-our-relationship were the beginning and end of everything in life?

The most important relationship for me right now, I am sorry to tell you, is not my relationship with you. It is my relationship with wood! Were you ever curious about my relationship with wood? Have we ever discussed the beauty I feel in the golden reflection on freshly varnished oak, the red veins of cherry wood, the pearly whiteness of birch, the clean smell of cedar, or the indolent softness of linden wood? The family of trees is the family with whom I spend my days. You refuse to expand your theory to include horse, teacher or wood in your definition of "family history." You analyze me in order not to hear me, to neutralize me. You interpret my life to justify your theories. You are too lazy to examine your thinking or consider new possibilities. Everything has to go into your analytical funnel because your perspective has become the wall you've erected to avoid the unsettling effect I have on you. You use theory to attempt to convince yourself (and me) that you understand me better than I do myself. You think you are a better judge than I of what is trauma and what is healing, what is valuable and what is not. I received a gift from my horse, an instinct that tells me to avoid your interpretations. They are not a good pasture for me.

In a family torn apart, who will be declared the number one victim? The person who convinced the therapist/judge that he or she was abused? What happens when one person begins asking for psychological indemnity from the others? The temptation of many inexperienced therapists is to deal with these problems in a very expeditious manner, to award the prize of victimhood to the person who had the best "defense," or sometimes – which is more perverse – to the person who is paying. The judicial model, when imported into the psychological realm, can imprison a person in the victim scenario forever.

# Chapter 6

# Therapy as redemption

Humanity redeemed! The myth of redemption is so pervasive that it permeates global politics, education, ecology, feminism. Depth psychology is not exempt. Ostensibly the analysand starts an analysis in pursuit of consciousness, but covertly the process can conceal a quest for redemption, masquerading as individuation, actualization, psychological health, wholeness, centeredness, mindfulness, or whatever new jargon accommodates the old myth. The smell of redemption is easily recognizable. It is the belief that analyzing the unconscious will lead to a clean, pure, healthy psyche and that one will evolve into a luminous, loving, dignified, pacified soul. Having attained this level of enlightenment, this cleansed soul wraps itself in a (metaphorical) white robe and awaits initiation into the world of the resuscitated, the individuated, the Elysian fields of psychological saints. Such a utopian dream would be nice were it not for the fact that it produces an odious, sanctimonious persona. To break the trance, one needs to differentiate redemption from individuation, salvation from wisdom. The following letter from a friend, a former colleague, shows somebody who suddenly understood that the time allotted for our life is finite, but the quest for perfection is not. His ego-driven pursuit of perfection was causing exhaustion. With his permission, I reproduce his letter.

## Off with my halo

I have finally put an end to my years of pilgrimage en route toward what I thought was individuation. There is a subpersonality in "me" – let's call it the missionary –

that has always wanted to "sanctify" the immature me. The missionary-in-me kept imposing noble goals such as individuation, illumination, compassion, detachment from ego, and the like. At the same time, this missionary kept refusing me the medal of individuation, on the basis that my relationships with my children, as well as my relationships with women, are still pretty neurotic.

I have been trying to please this inner figure who obviously refuses to be pleased. He doesn't understand that the process of individuation is an endless process, not a state of purity to which one can aspire. My inner missionary was after redemption, perfection, and sanctity. I am an exhausted pilgrim, out of spiritual wind from the long ascension towards an apotheosis of individuation, which seems to be non-existent, as I have never found it in myself or anyone else.

My missionary was impervious even to Jung's warnings that individuation can never be complete, that one can never be freed from the grip of the ego and the internal demons. I have tried admonishing him: "Shut up! Don't you see that individuation is like any ideal – democracy, justice, freedom, or charity? Noble ideals, all of them! We need them; we try to follow them, but no one attains them completely. Stop your proselytizing!"

Maybe there is something inherent in Jungian theory that invites such devotion to the principium individuationis. As far as I am concerned, the result is pitiful. My "illuminations" are mostly sparks from the ego. Well, the saint in me is resigning, and I am declaring spiritual bankruptcy. End of quest for sanctity! I want my humanity back. I want to honor Dionysos, not Augustine.

Sometimes it is almost irresistible to consider depth psychology as a new form of spiritual asceticism, a redemptive quest. The prose in which both Freud and Jung wrote is lush and powerful enough to open the door to that kind of fantasy. Just as the spiritual need is real, so is the danger of inflation. To avoid spiritual puffiness, I have found it useful to move away from imagining analysis as a spiritual discipline, to entertain instead images of a conversation between friends, like the exchange of letters with this particular friend. Conversations between friends have been going on for generations, discussing how to become more enlightened. The nice thing about being with close friends is that the ego can take a rest and humor is possible. The image of befriending the psyche can inspire analysis. My psyche and I are going on an excursion into a territory other than that of the ego, widening one's panorama and nurturing a sense of humor about one's own foibles.

The character of mythology that most aptly suggests a humble attitude toward "individuation" is Hermes (Mercurius for the Romans), the endearing Greek god who has a nose for puffed up egos. God of travelers and champion of paradoxical thinkers, Hermes embodies the possibility of double, triple, and multiple significations. Analysis is such a mercurial adventure, a sojourn into the land of paradoxical truths and multiple significations. When the ego has to travel, it prefers package deals and spiritual organized tours, religious traditions and well-worn paths. But to experience Hermes one has to outwit the ego and slip away like a con artist evading the sheriff. Depth psychology is at a place in its evolution where it can justifiably call itself post-Freudian, post-Jungian, post-Lacanian, post-modern – post anything that pretends to delimit the territory of inner life. For depth psychology to emerge as a form of wisdom, a revivification of the imagination, it needs to escape from inflation about the quasi-divine principle of the "Self."

Aren't we all seeking an escape from ego fixations, including theoretical fixations upon the masters that have trained us? Deification of the masters is, in itself, a sign that the myth of redemption is active. The masters who ask to be "adored" by their disciples are usually in the business of selling redemption ("Think like me and you'll be saved!"). For many adoring disciples there comes a day when they notice that their idol has feet of clay. The "master" turns out to be not the omniscient redeemer but merely human. Having placed him on a pedestal, the disciple now feels that he must knock him off. The critique then becomes vicious, fueled by a sense of betrayal and disillusionment. However, such decanonization would not have been necessary had they not deified their master in the first place.

One of my doctoral students, a brilliant woman of 40, had made Jung her redeemer, and was convinced that another round of analysis would finally resolve the conflicts in her marriage. What happened instead is that her husband asked for a divorce and she was devastated. She shared with me the note he left on her pillow the day he left.

### Lost in a mandala

You have been in analysis for the past ten years. You seem to be telling me, "Wait, there is this little corner of my mandala that I still have to explore. As soon as I complete my puzzle-mandala, I should be able to have a non-narcissistic relationship with you." Where do you think you are going with this mandala trip? I think you have already reached your destination and that is nowhere! Your principle of individuation is like madness; you remind me of those saints intoxicated with vanity about their performances of auto-flagellation. I have rejected the Church, why should I put up with your kind of religiosity? I can put up with the cost of ten years of analysis, but I can't bear the loneliness anymore. I can't wait until all is clean and smooth in your inner landscape. I prefer solitude, or the company of people less ambitious in their spiritual goals.

The problem here is not the length of the analysis but the fact that the wife was caught in the very Christian myth of a redemptive ideal, a myth she did not recognize because it presented itself in the language of psychological goals. She has lived the life of a deportee from paradise. We all do, to a certain measure. Neither Voltaire, nor Nietzsche, nor Freud, nor Jung, nor Sartre, nor any of the modern philosophers of atheism are completely free of the redemption myth. God may have been declared dead, but the mourning is not finished; it is too big a loss to be completed in just a few generations. Jung's nostalgia for God resurfaces at times in his theory about the Self (capital S). The woman who lost herself in her fantasy of mandala amplified that trend and believed in Jungian theory as one believes in a savior, because she too misses the certainties of faith.

Until our mourning is done, the fantasy of redemption will grow out of all sorts of grounds. I know for one that I am not immune. For sure, like most intellectuals of my generation and of my milieu, I endorsed the Nietzschean revolt against the religious traditions of our culture. Disgusted by the shadow of faith, we felt that our intellectual mission was to teach and write in such a way as to reveal the insufferable racism and sexism and authoritarianism of institutionalized religions. We fought against the very idea that humans would conceive and then submit to divinities such as Yahweh, Christ, Allah, tyrannical prima donnas who insisted on being the one and only. We were morally shocked to discover the viciousness of the wars between the three monotheisms, each demanding of their devotees that they sacrifice their lives in ugly wars. Our rallying cry was Zarathustra's "God is dead." This intellectual revolt provided me with an enduring motivation to practice psychotherapy: I felt then – and still do today – that a world without God need not be a desperate world. The work of psychotherapy is a daily battle against despair.

Nevertheless, the deconstruction of conventional religion does not alleviate the need for a sense of the sacred; but where is it? Surely, life is about more than the individual's journey from birth to death? The myth of redemption resurfaces in every cause that is dear to one's heart. Some feminists dream of a world redeemed by matriarchy (when women rule, all will be fine.) I know many ecologists who envision a world redeemed by nature (nature is good and, left to herself, all should be fine). Others seek political redemption (this party will change everything); financial redemption (as soon as I have enough, I'll follow my bliss); romantic redemption (one day my prince or princess will come); psychological redemption (one day I'll be individuated, one of the illuminati). Each of these fantasies stems from the monotheistic mythology. Even the ideal of Buddhist detachment can conceal a typical Christian fantasy where the guru replaces God, and an all-encompassing philosophical system serves as faith.

I like to tease one of my doctoral students, who is a Jungian analyst, that his unshakeable faith in Jung makes him a *Jungiodule* (adorer of Jung) instead of a Jungian. Who is immune to this kind of temptation? The atheist thinks God does not exist, the agnostic thinks there is no possible way to know, the faithful believes God definitely exists; what we all have in common is the desire to find meaning in life, and for meaning to manifest, we all need to imagine something beyond ego, something that transcends personal fate. Our life stories, if not inserted into a grander narrative shared by a community, are too insignificant to register as consequential. We crave art, literature, and music to give some amplitude to the banality of our existences, to attach importance to the ancestors who preceded us and to the progeny that shall continue sprouting branches on one's family tree.

When a talented historian writes the stories of a people we call that activity "history" and we derive a sense of tribal identity from reading it. Wars, won or lost, are elevated to historic grandeur, tragic but glorious battles fought in the name of some great value. Similarly, to make sense of my small life, I need the amplification of my ordinary life journey into something I can call an odyssey. I want the magnification of my battles at the office into an Iliad; I know my house is not a castle, but in a way it is. This aggrandizement of our story, which is not at all an aggrandizement of the ego, is a valid protection against feelings of absurdity.

Lives sacrificed in defense of a country, empires rising and falling, populations swelling and diminishing – all these stories, once historicized, have a narrative logic, a kind of consistency in the thematic structure. But in the lives of nations, as well as individuals, in times of great difficulty, the narrative logic breaks down and the transformation of facts into history fails. One tries to tell the events this way and that way, from this or that perspective, but the collection of facts remains absurd. The wars turn out to be pointless – so many dead, and for what? – and the trajectory of one's life seemingly random – what was *that* all about? The breakdown in the narrative capacity is often interpreted as a form of despair, like the despair of losing one's faith. Yet it can also signal a very different kind of breakdown, that of the redemptive myth, not the narrative capacity. Only then can the loss of the redemptive hope appear as a necessary loss.

## Life is absurdly, awesomely ugly and beautiful

Having witnessed the disorientation of meaninglessness in so many of my own patients, students, friends, I had my own turn at life as an incomprehensible absurdity. In the months following my brain injury, every possible variation of my life's trajectory appeared to be equally nonsensical, a pointless story filled with absurdist tropes à la Beckett, a sadistic play with neither tail nor head. I finally understood why the existentialists linked that feeling of "life as absurd" to the loss of God. It does not matter much if the loss of faith is in God, in love, in the nation, in progress, in family, in nature, or in psychology. Existential angst can happen with whatever value, theory, mission, ideal that has been elevated to an absolute in order to generate meaning.

When I left intensive care, I was the recipient of a very generous offer to stay in a magnificent house in the desert of New Mexico. It was a grand luxurious mansion, surrounded by cacti and many newly planted miniature weeping birch trees whose gracious tiny leaves seemed to caress the glass of the windows of the room where I stayed for 10 days. The owners were generous strangers, friends of friends, whom I have still never met. They were leaving town and offered my daughter and me a place to stay until I was fit to travel. From the day of my accident onwards, I had the feeling that I had walked onstage of the Theater of the Absurd. How is it that I am not dead? Why was I spared trepanation, paralysis, death? What did I do to deserve a second chance? This sense of unworthiness and unreality was intensified by the act of surprising generosity by the owners of the house, people I did not know. Why are they so good to the stranger I am to them? They are generous because they are generous which does not make sense, but it does.

I also discovered that a total absorption in observing the beauty of the tiny birch leaves catching the desert light and the desert breeze could be infinitely more potent than painkillers. The beauty of these young fragile trees, seen through the six windows of my room, was uncanny. Life itself felt like a coincidence. The fact that the beauty of the surroundings was more analgesic than morphine only added to the feeling that nothing made "sense" in the usual way, especially being alive. The most interesting aspect of that absurdist feeling was that my near-death experience was not at all what some have described as a "renewed sense of the meaning of life." Not for me; logic escaped me more than ever. Instead of a "renewed meaning" I was experiencing an increased tolerance of absurdity. Instead of existential angst, I felt an existential lightness, a sweet appreciation for the random mercy of survival, the unsolicited generosity of strangers, the incomprehensible power of beauty, the healing quality of a beautiful home (as compared to the cockpit décor of intensive care.) The realization that life is fragile, short and chaotic ended my fantasy of redemption; life does not require it. I was suddenly finished with the list of things to do, to be, to get, to improve upon before I allow myself to contemplate the beauty of everything that exists in the world. There are already – every day, every minute – plenty of immediate reasons for jubilation, and no need for the fantasies of redemption, of paradise after death, of bliss the morning after the revolution. "You are telling me, Madam Death, that it is not yet my time to die? I can play a bit longer before night falls? Alleluia!" Random, absurd, incomprehensible, but delicious.

Christians come from a culture that has millennia of religious indoctrination in which meaning was defined by hope of salvation in the afterlife. Even with the combined efforts of five or six generations of non-believers, the task of dismantling that system of beliefs has barely begun. Nietzsche and many others bulldozed the field, but the efforts of many more generations may be necessary to dig up and demolish the deeper levels of those foundations before we can start building an atheological tran- scendent myth that should change not only our religious attitudes, but our psychological makeup as well. We have only begun to expose the racist, sexist, oppressive, violent, hypocritical, para- sitic, exploitative cowardice present in the cement of all institu- tionalized religions. Religion is not without merit, but the denial of its shadow has resulted in distortions and atrocities in the name of the spirit. Philosophers as well as depth psychologists are exploring non-religious ways of transcending the ego; for example, lives filled with devotion to justice, love, science, nature, wisdom, beauty and truth . . . are lives filled with values that transcend the ego.

The usual promises of human love – "I'll love you forever" or "I'll never abandon you" – may be sincere, but these promises are absurd if one considers that mortality is an absolute limitation to the infinite depth of the experience of love. Nevertheless, this limitation, with all the sweet lies around it, is not reason enough to waste the spiritual value of love. We bring children into this world, and we love them madly, even if we know they will suffer and die. We love them with an intensity that is almost painful, even though we know, despite all our efforts, that they, like ourselves, will suffer and die. It doesn't make much sense, but not loving makes even less sense. The sense of the absurd, which is a consequence of the loss of religious faith, may come to be experienced as something as natural as the limitations of human love, a reality that simply is, like other realities that cannot be logically explicated.

Since my second chance at life began, the existential feeling of the absurd has not left me. In the cramped space of the intensive care unit, I prepared for the final voyage, but my departure was delayed. There I lay, with the baggage of my old values like so many suitcases packed with stuff I no longer needed. To go back to life felt like a silly return after a fake departure. For the first time I experienced the full meaning of what the early twentieth-century existentialists considered so important with respect to the experience of the absurd: a dissolution of all the meanings that had been taken for granted. I had unquestioningly accepted that life is good and death is bad. I now know the value of destruction and death. I had taken for granted that love means "being together." I now see that there can be love in separation. I believed that a high intelligence was preferable to good legs to walk with. No more. I thought that nice looking legs were as important as legs that can walk without pain. No more. I thought eyes were the mode of perception of the world. I find the faculty of imagination "sees" more deeply than eyes. A dose of death was needed to feel the orgasmic experience of waves of pure life that wash over our body with each breath. "Absurd" used to mean "nonsensical." It now means "mysterious."

Camus' sense of the absurd was influenced as much by Kafka as by the existentialist philosophers. He was a major literary influence on Beckett and Ionesco and others (like Pinter) who suggest that the detour into absurdity may be a necessary one[1]. Camus' interpretation of the myth of Sisyphus proposed a psychological solution to meaninglessness, which was to imagine Sisyphus as a happy man, regardless of the absurdity of his daily task. I don't quite agree anymore and I am having this little chat with the ghost of Albert Camus: "Yes, Monsieur Camus, I get the picture. You are suggesting that Sisyphus is the ordinary man faced with the daily task of living, only to die in the end, very much like you and me, and we should be fine with that. There are, however, other myths, other images that are equally absurd yet less depressing. Every day, when I do find myself absurdly alive, I feel more like a cat than Sisyphus, a cat presented with yet another delicious bowl of cream to lick. I have no idea where this crème de la crème comes from everyday, it seems to roll down the hill just like that, but I won't waste it. Life is indeed absurdly generous."

While Camus' loss of religious faith brought him acute distress, which may have influenced his image of life as a Sisyphean task, Jean-Paul Sartre's philosophical take on the absurd was very different. Re-reading Sartre now, I get a sense that his was a futuristic style of consciousness, one belonging to the post-mourning of God generation. I find my interest in his intuitions renewed. Regardless of the heaviness of his style, Sartre was clear and simple about a few foundational concepts:

1   We humans create our own values.
2   We are each responsible for our decisions.
3   We cannot excuse ourselves from responsibility by blaming the unconscious.[2]
4   We don't need a god to authenticate the highest values of humankind. Holding on to values is what makes us human.
5   We are equally free to damn ourselves. We don't need satanic dogma.
6   Hatred is the path to damnation. We are free to travel that path. The "Other" becomes hell, because the Other lives in my consciousness, is my consciousness. If I hate the Other instead of loving him or her, I have created my own hell. Hell is Others, just as bliss is Others.[3]
7   The relationship with myself becomes unbearable when I try to deny my freedom. Placing the blame (or responsibility) on others, proclaiming myself a victim, choosing to remain trapped by narcissism, destroys my freedom and, therefore, my life.
8   All "faith" is "bad faith" (*mauvaise foi*), a regressive abdication of reason. The problem with religious faith is not that it is arational (like love or poetry), or irrational (like superstition or defense mechanisms), but anti-rational, which is the most destructive value to be held by any culture.

The task of psychoanalysis seems to be to attempt to answer Sartre's question: What do you do with what was done to you?

Camus was aware that his angst was a consequence of his mourning the death of God the Father. Sartre's psyche was different. He wrote in *Words* how he never mourned the loss of his personal father, who died when Sartre was still a young child.

Sartre declared himself happy about his fatherless situation[4] and seemed to have had an easier time than his contemporaries with mourning for the Cosmic Father. The loss of faith was torturous for Camus. It was equally painful for Jung when he discovered that the symbol of the village steeple had lost its power. It was problematical for many in the generations of intellectuals after Nietzsche. Camus conceived of the sadness of losing God the Father as a part of the human condition, the price to pay for lucidity. Some of my generation think it need not be so.[5]

The existential angst at the loss of faith in a redemptive god may very well be simply a consequence of a very long domination by the monotheistic God. Religious sentiment, like the sentiment of love, has a history. Building cathedrals was a task carried on by many generations; deconstructing the faith behind the stone buildings will take at least that long. It can, however, be done – not stone by stone, but idea by idea, symbol by symbol. Like Sartre, who was not so attached to the Father image, feminists (male and female) may be more ready than most to give God the Father his pink slip. The departure of a misogynous and racist tyrant may come to feel like a formidable spring cleanup for the psyche, a welcome death. Post-modernism, with its unrelenting attack on single meanings, has acted as a sort of collective therapy. It took us to a place in our consciousness where the loss of the redemptive myth is simply equal to the major absurdity of most of life's trajectories.

An acute sense of the death of God can stir up feelings as painful as when experiencing the death of a child, or the loss of a loved one in a stupid accident. It seems so absurd, so meaningless, the anguish is so acute. The danger is then to invest all of one's psychic energy in explaining the absurd. (Why? Why? Why?) We become obsessed with a search for meaning to redeem the tragic, and because there is no redemption that search itself becomes tragic. This is where I find that an archetypal approach can be of help, because it moves away from explanations, starts in the territory of the tragic, and goes from there into the deepest layers of the imagination, where psychic regeneration can occur. The opening of the deep layers of the psyche offers not redemption but a map of the journey through psychic devastation. Instead of the usual prescription, which is to head right back into traditional faith, the psyche can provide other ways of experiencing the connection to humanity – rather than appeals to an absent god.

New Age spirituality, supposedly a post-Christian alternative to spirituality, presents itself with the qualifier of "new" as a new myth of God. I am all for renewal and renaissance because, frankly, the traditional religious symbolism, with its inherent racism (the chosen people) and sexism (the chosen gender), feels beyond resuscitation to me. In all renovating projects, a contractor friend of mine convinced me that there comes a point where it is wiser to bring in the bulldozer than to attempt renovation. I agree, and apply his wisdom to the examination of the edifice of Christianity. I think it is beyond renovation. I prefer to take my spiritual material from the cultural memory of the paganism of the Greeks, mainly because it is a mythology and not a religion, one that did not ask for belief in their gods.[6] Although New Age spirituality may look like a new and improved product, one has to be vigilant. Much of what is presented as "new" is in fact a recycling of a religious reflex worthy of Augustine. He asked himself the age-old question that historians have in common with depth psychologists: can one find meaning in history? (And the corollary: can I find meaning in my story?) Augustine's answer constituted dogma for a very long time. Yes, history has meaning, says Augustine. It is the meaning given by faith. If one loses faith, one also loses meaning. Problem solved.[7] By remaining unconscious of our Christianity we tend to apply that same logic and replace one bible with another (for example, replacing a patriarchal bible with an equally exclusive matriarchal bible), falling right back into Augustinian dogma. As long as one is asked to believe in some sort of godlike redemptive principle, it is the same old Christian goods and services, only the packaging and marketing are New Age.

One of the current tasks of depth psychology, as I understand it, involves dumping the last residue of that Augustinian style of consciousness, based in faith. Not that there is a need to bring up Augustine's case again. He has been tried and found guilty over and over. Nevertheless, Augustinian debris is blocking new construction. Depth psychology is experimenting with the next style of consciousness, one that allows a person to endure the absurd, to cope with the insufferable, to lose one's innocence and, instead of turning to Augustinian redemption, to learn to swim in the Styx, imagine life differently, making room for its tragic element. Depth psychology suggests that you are free to jump off a bridge, if suicide is what your soul ultimately wants, but before you literalize death into physical death of the body, try a metaphorical death. Try an imaginal trip to the Underworld. Try a form of loving through pain, living with loss, aging in character. Try imagining another self, inventing another myth, writing another chapter in your story. Travel first, see the inner world, and then decide if it is literal or metaphorical death you want.

I have a friend whose son became psychotic in late adolescence. My friend was a devoted and competent father whose patience his friends (and I) all admired. His son had an episode of psychotic rage and killed my friend's wife, the love of his life. I knew her. She was joy and compassion incarnate, a radiant human being. The psychosis of the son destroyed that human masterpiece. It is only now that I understand why my friend is so impatient with acquaintances who try to "make sense" of his immense tragedy. He cannot bear those trying to explain the tragedy in terms of predestination, fate, or any other religiously or New Age inspired consolation. What might have helped him, and what he did not get, was a community with a sense of the tragic. In his milieu, a person going through such tragedy is expected to complete the mourning process according to the theory that says a one-year cycle should be sufficient. Beyond the so-called "norm" of 365 days it is renamed and on day 366 it should be coded as a clinical symptom or self-indulgence. Not so for my friend. He had two choices: either he killed himself in despair, or he learned to live with this tragedy in his heart for the rest of his life. There is no redeeming of what happened; it will remain tragic forever.

The desire to find meaning is a human one, and is given expression in the creation of a narrative, but there is often a contamination with the belief in a redemptive principle, where bad turns into good. "My baby is dead, but she is now an angel in God's paradise" is a frequent defense against despair, a direct consequence of not having completed the mourning for one particular long-lived God. Nietzsche was justifiably upset with the many people around him trying to extract moral lessons from a philosophy that did not contain them. The almost irresistible reflex of turning everything into morality of good and evil belongs to faith, belongs to a God that dictates right from wrong. The adventure of a depth-psychological analysis is at the same time a move away from this kind of religious conditioning. The need for redemptive ideals is replaced by another style of consciousness – the capacity to value the awe-inspiring mysteries of the psyche. As one opens up to the possibility of living a full and generous life, the thirst for redemption diminishes and the need to be of service to others, to culture, and to nature increases.

Since Nietzsche, the necessity for a God who dictates morality has been partially replaced by a global recognition of the universal principles of respect for the rights and dignity of the Other, by a sense of responsibility for one's actions, of responsibility toward the preservation of nature, as well as the preservation of the cultural heritage. Nonetheless, each of us, individually, struggles to answer the personal question "Why should I live?" As an agnostic, I do not wish for a world devoid of spiritual values. Who would, really? Rather, I wish for a world where the need for spirituality would be definitively dissociated from the imposition of pre-fixed meanings and pre-defined values. This is why the Jungian and post-Jungian approach (particularly the work of James Hillman) feels like an alternative to religion for me. It recognizes the human need for something bigger than ego, but refuses to let religious orthodoxies manipulate that need.

My generation is perhaps the first in history to have been so freely agnostic, without the risk of being shunned, condemned, tortured, or burned at the stake. I am immensely grateful, for example, that my academic milieu, although at times as constricting as a tight girdle, has allowed me a long excursion to rediscover the pre-Christian gods and goddesses. I find in the study of the classics a richness of imagination, a magic, an esthetic sensibility that is deliciously contrary to that of the constrictions of Christianity. A different spiritual posturing can be truly relaxing. Be it the bison of Lascaux, the Greek Aphrodite, or the Amerindian figure of Coyote, all these non-Christian images of the divine serve the spiritual need to see things "big" and to see "differently." Human glory, health, and fortune do not suffice to fill the vast inner space. We need to imagine a wider world, one of archetypal dimension. All humans, once they take care of survival needs, feel that there is a beyond-the-ego realm. Many still choose to call "it" God, or Goddess, or Love, or First Principle, or "any other term of your choice," as they say in Alcoholics Anonymous, with impressive success.

This God-image or God-principle, this beyond-the-ego realm of the archetype is truly different from traditional religious faith. It does not demand the kind of obedience that traditional religions have tried (and are still trying) to impose. It is a radical move away from a posture of belief. It is an opening of the whole being that allows one to serve one or the other of the archetypal values of humanity. Those very human values – justice, truth, love, compassion and so on – don't need to be handed down from a priest, a guru, or a preacher to have transcendental value. Transcendence, which means a sense of value above, beyond and apart from the material world, doesn't need to be packaged with religious dogma. Monotheistic religions tend to place all good in God and most of the bad in humans or in the devil. They have traditionally claimed that transcendence comes from their God. Pagan religions were considered inferior forms of worship, good for peasants, lacking in sophistication. One of the interesting outcomes of the globalization of culture may very well be that Christianity's claim to transcendence will be revealed for what it is – an artificial monopoly that needs to be dismantled. Depth psychology is part of the demolition crew. It facilitates and accelerates the mourning of God.

Rather than the relentless pursuit of an ideal of flawless psychological health (which exists no more than God), I prefer the via negativa, taking the road away from that which destroys. We all have the option to develop an aversion to cruelty, a skillful avoidance of narcissistic indulgences, the rejection of manipulative, controlling, oppressive relationships. In other words, the psyche can use a negative compass, one that points away from forces that have the power to cripple. It is a reversal of the Christian fantasy. Rather than gazing aloft at the sanctity of God, the via negativa suggests a prudent tiptoeing away from the nastiest human monsters.

## Psychic monsters don't need redeeming

In order to travel the via negativa and move away from a destructive force, one needs a clear vision of what is to be avoided. We can draw inspiration from a literary or cinematographic tradition and imagine those destructive forces as monsters, demons, beasts, bug, viruses, alien subpersonalities – whatever seems appropriate as long as it is an image. What others call a neurosis, let's call a "monster." The difference between the concept of neuroses and the image of a particular monster is a huge difference; it marks the boundary between science and the humanities. Symbolic images develop into a story, whereas the concept of neurosis is a dysfunction described in a medical lexicon. The abstract concept of "neurosis" flattens the imagination and requires a clinical cure. The challenge of a story with a monster in it calls for a heroic adventure. We all have to meet our monsters, mini or maxi, ordinary or extraordinary. A monster, in mythology as in cinema, is defined as a malevolent creature that has a great power of destruction and is a threat to the community. The presence of a psychic monster calls forth a hero to battle or outwit the monster until the community is safe again. In a family, for example, the first person who manages to break an old pattern of destruction – be it the serpent of addiction, the giant brute of domestic violence, the wicked curse of self-absorption, or the demon of hypochondria – qualifies as a mythological hero.

All forms of psychoanalysis begin with a meeting with those inner monsters. First, I become aware that this "thing", this psychic virus, is in me, can destroy me, and us, and them. If the monster reigns, the forces of destruction break loose. A time of preparation is needed before one is ready for the heroic encounter and that is one of the reasons why an analysis takes time. Joseph Campbell[8] has shown how the hero often at first refuses the task and wants to stay at home. The safety of home, however, is not really an option; Dorothy and Toto are not in Kansas anymore.

The romantic poets, from whom Jung took inspiration, imagined the psychological monsters as shadows, that part in us that the light of reason does not seem to reach. Psychological monsters dwell in the shadow because of their irrational nature. They are the skeletons in the closet, the bugs in the programming, the night of the living dead, the invasion of the aliens, the creepy crawling things under the rock of unconscious repression. Our monsters feed on cowardice and unwillingness to acknowledge them but can never entirely be eliminated. The Christian strategy of war and triumph over the devil is limited compared to the range of possibilities offered to mythological heroes, whose strategies include wit and wisdom, curiosity and intelligence.

The Christian attack and denial of the shadow is based on a denial of the human body and desires. Such a tactic may have had a powerful civilizing function when Christianity was converting hordes of barbarians, but it soon turned into an inhuman fantasy of the elimination of the monsters. It started with the demonizing of the figure of Dionysus, who, before he was transformed by the Christians into a devil, had been a god. The Greek Dionysus had been a troublesome character, dangerous, tragic, destructive, but divine nonetheless. Dark as he was, he was an essential representation of the animal vitality of all life forms.[9] Depth psychology allies with paganism when affirming the polytheistic nature of the psyche, pointing out that God has never had final victory over Satan. The irrationality of the psyche is to the ego what Dionysus is to Apollo; not an opposition between a devil and a god, but one between two gods, two essential principles whose opposition is part of a necessary equilibrium. Moreover, they are not the only divinities either, they share the stages with many others.

The fantasy of one god triumphing over one devil has not only created the huge shadow of Christianity but has also permeated many of our psychological attitudes. A religion of love that is blind to the fact that it is one of the most violent in history[10] obviously has a problem with the shadow. Similarly, a person who won't face his or her shadow will burden others with it, insisting that others carry those uncomfortable feelings that their image of a perfect self cannot accommodate. Psychologically speaking, there is another approach, one that does not suggest going to war with one's monsters, nor seeking to purge and exorcize the demons. Rather, it suggests a polytheistic strategy of balancing the energies, balancing Dionysian irrationality with Apollonian self-discipline; balancing authoritarian Zeus with witty Hermes; giving his due to workaholic Hephaestos, to belligerent Ares, to strong Poseidon, to dark Hades but also showing our respect for sexy Aphrodite, nature lover Artemis, homey Hestia, wise Athena and regal Hera. Those divinities (and many more) are all archetypal representations of aspects of life; when we don't pay attention to the principle they personify, we maim ourselves and waste a fantastic amount of psychic energy.

Just as we study a child with learning disabilities, we can study our personal monsters and consider the problems we create for them by wanting to "redeem" them. Psychic monsters resist both demonization – "curse me all you like, it is like water off a duck's back" – and they also resist redemption – "a halo won't fit on my horny self." Nevertheless, there is a way to reach them: monsters want recognition, education, participation. It is as if these virtual beings who live in our imagination want us to acknowledge them, to give them a temple in our inner city, to include them in the psychic community. Psychoanalysis is precisely that: an invitation to gather in the analyst's office, where even the wariest, wartiest, sexiest, silliest parts of our self are welcome. It is an opening of the closets to bring out the skeletons and the demons. The monsters under the bed are dragged out and given a place at the table. We get to meet them all, up close and personal. The psyche is vast enough to host a multitude and the manner in which one hosts them is what archetypal psychology calls the possibility of developing a psychological polytheism.

## A monster can be contagious

By belonging to a family, a group, or even a couple, we necessarily exist within a psychological network, a psychological environment that has a psychic atmosphere. A heavy atmosphere is like a psycho-dictatorship. A few powerful monsters impose their style (paranoid, depressive, hostile, frigid, manipulative, mean, victimizing) and make misery because psyches are much more contagious than we like to believe. Throughout an analysis, we put a lot of effort in establishing our "psychological boundaries." ("This feeling belongs to you, please don't project it on me. Would you mind picking up your dirty socks that are all over the bedroom, and while you're at it could you pick up your projections as well?"). Nevertheless, hard as one may try to erect boundaries, most feelings are highly contagious. There is no perfect filter. The following vignette illustrates the fact that just as laughter, joy, and love are contagious, so are hatred, fear, anxiety, depression, and paranoia.

### Psychological viruses

When my wife is angry with me, she says nothing. Her face is blank. She goes about her daily chores with a subterranean coldness, waging a silent, undeclared war. Looking at her, one might think that she looks like someone watching TV, or thinking about something. I know she is brooding, emitting particles of hostility like those micro-bubbles of water from the humidifier. I breathe in each one of these particles of resentment and they infect me. There is no wall, no door, no headphones that will protect me against these moods. Sooner or later, I appear like the attacker, because I will bang a door, snap at her, or become agitated, trying to release the vice-like grip around my heart. I am the one who appears to be hostile, but my feeling is that I am defending myself against a coldness that is death-like, disproportionate, monstrous, and dangerous for me.

This man asked his wife, as a last resort, to go into couple therapy. She agreed to a consultation and at the second session was willing to invite her resenting monster to come center stage, to appear in the room. She named it: "I know you, brooding monster. You are my silent anger." She had a question for the monster. "Why do you want to destroy my marriage?" The conversation with the monster was a revelation for her. Later on, the husband discovered an interesting monster of his own. "I know you, you big flattening machine. You are my inferiority feeling. I know you are there in the shadow, giving me angry prompts when I feel unseen."

When I was an adolescent, every Christmas I would see one of my cousins at the annual family gathering. This guy annoyed me more than anyone on earth. He would pursue me, insisting on talking about cars and money. He wanted to tell me how much he had paid for his car's tune-up and wax job, or he would detail all the bargains he had found in the last month of shopping. Not only was he the most boring person I ever encountered but, for some reason, his talkative, invasive, insisting persona distressed me. I evaded him with all possible excuses, but he would catch up with me. None of my evasion strategies – bathroom, buffet, babble, blurting, blushing – ever worked. A monster is just like this cousin – inescapable – part of the family, unavoidable. Whatever you do, wherever you go, he'll show up.

We can no more dodge a monster than silence the ego. The only thing that finally worked with my cousin was to become curious. Why, I finally wondered, is this guy so interested in small bargains when he is loaded with money? What is a car to him? Why doesn't he perceive that I don't give a flip about the care of cars, or the price of a wax? What in him and what in me makes his presence so excruciatingly boring? Why is it excruciating for me to be so bored by him? What do I find so terrible about boredom? From then on, his presence stopped being a problem; it became an interesting psychological puzzle. When he died I was sorry, because I had become interested in his particular way of being-in-the world, I had developed a weird kind of affection for him, a familiar family bugbear.

A similar strategy works pretty well with psychological monsters because the possibility of educating the psyche begins with curiosity. Curiosity makes a good detective, a good scientist, a good student, a good analyst and a good analysand. To educate the psyche, we have to become curious, psychological magnifier in hand, looking very carefully for clues about the nature of a particular monster. The psyche will not learn if it is approached with impatience, aggression, or contempt. Beating a child to teach him a poem won't work. Our demons are just like that child. In the following example, the technique of active imagination helped a patient imagine a way to "educate" his monster, with the respect and patience that one would use with a recalcitrant child.

## My monster is an accountant with a moralistic attitude

My inner torturer is an accountant who knows how to push all my guilt buttons. He whispers to me, "You've wasted the family fortune . . . you've wasted the family fortune . . . you've wasted the family fortune. . . . Look at your portfolio, look at how little the money you inherited has grown, all your investment strategies failed, you have a negative growth. To be poor is to be nobody. Your brother invested well and look how rich he is. To be poor is a shame. Shame on you!"

I had a talk with this inner abuser. "Do you realize that you speak to me as if you were the voice of conscience? Do you see that you ignore the fact that I am the only one in the dynasty that has broken the pattern of alcoholism? Do you really think it is wise to reduce everything to the growth of a portfolio? Let me show you another kind of balance sheet. You may like to learn a different approach to life. You may like what I want to teach you."

To do active imagination with the subpersonalities one may start by imagining their voice, their posturing, their habits, and then to interrogate them – not as if we were conducting an inquisition, but rather like the curious questions of a traveler. A tourist doesn't act like a detective interrogating a suspect, but asks questions like: "Why are the apartment buildings in Paris, Rome, and Madrid turned inward, around a courtyard, while in New York, Dallas and Chicago, the preference is for a high panoramic view? Why is it polite here to burp after a good meal, whereas at home it is considered vulgar? Just asking! Curiosity. Monster, tell me: why are you upset when this guy talks about cars?"

## Unredeemable Narcissus

Narcissus is one of those psychological monsters about whom there is an abundance of literature. The myth of Narcissus is extremely useful to illustrate how walking away from a negative ideal can sometimes work better than aiming at a positive ideal. Instead of asking oneself, "How can I redeem Narcissus; how can I be more altruistic?" one starts with curiosity: "Hey Narcissus, how did you get into my psyche? Who put you in charge? What tricky things are you up to now? How, when, with whom, and in what kind of emotional context do you take hold of me?" The tragedy of letting Narcissus invade the psyche is most common and the damage is always the same. Narcissism inevitably destroys the possibility of joy because joy is always in relation to the Other, even if that Other is a tree, the ocean, a puppy, or tulip bulbs asking to be planted before they rot. To feel joy in any kind of accomplishment there has to be some sort of connection with whomever the accomplishment will benefit. If I send my check to an organization that helps heal the ocean, I will feel joy when I read that the ocean's health is improving, because I previously felt my connection with the ocean. Narcissus first experiences joy when he beholds himself in the mirror (the still water of the pond). He thinks he is finally meeting that Other whom he can love. The joy disappears with the realization that connection with this Other is impossible. The narcissist is always trying to connect with his own image of an idealized self, his own most wonderful, godlike self-image. Half the time the narcissist is in love with himself and for the other half he loathes himself, but it is still all about him.

What is godlike in ourselves gives joy only when shared. Even the most reclusive scientist, the shyest artist working in seclusion, can feel joy if love for science or art connects them to the world, to an imaginary Other who will benefit from their accomplishments. As vitality and joy can only come from connection, the consequence of letting Narcissus – or any other monster – rule is a desiccation of the heart (the fate of Echo who falls in love with him). Narcissus does not know that his self-absorption is lethal, to himself and to Echo. He does not recognize that all his gazing into the face of the beloved is only a reflection. In love with himself, he can only suffer his tragic fate, which is to disappear into the mirror. He never gets the message – look buddy, there is nobody but you in this game.

Lost in the mirror is a perfect image for the narcissist, but there are a great variety of them. A patient of mine dreamt of a chrysalis that never transformed.

## My sealed cocoon

I spent years creating a cocoon supposedly to protect myself from the Invaders, which meant everybody! I imprisoned myself by spinning more and more layers of protection, the filament being incessant thoughts about me, me, me. I never learned what joy is, or is not. I usually "buy" love in one form or another of an emotional deal. I've had three marriages that were all contractual arrangements. I do not trust that I can reach out, grow wings, and fly. I don't believe I can experience the reciprocity of love.

This narcissistic monster kept this man captive in a cocoon, not letting anybody come close to him. Like a child kept in a closet, Narcissus is infirm in his capacity to connect. Narcissus is but one figure, one myth. The variety of monsters and the brand of narcissisms are as wide as the characters in mythology. The beautiful Aphrodite can be pretty obsessed with the mirror and she too can provide images of self-centeredness as well as Zeus, Apollo, and all the others in the Greek pantheon. All quests for wisdom initiate some form or other of that conversation with the weak, primitive, dangerous person in us. The fantasy of redemption is one of getting rid of monsters. Such an attack on the inhabitants of our psyches would deprive us of a partner in the inner conversation, one that we need for our development.

As I promised the patients who agreed to have their stories included, I will disclose something about one of my familiar monsters, whom I long ago baptized the "Little Match Girl." This imaginary character, with whom I have an ongoing dialogue, will not go away. Yet, through the technique of active imagination, it seems that she benefited from a sort of "education." She used to appear in moments of perfectly fine solitude, the kind of solitude a writer absolutely needs to write and read; she would instill doubt suggesting that I was not alone, but lonely, or maybe, even an abandoned orphan. This monsterette now exerts less tyranny on my psyche, thanks to analytical work. Here is an example of an imaginary dialogue with her (LMG).

### Educating Little Match Girl

*Ginette:* Is it you again, infantile girl-monster with your whining voice?

*LMG:* Yes, I am your fear of being abandoned in boarding school.

*Ginette:* I know your tactic: you paralyze me with panic, making me think, feel, and act as if I were a poor lonely orphan, the kid who remains in boarding school when all the others have gone home for Christmas. Can you tell me why you instill nostalgia in me whenever I decorate a Christmas tree? It's odd. Where does this scene of the perfect Christmas come from, this scene that evokes such melancholy? This perfect Christmas never happened; how do you manage to create nostalgia with something that is not in the memory?

*LMG:* Simple: I push the pathos far beyond the reality of what is happening. For example, you are pleasantly alone in a comfortable silent house, seated at your desk, fingers on the keyboard, focused on writing, and I come in and put you in a trance and from then on you feel as if you were famished, lonely, abandoned, shivering with cold, on Christmas Eve, with not even a match to hold on to the fantasy of the banquet that is being served to those who,

unlike yourself, have perfect lives and plenty of good
company.

*Ginette:*  You are indeed a poor little monsterette! I think it is you
whom I have abandoned! I can see why you want to
instill in me those sorrows, but really they belong to
you. I apologize for having been ashamed of you. I have
ignored and suppressed your voice for many decades
because you are so extravagant in your pathos.

*LMG:*  Yes, you did abandon me. Your act of the "queen of
autonomy" was an insult to me. I want your attention. I
want you to help me grow up. I want you to educate
me. I am primitive, hungry, lonely, poorly dressed,
poorly fed. I have no social skills, I am shy and, most of
all, I am tired of my drama because there are much
more interesting things in this world than fantasies of
unreachable cakes in a shop window.

*Ginette:*  Okay. Get ready for a change, sweetie, because I am
tired of our drama. I am definitely not an orphan but a
grown-up woman with a pension plan and an almost
paid-up mortgage. Famine and homelessness are
unlikely to happen at this point in my story. I may
not be the queen of autonomy but I am not the lonely
orphan either; I have friends, passions, a garden, and
lots of very good books to read.

*LMG:*  You like books more than cakes?

*Ginette:*  I do, and I have access to more books then I can ever
read in the time I have left on this earth.

*LMG:*  What is your plan with me? Will you feed me or read to
me?

*Ginette:*  I'm adopting you, Poor Little Match Girl. Come, take
up residence in my heart. My heart is your home.
Believe me, cakes and books and company you will
have, but stop the tyranny on my soul. Take a look
around. Life can be good, warm, and delicious, and you
are welcome to the banquet.

To be honest, I have others, much shadier characters in my psyche
than this monsterette, but she is real too and has taught me a thing
or two about the necessity to avoid the Christian ambush of
redemption. My psychological creativity comes from the respect I
now have for those unredeemable figures of my inferiority feelings.

All monsters ask for a chance to evolve, an occasion to appear on stage and react with disgust at fantasies of redemption. What they are asking for is much simpler: to join the living. In exchange, they will do some of the living for us; they love to participate, to play, to write a few chapters in our life stories.

# Chapter 7

# Boundary issues

## "You, science. Me, humanities."

Economic models are entirely adequate for doing business. Legal models represent centuries of refining processes for maintaining law and order in the land. The medical model is effective for healing illnesses. The model of religion makes sense as long as one has faith in the redemptive power of the deity and trust in its institutions. All of these models have influenced the practice of psychotherapy, but are not meant to address the passionate, irrational, Dionysian aspect of psychological life, in its destructive as well as constructive movement. The promise of healing (medical model), the desire of multiplying one's psychological investments (economic model), the negotiation of one's psychic territory (judicial model), the hope of redemption (religious model), all play a large role in every analysis, because they are significant components of lives and cultures. Nevertheless, if we limit ourselves to a rational, non-Dionysian approach to psychological suffering, we lose the sense of life as an adventure and replace it with life as a series of medico-scientific problems to be solved.

When I was nine years old, one day my father and I were sitting on a bridge stalled in traffic. I saw a man, dressed in a black cashmere overcoat, white silk scarf and a perfect felt hat, leaning over the railing of the sidewalk of the bridge, looking down into the waters of the mighty turbulent river below. I had the sharp intuition, a certitude, that he would throw himself from the bridge and said so to my father. Moments later he did; I saw him jump, his hat still on, the white silk scarf unfolding in the air like soft wings. The next day the paper told his story of heartbreak. To the child that I was, this tragedy proved the reality of the soul. There exists something in us, invisible and intangible, that distills suffering and joy. Loss of love, lack of love, failures of love can attack this invisible organ of feeling and we want to jump off a bridge. I had found my vocation and a definition of the soul: that which is invisible, yet experiences all feelings.

At 55 years old, after a brain injury and eight months of rehabilitation, I felt the same certitude: the reality of the psyche is invisible yet it qualifies all our experiences; it can turn pain into a gift and a gift into a curse. But knowing something from the heart and finding the language to communicate the experience are two very different things. When the time came for me to get back behind the podium and resume my work as professor of psychology, the panic was intense because I had to relearn how to teach, this time from a place of uncertainty. I had to leave behind the gnostic stance, to stop posturing as the psychologist who knows about the psyche, and to assume the position of the agnostic, of one who does not know for sure. When I confided this to a friend, himself a professor of literature, he gave me this advice: "I never know for sure the meaning of a poem. Still, I can talk with my students about the poem's evocative power." That was excellent advice and I followed it. The psyche really is like a poem; it has evocative power and it can be trained to perform with even more power. I finally understood the intellectual liberation that comes with the idea that the entire field of depth psychology can now move back to the original goal, which is to evoke, a verb which means: "1. to bring to mind a memory or feeling, especially from the past; 2. to provoke a particular reaction or feeling; 3. to make beings appear who are normally invisible."[1] Symbols are evocative, stories are evocative, art is evocative, literature is evocative, myths are evocative.

The reality of the psyche is a virtual one, based on the psychological imagining or "imaging" we do daily because we need to symbolize events that move us. The goal of an analysis is to become aware of that evocative process, aware of the virtual script we create every minute, aware of the flavor of today's ordinary hypnotic trance, or – to use Joseph Campbell's words – to become aware of the myths we live by. A myth is a powerful suggestion, just like a post-hypnotic suggestion, and it is based on a fiction. A metaphor is a fiction, a symbol is a fiction, just as a sad movie is just a fiction but it can move us to shed real tears. As Jung described it, a symbol is true inside and false outside. A movie script is true inside (it can move me to tears), yet it is false outside (an invented story). A poem that suggests my heart is a violin playing its sad melody in minor mode is true inside and false outside; a guided relaxation exercise (auto-hypnotic technique) that helps me relax at the dentist by listening to a tape of the sound of the ocean offers only a fictive ocean. All this imagery is made up, but the evocative power of the images is as powerful as the still incomprehensible magic of love.

A myth is never factual in the sense that a detective or journalist needs a fact to be just a fact. A myth is a fantasy, a preferred lie, a foundational story, a hypnotic trance, an identity game, a virtual reality, one that can be either inspirational or despairing. It is a story in which I cast myself, it is my inner cinema, the motion picture of my inner reality – one that moves all the time. No diagnosis can fix the myth, no cure can settle it, because our inner life is precisely what, in us, will not lie still.

Our personal story is the product of our imagination, a faculty that used to be synonymous with what we now call the unconscious. Imagination is just as good a word as unconscious, which, as Freud himself insisted, is and remains a hypothesis, as unproved and unprovable as the concept of "imagination." It is just a word to point at our tendency to amplify stories and expand them into myth. Myth contains no certainty, no sure knowledge; it is a product of our imagination. Yet, we cannot live without myths, any more than a culture can survive without literature, art, music, poetry, storytelling, or the form that mythic imagination now takes: cinema, songs, advertisements. It is crucial, however, to know that a myth is only a myth; it presents itself as truth, but knowing its fictive aspect gives one the power to edit the story.

Just as one has to be really naive to confuse an infomercial with information, all the same we don't like those who insist on presenting their organizing myth as the source of causality: "You want me to believe that if you beat your kids today, it's 'because' your dad was an alcoholic? Sorry! I am not buying into your myth." Such oppressive myths can be deconstructed while useful ones can be amplified. Falling in love is an uplifting myth: "You want me to believe that you are a beautiful, creative, interesting, generous, capable person? Yes, I can relate to you from that script." Certain movies have the power to transform us and it does not matter if we know they are invented stories, because we still feel they are internally true. Their artistic and psychological truth resonates with us; that is why we love the cinema. Nevertheless, as rational beings, we also need a clear distinction between the categories of truth. Factual truth is not the same as artistic or psychological truth, and the difference is crucial. The idea of a reporter who, instead of reporting facts, would weave a plausible fiction, is immensely troubling. A fact should, in principle, never be confused with a fiction, although, as all studies in communication have demonstrated, the confusion is more frequent than we like to admit.

When a myth no longer serves, the first move is usually to label it just that, a myth. We declare something to be "only a myth," when the "lie" in it (the metaphor) no longer works for us. The invented story, the scenario, is then deconstructed. Feminism, anti-racism, ecology, atheism have performed such spectacular "deconstructions." The oppressive myths were revealed as lies: black is not ugly, female is not weak, natural resources are not infinite, religion, churches, priests, and obedience are not essential to spirituality. This process has been called deconstruction, a fascinating demolition derby to scrap oppressive myths. The joy of myth debunking can be intense. The deconstructionists did not invent the concept, just a refreshed theory for it. Deconstruction can also be called the work of intelligence and rationality, as opposed to belief and propaganda. It is a form of lucidity, a seeing through fictions that pretend to be facts.

The first step of myth debunking is usually to produce arguments of reality as evidence of the falsity: "You say that women should not get pilots' licenses because their hormones make them unstable? False! Take a look at the statistics!" We are not yet in myth debunking, just getting the facts right, a first step, because rationality is never enough to get rid of a negative myth. Only a fresh, lively, charged new myth will carry enough magic to replace the old, negative, tired, abusive, retrograde, finished, exhausted myth. Facts are contradicted by facts, statistics by statistics, data by data, and that is called the scientific approach. But a myth can only be replaced by a myth, a virtual reality by another virtual reality, a symbol by a symbol, a story by a story. Along with the rational arguments aiming at the logical deconstruction, a fresh set of images has to appear, exciting new stories, new interpretations, new episodes in the collective script. The new myth reverses the old values and suggests, for example, that black is beautiful – or female is beautiful, gay is beautiful, old is beautiful, fat is not abject, atheism is virtuous – and so on with each value that was part of the old oppressive myth.

If one reads nineteenth-century novels, any plot involving a woman who chose divorce had to suggest that the price of such freedom might be more than she could bear.[2] The cultural programming of the time was such that the only virtual game a woman was allowed to play when imagining her life was that of selfless wife, obedient nun, or sexless old maid devoted to church, aging parents, cats, begonias, and goodwill. Divorce was legal but the literature was undermining the legal gain. Every popular novel involving a divorcee had to show her doomed, a pariah, destitute, a lost soul. By comparison, a slew of movies appeared around 1960 exemplifying a very different script; they depicted women who were not only surviving, but thriving and – oh surprise – enjoying their freedom. The legal, factual option of divorce was making its way through literature and movie scripts, some of it written by women as they began expressing themselves as writers and directors and some written by men attuned to the new myth. Every collectivity is always updating its myths and if it ever stops doing so there is stagnation.

The same process goes on in the personal psyche: it has to constantly add, cut, paste, save, delete, and sometimes reformat the whole psychic disk, or else it stagnates. A destructive myth should be treated like a deadly enemy. The psychic space between the new myth and the old myth often feels like a deadly zone. It is. This is the zone for which depth psychology offers a map, one that shows a completely different topography than the map used for a medical diagnosis.

## The confusing definition of depth psychology

Depth psychology is a general term that remains confusing because it defines all approaches that take into account the unconscious dimension of the psyche. Depth psychology was first presented as a victory against the debilitating symptoms of neurosis. Freud's initial positioning was that of a medical doctor looking for causes: if the patient's arm is paralyzed because of a repressed desire to slap somebody in the face, then the psychoanalytic talking cure, in lifting the unconscious repression, would cure the paralysis. It was crucial for Freud and Jung, and the immediate followers of depth psychology, to ally themselves with the medical profession, in order to break the Church's monopoly on the care of the soul. The insistence of the first two generations of depth psychologists on being "doctors of the soul" was a strategic necessity, a useful alliance, a wise posturing. Only the medical model was legitimate enough to allow them to talk about a topic such as sex or a concept such as the unconscious. The title of medical doctor offered the prestige needed to challenge the religious monopoly on moral counseling. But today, many, but not all, depth psychologists (including myself) feel that the need for that strategic alliance with the medical profession has passed. This split is responsible for a real tension, and at times an incompatibility, between approaches which, technically, belong in the category of depth psychology, because they all consider the unconscious dimension of the psyche, but take residence in different academic houses. For example, such psychodynamic theories as those of Kohut, Kernberg and Gunderson cling to a rhetoric of trauma and treatment, a choice that situates them in direct opposition to many Jungians, post-Jungians[3] and archetypal psychologists such as James Hillman, who is joined by theoreticians from religious studies, philosophy, literary criticism and mythology[4] – all of whom radically place themselves outside of the medical logic.

Throughout this book, I exclude psychodynamic approaches whenever I refer to depth psychology because I believe their trauma-treatment rhetoric places them with the nineteenth-century perspectives. Although fascinating to read, I am arguing that they belong to the history of depth psychology but not to its future, because to do science one has to follow its method. Advances in neurology and psychiatry invite a clear break with pseudo-scientific theories about the unconscious psyche.

The deconstructive–reconstructive approach of archetypal psychology[5] examines the reasons for dropping the medical pretense and the benefits of getting rid of the whole lot of useless, unprovable hypotheses by radically separating depth psychology from the field of medicine. It was Freud who began the game of fabricating one hypothesis after another, consistent with the medical persona which was crucial to acceptance within the medical milieu that was his. Yet at the beginning of his career Freud had been careful to mention that the unconscious was only a kind of useful hypothesis, still unproven, that the unconscious should never be posited as "real," that it was only a useful concept to start thinking about inner life. Freud also expressed that medical training might be the worst possible preparation for being an analyst. He argued in favor of lay analysis, pointing out that the best training was a culture, especially a knowledge of literature, philosophy, anthropology. He admitted that his case histories were more like short stories than medical reports. He explicitly said that his theories were not amenable to experimental confirmation or disconfirmation. It is regrettable that later psychoanalysts weren't able to acknowledge this part of the Freudian legacy. They would have felt more at ease with the fact that depth psychology is mostly literature, but a vitally important and rich form of literature. Freud, after all, got the Goethe Prize for literature, not for medicine.

The production of pseudo-scientific explanations about the psyche – adding to the impressive stack of unproven, unprovable psychological hypotheses – has slowed down in the last decade, mainly because the development of neuropsychology is producing research that is truly amenable to experimental confirmation or disconfirmation. Yet, every year, more of these pseudo-scientific explanations are published, only to be later discarded as junk, as is most of the theorizing about homosexuality, frigidity, hysteria, depression, mood disorders, personality disorders, post-traumatic disorders and most afflictions of the psyche that are not evidently based on a general medical condition.

This intellectual waste is revelatory of a complex of inferiority toward hard science, cluttering the field of depth psychology with the wrong rhetoric. I find it more fruitful to work toward an acceptance of the fact that depth psychology is not a natural science, never was, never will be. It was, is, and shall remain a part of the humanities. The mimesis of science, the language of hypothesis, the obsolete conceptual abstractions, the fake complexity (when the real one is that of the psyche), the battles between schools (hiding a battle of egos), all of it is coming to a full stop as depth psychologists begin to speak evocatively instead of dogmatically. Theories that borrow the language of science but without the rigor of the scientific approach are useless as science and useless as literature.

After almost a century of trying to prove psychoanalytic theories right or wrong, depth psychologists have no other choice than to take into account the conclusion reached by their own community of researchers. A former president of the American Psychiatric Association, Alan Stone, professor of law and psychiatry in the Faculty of Law and the Faculty of Medicine at Harvard, in his keynote address to the American Academy of Psychoanalysis in 1996,[6] voiced the consensus: depth psychology belongs to the arts and the humanities, not to science and not to the medical model. He did not specify which of the arts, which of the disciplines of the humanities, but he says this in his conclusion that "psychoanalysis will survive in popular culture as a narrative by which we understand and reflect on the moral adventure of life." In other words, he is saying, without using the word, that psychoanalysis will survive as mythology. A mythology, to take his very words, is precisely "a narrative by which we understand and reflect on the moral adventure of life."

Depth psychologists, as well as their patients, can get back to the task of becoming psychologically wiser, philosophically brilliant, rhetorically inspired, and renew their alliance with the arts. We can, at last, stop trying to cure what will not heal, and fix what will not lie still. We can finally afford to stop the pathetic effort to surpass the Joneses (the scientists). Depth psychology has a niche: the art of creating virtual reality. It does not need to lay its eggs in somebody else's nest. Just as there is no denying the progress of medical research, there is also no denying that the richness of a culture is grounded in the humanities, which nurture the capacity to think deeply about things. Depth psychology, as a theory, is just that: a deep thinking about the life of the psyche and, as such, belongs to the arts and humanities.

## Schools, labels, egos, copyrights, money

Another factor of confusion when defining "depth psychology" comes from the fact that, over the past decades, the theoretical boundaries between the many depth-psychological schools following Freud, Jung, Adler, Reich, Rank, Lacan, Hillman, Klein, Bion, Winnicott, Bowlby and Kohut have broken down under the influence of the eclectic range of practitioners who are all interested in the unconscious dimension of the psyche, but reject the theoretical strictness of the founding fathers. Training institutes, in opening their doors to social workers, educators, philosophers, have fostered a climate of openness. As these new practitioners are trained in more than one approach, the traditional distinction between the concept of psychotherapy and that of psychoanalysis has also softened. Many practitioners are reluctant to label their approach because they want to avoid cultish overtones of schools based upon one founding father (are you Freudian or Jungian?) or one founding mother (are you Kleinian?).

Following that deconstructive mode, psychotherapy from a depth-psychological approach appears under many names: psychoanalytic psychotherapy, psychoanalysis, psychological analysis, analytical psychology. For the sake of simplicity, when in need of exploring differences between schools (such as that between the strictly Jungian approach as compared to the post-Jungian archetypal approach) I prefer to insist on the theoretical nuances in the thinking, rather than differences in the labeling of the approach.

This vagueness around the label of "depth psychology" echoes the vagueness around the word "psychology." First-year students in psychology are invariably confused by the fact that the word "psychology" can be affixed to almost any trend, any problem, any discipline: take the word "neuro" and affix the word "psychology" and you have "neuropsychology" which clearly belongs to science; but then you can also take the word "sport," or "music," or "parenting," or "aging" and affix the word "psychology" and you have four more psychologies: psychology of sport, psychology of music; psychology of parenting, psychology of aging. For some of these "psychologies" it is easy to see how they clearly belong to science: neuropsychology and neuropsychological assessment of memory disorders (such as amnesia, aphasia, apraxia); cognitive neuropsychology and assessment of speech and language disorders; neuropsychological rehabilitation; psychology of learning disabilities (such as dyslexia); psychology of motor development; experimental research in clinical and social psychology; clinical assessment and treatment; developmental psychopathology and gerontology; statistical research in mental health disorders.

It is also quite easy to identify the psychologies that belong in the mixed category of "social sciences": behavioral and cognitive development; social psychology (intergroup behavior, group dynamics, action research, participatory research, attitudes and persuasion, gender identity, sex roles, delinquency, prejudices, styles of leadership, social psychology of organizations, verbal and non-verbal communication, self and social identity); developmental psychology of early attachment (childhood, adolescence, adulthood, lifespan development, transitions, aging); comparative and intercultural psychology; psychology of moral development; psychology of animal behavior; economic psychology; political psychology, sport psychology.

And last, there are the psychologies that read like essays in the tradition of the humanities, although many of its authors still cling to a rhetoric redolent of social science: environmental psychology, feminist psychology, evolutionary psychology, psychology of religion, psychology of music, transpersonal psychology, ecopsychology, Freudian and post-Freudian psychoanalysis, Jungian and post-Jungian analytical psychology, imaginal psychology, archetypal psychology.

New "psychologies" are added every week, some of them little more than the product of ego-inflated authors trying to sell their copyrighted brand of psychology, others showing real innovation and answering the need to better understand the psyche–soma connection. Publishers' catalogues come up every year with more classifications to organize the genres in which their authors are writing. Students drink it all in and later make their own menu from all those approaches.[7]

This proliferation and specialization can be interpreted as a byproduct of the growing psychology industry but it may also signal a turning point in the history of psychology. I believe that the next psychologies will present themselves with clearer identities: on one side the psychologies that belong to science, and on the other side the psychologies that belong to the humanities and are concerned with becoming wiser humans. The richness of any culture is so obviously grounded in scientific progress that we have been inclined to take for granted other kinds of progress. Nevertheless, history is a demonstration of how advances in the humanities are determining of the quality of our existence because they bring a capacity to think deeply about things. Depth psychology, as a theory, is just that: a deep thinking about the psyche.

## What is deep about the psyche?

The power of depth psychology lies in: (a) an idea, (b) a technique, and (c) a quality of presence. The idea is simple: if I, the patient, refuse to examine the myths that organize my perceptions, I lead my life on automatic pilot, unaware even of a personal destination. As a result, I may end up in a disappointing land. An analysis may help me become aware of my navigational programming. The technique is also quite simple, although it takes some serious practicing. The therapist/analyst listens attentively, respectfully and in a non-judgmental manner. When he or she speaks, it should not raise the patient's resistances. There are other techniques, such as active imagination and dream analysis, but they only work when the listening and the speaking are just right.

The third element, the quality of presence, is not as simple as the first two. It is the one invisible and absolutely essential quality, almost impossible to define, and difficult to teach. The quality of presence differentiates a talented therapist from a mediocre one. That elusive quality is part of what makes therapy an art, the art of seeing through to the interior cinema projected upon the psyche. This art involves a nose for the lies that patients are telling themselves, an ear to detect a quaver in the voice, an intuition for what is unknown, even to the patient, a heart to host the suffering, and an intelligence to perceive the leitmotifs of the dramas being enacted. Needless to say, the analyst must have learned to identify just such factors in her or his own life.

The analyst brings to therapy some ideas, some techniques, and a quality of presence. The patient arrives at the first session with a similar set. He or she holds ideas, has developed survival techniques, and exhibits a quality of presence. The ideas that are usually discussed in therapy are the invalid inferences that make the patient's life so painful. For example, in most advanced societies, sexism and racism are now considered philosophical and moral errors and have been replaced by more equalitarian attitudes. Nevertheless, they linger in the psyche like toxic waste. The violent husband who lives in an antiquated mind set rages because his pay check does not buy him control over other human beings. The idea of equality between the sexes does not fit his beliefs. He does not see the advantage of such an ideological shift. Even if he gets past his resistance, he does not know how to "think" or "imagine" an equalitarian, reciprocal relationship between a man and a woman. It is his ideas that need therapy.

His ideas are sick, but sick ideas are not listed in the *DSM*, so the clinical label is attached to the person instead – one that locates the sickness in him and creates another problem. Most likely, the wife of that man is also trapped in rancid ideas, thinking that her submission precludes her taking responsibility for herself. If he beats the children, she may settle into the role of victim. Her thinking does not go far enough for her to conclude that she is a coward for letting him beat the kids. Sick ideas need therapy, which translates as enlightenment of the emotions, the intellect, the imagination. We are all sometimes unaware of the rotten ideas we have been fed. Regularly, we have to vomit them up. It might be healthy to think for a while not of glorious and happy things but to squeeze our eyes and catalogue all behaviors we are most terrified by, what psychic shadows hide in our uppermost attic closets.

The patient also has his or her set of coping techniques, a psychic survival kit that contains healthy as well as neurotic techniques of self-defense. All defense mechanisms are "techniques" to avoid psychic destruction. The problem is that the techniques are often outdated and have become too costly to perform, like a triple heart bypass to treat the arrhythmia of a panic attack. The patient's quality of presence to himself or herself as well as to others has usually deteriorated into a state of abuse and internal violence. One of the immediate benefits of psychoanalysis is that the patient comes to understand that this relationship to himself or herself can be improved, and that it is the basis for the relationship with others. The analyst educates the soul by showing, in practice, how presence can have a different quality. Analysis is not so much a cure as it is an education, like learning a new language, a philosophical adventure in self-discovery, an art of living more lucidly and intensely.

Psychological wisdom is the goal of an analysis. If wisdom is replaced by formulaic diagnoses and inflexible treatment plans, the quality of presence is lost. There is among young psychologists fresh out of school an optimism, an innocence, a naivety, and an inflation that is one of the results of an overly technical training. They are led to "believe" in their theories. They are taught to approach psychological suffering through all sorts of theoretical grids, processing all human emotions and life's complications as "problems" that this or that theory can solve. All the stories they hear go into a theoretical blender and come out in the form of a slush of "should" and "should not." Just as we have the techno-optimists, who believe that new technologies will bring the planet together, we have the psycho-optimists who believe that loss, angst, heartbreak, love triangles, fear of pleasure, fear of freedom, fear of life's adventure are all wounds that can be healed with the proper techniques.

The growing insistence on the code of professional rules of conduct (such as: no physical contact with the patient, no socializing, an office with two doors, not giving the patient information about your personal life, etc.) receives a lot of attention from students of psychotherapy. However, the more profound ethical issues of analysis are barely discussed. Rules are useful, but, more often than not, they are a set of legal guidelines to protect the therapist from litigation. The professional code of conduct provides a model that maintains a minimal kind of order. A model does not, however, ensure a positive result. Just as good table manners don't reveal anything about someone's ethical judgment, the ethics code of the American Psychological Association (APA) primarily reflects the technical, legal, and economic concerns of a corporate body. But a model that persists in ignoring the Dionysian aspect of the psyche cannot go very deep toward understanding the fury, anger, jealousy, betrayal, playfulness, tragedy, and complexity that are part of psychological life. As much as we may need more and more "fix-it" techniques in the service of productivity and mental health, a rich culture will also want to develop the art of dancing in sync with the psyche.

# Chapter 8

# Brother philosophy, sister psychology

Philosophy, rather than psychology, first had the reputation of being able to teach us how to grow up and live wisely. Psychology stole that role from philosophers. Brother philosophy and sister psychology might benefit from a good talk about their mission in the world. Since my own brother, Claude, is a philosopher, I am starting with my own personal effort at territorial reunification.

I am not one of those intellectuals who has read everything. Before reading Freud and Jung, I did not, as my brother Claude recommended, read the authors who had inspired them: Plato, Aristotle, Goethe, Kant, Kierkegaard, Heidegger. Claude is the philosopher of the family. Two years my senior, he was my first intellectual hero and a true brother. I saw him only on weekends and during summers, since I was in boarding school from age 7 to 20, but his influence was formative. The reciprocal influence of siblings has received very little attention in psychological literature, as compared to the study of the parental influence. That oversight is part of my motivation in exploring how my brother and I shaped each other's minds and psyches. It is also my way of expressing the necessity for philosophy and psychology to reconnect, as brother and sister can do. If he, a typical philosopher, and I, a typical psychologist, can talk and understand each other, so can our disciplines.

Claude read very systematically, with a logical progression and an impeccable discipline. He read the chapters in the order they were presented, noting quotations on cards, with full reference and a summary of the main ideas. I read right and left, here and there, this and that, with a voracious appetite and no logic. My brother intensely disapproved: "You read like a cat that follows the smell of spilled sardine oil on the kitchen floor!" I accepted his judgment on the inferiority of my method. I also accepted the metaphor of cat. Having interiorized the notion that I was a bit animalistic and of an inferior mind, I went on following my nose and read with feline pleasure, because I was truly incapable of his disciplined approach. Psychology felt like a better choice because there was more chaos in the theory and I could hide my own intellectual disorder.

Thus I read Jung before Freud, Proust at the same time as Bachelard, Lacan and his groupies at the same time as Jean-Paul Sartre and Simone de Beauvoir, humanistic psychology mixed in with existential psychology, Fritz Perls and his hippy friends at Esalen at the same time as English anti-psychiatry (Ronald Laing and David Cooper).

To get licensed and start a practice, I learned the coding systems and the dry language of the *DSM*. I initially liked the logic of such a neat system of "categorical classification that divides mental disorders into types based on criteria sets by defining features."[1] It certainly gives any young practitioner a sense of order and competence in being able to put a tag on human frailties, although when my classmates and I discovered that we all had many of the traits that were supposedly pathological, we began to question the status of the *DSM* as "the bible." From then on, most of us took it for what it is: a sometimes useful taxonomy to develop an eye for severe clinical pathology, an educational tool, an elaborate statistical survey of mental disorders with a huge caveat because "there is much physical in mental disorders and much mental in physical disorders."[2] Yes, indeed.

To wash down the dryness of the *DSM* approach, I read a lot of mystical teaching from all kinds of esoteric traditions and tried everything (chemical, intellectual, mystical) that could open the doors of perception. These turbulent years were like having a room with a view on that border between the mental and the physical. I also read a lot of pop psychology, because I earned good money writing articles for two different women's magazines. I earned even more money writing term papers for affluent students. I delivered papers on command: Szasz, Foucault, and the "post" (post-Freudians, post-Marxists, post-Lacanians), transpersonal psychology, Gestalt psychology, Rogerian psychology, transactional analysis. With the money I bought books and kept myself satiated, gobbling one sardine after the other.

Because I am a woman, I wasn't sure I had the right to have my own thoughts like a philosopher does. But as a psychologist, I could specialize in feelings. When depressed, I would buy lacy underwear as a reassurance that, at least if my brain wasn't good enough to philosophize, I had a good enough female body. Lacy underwear was never as helpful as reading liberating ideas. Reading was truly the source of the numinous for me. My gurus were all paper gurus – and still are. I met all my "masters," not in a temple or monastery, but in the library. The ideas found in books were more valuable to me, as a woman, than diamonds; they gave me permission to be fully human. Since my brother (who was always reading) was the one who pointed me in the direction of those brilliant thinkers, his influence was greater than I realized at the time. If Freud had been a woman, with such an interesting brother as mine, and as much in need of intellectual training as I was, maybe he would have balanced his theory about the influence of parents with a theory about the influence of siblings.

My brother's disapproval of my intellectual methods (and of my whole intellect in general) was a wounding that turned out to be a useful initiation. It prepared me for the critical reception of my colleagues in a department of communication at a state university in Montreal, Canada. Here I was, a 30-something tenured professor (with the face of an 18-year-old, and female), teaching – oh anathema! – some of Jung's ideas, in a course I had created on symbolic communication. My defense was that symbols are, after all, the only universal form of communication. A symbol does communicate, doesn't it? For example, the image of a tree laden with ripe fruits is consistently interpreted as meaning fertility, hope, joy, and never as death and decadence. Even when the symbolism is reversed (for example, a fairy tale with a poisonous apple tree that attracts innocent children) the effect of horror works because it reverses the customary meaning.

It is undeniable that Jung's exploration of symbolism contains many ideas extremely relevant to theories of communication, but the word in my milieu was that Jung was a mystic who did not belong in academia, and could at best attract a young faculty such as myself. It was admissible to teach Freud, as an influential historical figure – the founding father of depth psychology – but even with Freud the intellectual dogma was that soon "all that" (the depth psychological perspective) would be replaced by cognitive-behavioral therapies and neuroscience. I began teaching just the opposite: depth psychology is not in competition with neurosciences, any more than literature is in competition with dentistry.

The separation from the neurosciences is just now giving depth psychology its first chance at being itself. There is excellent neuroscience, and there is excellent experimental psychology, and there is our cultural history of the psyche and there is the crucial art of listening to the voice of the soul. All avenues have value if we differentiate them properly.

As for Jung's exploration of the spiritual aspect of inner life, it does belong in academia because it presents a rational argument for a psychological alternative to faith. Isn't academia the house of rationality? Jung's God is the Self, with a capital S and a useful reminder that there are realities bigger than the ego. For sure, Jung's language is often ambiguous. An atheist browsing through his work randomly may take his outpouring of religious emotions as the nostalgia of an ex-believer, or as a strategy to repackage the same old faith (God) in psychological wrapping (Self). One may agree (as I do) with much of the critique of Jung's mysticism, and still appreciate how his approach does offer an alternative to faith. Instead of prayer, active imagination; instead of redemption, individuation; instead of belief, the archetypal images of gods and goddesses – images, that's all! Instead of kneeling in adoration of an image, lie down on the couch, re-imagining all images that structure the experience of life. Instead of submission, analysis, lucidity, negotiation with the persistent desire to believe in the illusion of a powerful Daddy in the Sky.

Academia's vehement rejection of Jung has intensified over the years in curious ways, with numerous academics who have gone out of their way to demonize him and discredit the work of those who dare to find reading Jung inspiring. Negative reviews of Jung's work have consistently shown a suspicious intensity of rage at his inexplicable and enduring influence on millions of highly educated readers (clinicians, artists, scholars in the social sciences and the humanities, film-makers, novelists, architects, environmentalists, educators, and organizational developers). Jung's significant impact on the culture at large, as opposed to a specialized influence on a narrowly defined academic field, seems to be insulting to some academics.

The shunning of Jung is very similar to that of the mythologist Joseph Campbell, whose influence on the culture was immense despite its being ignored by the academics. There are many doctoral dissertations analyzing the cultural importance of the Star Wars mythology created by George Lucas, but anyone trying to write a dissertation on the author who, according to Lucas himself, was the intellectual inspiration for it, will be met with a list of unexamined reasons for the shunning. Campbell had the mentality and courage of a pioneer. A pioneer opening a new territory has to put up with rudimentary accommodations. Many of the theoretical critiques of Campbell are quite valid. Nevertheless, there is also some unexamined snobbery in a critique that says: what rudimentary theory! Maybe, but isn't this the case for all pioneers? The deceptively easy suggestion to "follow your bliss" was just the kind of formula that academia was only too happy to turn into a cliché, while it ignored the rest of his work. The fact that Campbell taught in a college (worse, a girl's college) instead of a major university is also part of what raised eyebrows.

To be able to teach some of Jung's – and some of Campbell's – ideas at the beginning of my career in academia, I found the following to be necessary: (1) a tenured position and relatively good evaluations by students; (2) a naivety regarding academic freedom; (3) a department that was so divided that no one cared or paid any attention to what anyone else was doing; (4) a field – communication studies – on which nobody has been able to impose a definition, because nobody really knows with certainty what "communication" or "communicating" means; (5) the advantage of unimportance; (6) the natural laziness of many academics who won't take the trouble of actually reading Jung – or Campbell – before expressing their opinion, which is usually the current intellectual party line.

Thus, I was at liberty to express, in polite academic words and with the good manners I had learned at the Convent of the Sacred Heart, the equivalent of: "Why don't you shut up? You haven't even read the author you are talking about." My tactic of intimidation worked well with the ignoramus; it did not work as well with a colleague who was one of the cognoscenti of Jung. This professor had spent years reading Jung, only to reject him at every occasion, his face flushed red from his outbursts of outrage at Jung's enduring success among the best of our mature students. This colleague was an interesting example of an emotional complex presenting itself as a logical demonstration. He inspired my canary test for academic air which consists in mentioning how much the work of Jung (or that of Campbell, depending on the context) means for me and my students, and then to examine the psychodynamic at work in the other's response.

If my interlocutor begins to choke at the very mention of those two names, I know I am dealing with an intellectual bigot. I am not saying their arguments are wrong, only that when the first reaction of an intellectual is an irrational outrage or a scandalized refusal to discuss, it signals a psychological complex, a notion first defined by Jung, and now part of everyday vocabulary. I don't even need a cage for this canary; it follows me, and it can even signal a lack of air in my own mind.

## Useful wounding

The academic milieu is indeed a minefield. The training I received as my brother's intellectual protégée was both wounding and helpful, another example of the paradoxical aspect of psychic reality. Claude's continual attacks on my lack of intellectual discipline were the best preparation I could have had to survive the rarified air of academia. Following the pecking order imposed on institutions of lower standing by those of higher standing, my milieu was dismissive of depth psychology in the same manner that my brother had been dismissive of my intellectual methods. Consequently I used the same tactics of survival and persisted in reading Jung for the abundance of tasty sardines. The company of millions of educated readers felt good enough for me.

My brother's criticism started in my adolescence, at the vulnerable age when I was terribly afraid that being "just a girl" implied that I might not possess a brain capable of serious thinking. Ever since Aristotle, women have been suspected of being closer to animals than to the rational citizen-philosophers of Plato's ideal city. I remember an acute attack of inferiority, at 15, when I asked Claude to give me feedback on a paper I had written with the title "The Symbols of the Night." He recommended that I change the title to "Nyctomorph Iconography," since it meant the same thing but looked more scholarly. I refused, finding it pretentious for one such as myself (after all, only a girl) to be talking in that style. He then predicted a life of difficulties for me. You will never be respected as an intellectual if you refuse to play the academic game. His prediction sent me into a state of panic, because, more than anything else in the world, I wanted to become an intellectual, as it meant for me somebody who has the ability to do his or her own thinking. It meant the world. It meant the triple motto of the French revolution: liberty, equality, fraternity (I did not know the term "sorority" then). It was not at all a desire to erase my animality, something Claude was fond of pointing out to me. It was a love of ideas that even the hormonally challenged mind of an adolescent girl can sometimes feel. One thing adolescents have in plenty is instinct. I was experiencing an instinctual refusal to be deprived of the human dimension of thinking. Nevertheless, when Claude insisted that becoming an intellectual meant playing the kind of "game" he was suggesting, I lost confidence, I wasn't sure I belonged. I refused to budge or to change the title of my paper, exhibiting what he then called a mule complex, because mules refuse to budge even if you beat them until they bleed. From cat to mule did not feel like a promotion, but at least a mule is capable of kicking back.

Five years later, the mule complex reasserted itself. This was the moment of Claude's greatest influence on my life. I was 20, and Claude declared that it was time I read Kant. To prepare myself, I found a book on Kant's correspondence, thinking it might be an easy introduction. By the end of the week, I felt as beaten as I had been at 15. I transcribed in my diary a passage from Kant's philosophical correspondence:

> In my judgment everything comes to this: that, since in the empirical concept of the composite, the composition is not given by means of the mere intuition and its apprehension but can only be represented through the self-active connection of the manifold in intuition and indeed in a consciousness in general (which is not empirical), this connection and the function thereof must stand under a priori rules in the mind, which constitute the pure thought of an object in general.
>
> (C II; 376)

The three girls who were my friends in boarding school were right: I should capitalize on my looks, not my brains. When I saw Claude a few days later, I showed him the passage from Kant, and told him that there was no way I could ever become an intellectual, and that finally, at 20, I was coming to my senses and giving up that ambition. We then had a crucial conversation:

*Claude:* What discouraged you?
*Ginette:* Kant is too obscure.

*Claude:*   Not so! Kant is difficult, but not obscure. Hegel is obscure, but not Kant.

*Ginette:*   Difficult or obscure, what difference does it make?

*Claude:*   The proof of the clarity of Kant's thinking lies in the fact that his commentators can agree on what he means. Such a thing is impossible when a thought is obscure, as opposed to simply difficult, or complex. The only obstacle here is your laziness.

*Ginette:*   Not so! It is not so much the difficulty that discourages me. I like complicated games. What really gets me is not the difficulty, it is the fact that Kant writes like this in a letter! Can you imagine? That kind of heavy thinking, that kind of style in a letter! A letter, not a lecture! Kant was writing these ideas to a disciple.[3] When I write a letter, I talk about the weather, my boyfriends, my new haircut, school anecdotes, silly gossip, perhaps dirty jokes. I end with lots of kisses and hugs and love love love XXX. My epistolary style seems to demonstrate that I am definitely not an intellectual.

Claude listened attentively. He was, at that time, developing a persona that I called King Solomon, because he was fascinated by Solomon's legendary wisdom and munificence, a splendid example of the wise philosopher. Claude's persona was still incomplete, like a website under construction today, but his budding wisdom had a determining impact on the rest of my life:

*Claude:*   Your letters are like all girls' letters! That is all there is to it. Girls are like that! Frills and kisses and silly giggling. That just is. No big deal. Wisdom starts with the acceptation of who, what, how, you are. You are a girl. Here is your homework: you are going to read, starting today, all of Simone de Beauvoir, and you will get it, once and for all, that a person can be a girl, and may care for dresses, cats, romantic movies, write letters with hugs and kisses, and still have a brain, still be able to THINK! To be a girl should never be an obstacle. Don't give me this excuse.

It was the admiration I had for the way Claude was using philosophy to think through psychological problems (especially mine) that convinced me not to renounce my intellectual goals. To be sure, Claude continued to use the vast repertoire of all my fears, but it worked out fine. Knowing how much I liked our intellectual games and how I craved access to his books, he would refuse conversation until I had done my homework. We were operating from an unconscious agreement that had been established very early in our childhoods.

As a child, Claude had been allergic to cats, dogs, hamsters, and many plants. He was not allergic to me, his little sister. I became his pet, to whom he taught intellectual tricks. I had to play by his rules. I was to look intelligent, ask relevant questions, to allow him to develop his ideas further, all attitudes that proved extremely useful to my survival later, as a woman, in an academic milieu. He was practicing his future role as a teacher of philosophy while I, the talking hamster, was learning to pass exams. We both became professors. His influence on me was definitely as determining as the parental influence.

I am grateful to him, as I am grateful to all my paper gurus, for orienting me toward the ideas that were crucial in enabling me to live my life on major chords, as I had imagined it. As Claude and I grew ready to go our separate roads, we had one last summer together. He was studying philosophy at the Sorbonne, and I too was in Paris, smoking Gitanes and drinking gallons of espresso coffee, going from the Café de Flore, to the Deux Magots, to La Coupole, to Brasserie Lipp. Like so many other admiring students, we waited for our intellectual divinities to appear: Jean-Paul Sartre, Simone de Beauvoir and their court. Alas, they had long abandoned the temple of our puppy-like devotion. Henry Miller, Beckett, Ionesco, Koestler, Merleau-Ponty, Camus, and Sydney Bechet were nowhere to be seen either.

That summer, Claude and I discussed Sartre's existential philosophy, page by page, ingesting, with the black coffee and the house wine that was then very cheap and very good, ideas by which we lived for the rest of our lives. That period crystallized into one enduring principle: to be free, one must be responsible for oneself. This one gem of wisdom is all that I really understood about Sartre, about de Beauvoir, about existentialism, and about feminism. Very little, but enough. At the age of 20, we are not as dumb as some insecure professors try to make us feel by hiding their ordinariness in esoteric fog. Youth is a time of ignorance. The raging hormonal battles and intense sexuality at times blur the mind, but also sharpen it because of the vital need for new ideas. Precisely because it is such a crucial time, youth also means that one is capable of ingurgitating, at a fantastic speed, really big and meaty ideas. Personally, I needed them as much as food, drink, and sex.

Later that year, like the unfolding of the first principle (one is responsible for oneself), I added to my personal manifesto three other big ideas from Sartre: (1) the ego is a construction, and hence can be deconstructed; (2) the existence of the unconscious does not contradict our basic freedom, because one can see through one's bad faith;[4] (3) love is not the desire to possess the other – it is a wish to see the other gain a maximum of freedom and a deep desire to contribute, participate, support, accept, share the freedom.

De Beauvoir's feminism was soon amplified by American feminists who were presenting these liberating ideas for women of the world and translating them into political activism. Their writing style was accessible and vivid, thus helping millions of women to rethink their values. I was so completely seduced by this typically American style that there and then I vowed to serve this ideal in my teaching and writing. Later on, other ideas came to contradict, deconstruct, or replace early existentialist influences. De Beauvoir's feminism was criticized by American as well as European feminists, who, like Luce Irigaray, believed it denied women their otherness (alterity).

Some of the best women film-makers (like Agnes Varda) took an anti-de Beauvoir view in their films, showing how being in a woman's body is determining, insisting on the sensual, bodily experience of being female. Post-de Beauvoir feminism was a time to claim the difference of femininity. Female students defiantly began doing things like knitting while listening to the teacher's lecture, flaunting their femininity like a symbol of identity. This insistence on otherness added a layer to feminist thinking and convinced me of the need for a pluralistic approach to feminism. De Beauvoir's feminism insists on our shared humanity (and all the issues of equal pay for equal work), while Irigaray's feminism explores identity, which needs the contrasts of alterity.

I now think a pluralistic approach to feminism reveals not only two opposing feminisms, but as many feminisms as the minds of men and women care to think of, as they are all modalities of freedom. One can imagine, for example, one feminism for each goddess of the Greek Pantheon, or one feminism per philosophy (de Beauvoir imagined an existentialist feminism, Irigaray a psychoanalytic feminism), or one feminism per culture.

Polemic and contradiction will accompany these intellectual constructions, but polemic and contradiction are part of what makes the life of the mind like the never-ending renovation of a magnificent grand mansion. Take that wall down. Add a window. Frame that door. Elevate that roof, open the view here, close it there, and then start all over again because the house of ideas that was fixed years ago is now crumbling and needs another round of renovation. Ideational structures need renovation all the time because the ideas and even more the vocabulary of which they are made ages as fast as a wood floor gets scratched and plaster joints crack.

Before leaving the family cocoon for good, Claude and I split the world in two. On one side, there would be the philosophers, whose task was to dust off the dry messes of contradictory ideas that battle against each other. On the other side, there would be the psychologists, whose task was to mop up the liquid messes of human tears about those same contradictions. It seemed obvious that philosophy belongs to the animus and psychology to the anima, which meant that I would become a psychologist, and he a philosopher. This parting of the world was as senseless as saying that women don't have ideas and men don't have emotions, but we did not see the problem at the time. Sometimes, at 20, one may have stupid arguments to justify a not so bad choice, one that instinctively makes sense. For the wrong reasons, we made the right choices and spent the next 30 years feeling respectively at ease in our fields.

However, since cracking my head and feeling all disjointed, I feel a renewed need for philosophy. Consequently, I have reconnected with Claude. We continue, via the internet, the conversation that was interrupted by the business of our growing up.

### Dear Brother: what is on your list?

Dear Brother,
You always insisted that the task of philosophy was not to answer questions but to refine them, to examine as many aspects of a question as our minds can possibly hold, to expand the intellect. I found this Bertrand Russell quotation in

a card you sent me for my sixteenth birthday: "Philosophy is to be studied, not for the sake of any definite answers *to* its questions, but rather for the sake of the questions themselves; because these questions enlarge our conception of what is possible, enrich our intellectual imagination, and diminish the dogmatic assurance which closes the mind against speculation; but above all because, through the greatness of the universe, which philosophy contemplates, the mind also is rendered great, and becomes capable of that union with the universe which constitutes its highest good." The card on which those words were written is half rotten because of the dampness in my basement. Yet, the words are still filled with the same freshness as when I first read them because my mind is now pondering anew some of those big philosophical questions.

I would very much appreciate it if you would give me a list of the most recurrent philosophical questions, those that are unanswerable but always reformulated. I would like to compare your philosopher's list with the list of questions that seem to arise for every person undergoing psychoanalysis.

Your favorite (because only) Sister

## Dear Sister: a list of deep questions

Dear Sister,
Here is my formulation of the "biggies." These fundamental questions are at the core of every philosophy. The list is potentially infinite, and each question has infinite depth, just like the unconscious. Let's start with one traditional set of: what, when, where, how, why.

1   What is a good life? What is the best balance, for me, of the quest for truth, love, justice, beauty? What are the values that are most likely to make me appreciate my humanity?
2   When should I strive toward "having" more, and when should I strive toward "being" more?
3   Where does my freedom begin and where does it infringe on the freedom of others?
4   How does one behave when there is a conflict between your freedom and mine?

5   Why is there something rather than nothing? This question
    is on everybody's list.

Your Brother

### Dear Brother: surprise!

Dear Brother,
Will you be surprised to hear that patients arrive in therapy
with a very similar list? Of course, I have never heard anybody
say, "Doctor, I am experiencing a philosophical dilemma. I
don't know where my freedom begins to infringe on the
freedom of another." No! I am much more likely to hear
something like this: "I feel trapped in my marriage. My wife is
smothering me to the point of psychic strangulation. I want a
divorce, but I know it will hurt her profoundly. I wonder if I
can bear the guilt of wounding anybody that deeply."
    Nor have I ever heard a patient declare: "I have come to you
to for guidance in the resolution of conflict between two
individual freedoms." The same conflict was formulated by a
woman who asked if she had a right not to tolerate it that her
husband checked the mileage on her car every morning, to
make sure that she was not going anywhere else but from
home to work and back.
    It seems that your profession and mine deal with the same
list of problems. I am sure it will come as no surprise to you,
because philosophers (in competition with clergy) used to be
the counselors of souls. Although I am glad that Freud and
company broke the monopoly of priests, pastors, and rabbis, I
find it a pity that philosophers and psychotherapists don't talk
shop anymore. Brother! You and I face the same problems,
your gang and mine!

Your Sister

### Dear Sister: you want global talk?

Dear Sister,
Not only is there a lack of communication between philosophers and psychotherapists, there is also a lack of
conversation between the different "sects" of philosophers;
there are tribal wars in all philosophy departments, in all

university campuses. Where, with whom, how do you think
you can have that global conversation?

Your Brother

## Dear Brother: the globalization of psyches

Dear Brother,
Global is the right adjective for the conversation I yearn for.
Or maybe I yearn for a war of words, not one of guns and
blood. I am angry that the incessant discussion about globalization is only about money and things. What is more
"global" than the need for a conversation about the big
questions, about inner life, and about human relations? Tears
are tears, joy is joy, anger is anger, love is love, oppression is
oppression, freedom is freedom, and the psychology around
these emotions is similar whether you live in the U.S., France,
Japan, Brazil, Argentina, India, Africa, Canada, or Australia.
Why would it be different when asking the big philosophical
questions? A global exchange of psychological and philosophical insights is as much needed as the exchange of goods.
Everywhere, all the time, with everyone on the planet, there is
a constant need for the examination of values, of philosophies
and of psychologies.

The next psychologies will have to be "global" and inclu-
sive of all cultures for the same reason that software capability
needs to be upgraded constantly for global business to work.
The actual need for assessment of psycho-cultural assumptions
is as crucial as assessing global capabilities for business. Just as
we all, regardless of our circumstances, have to come up with
a budget (even the very rich), a schedule (even kids and retired
persons), we also all have to come up with a value system, in
other words, a philosophy that orients our choices on this
planet.

If the language of both our trades wasn't so heavy, maybe
philosophers and psychologists could have their own kind of
globalization summit. The kind of philosophical jargon that
professional philosophers favor is extremely localized,
clannish, esoteric, making me feel I am back to square one
with having to say "nyctomorph iconography" instead of
"images of the night."

Let me tell you a moment of great unease I experienced in my recent effort to refresh my meager philosophical education. Last month, your old friend – whom you nicknamed Yep because of his way of pronouncing Yes as Yep – was lecturing at the University of Los Angeles and I drove from Santa Barbara to hear his talk. He was introduced with great fanfare, as a philosopher of great significance to our time, and the audience applauded enthusiastically even before he opened his mouth to talk.

He lectured magnificently on Schopenhauer and Spinoza, his specialty, but I am afraid that only a few people in the room understood what he was talking about. I could not grasp even one idea. It was a waste of my time, a waste of gasoline, a waste of a chance to educate myself. I don't object to the fact that, being a professor of philosophy, he needs to demonstrate his mastery of a complex conceptual apparatus. I don't really object that Yep requires his disciples to spend years learning his ultra-specialized vocabulary as such discipline forms the mind. I do understand that each specialty develops its own jargon and sometimes it is necessary. I do find it sad, however, that Yep, like so many philosophers, chose to speak exclusively to the linguistically initiated.

Are you aware that this kind of intellectual elitism is exactly what made it so easy for us, psychologists, to steal most of your devotees? The intellectually curious, who used to gather around the philosophers, as you and I gathered around our existentialist wise men and women, have been coming toward psychology because they can readily follow our conversation about the soul.

Your friend's intellectual haughtiness is such that it contradicts one of your dearest theories – that philosophy ultimately leads to intellectual humility and wisdom. Let me tell you, such is not the case with Yep! Following his talk, there was a banquet for all the presenters, the finale of that international conference. Yep was unaccompanied and he invited me to join him, for old time's sake, and because he wanted to hear all about you. We sat at one of those large round tables that are typical of hotel ballrooms. A woman that I happen to know and admire joined our table. She is a formidable woman who represents for me all that I like about Americans: she has great intellectual courage, boldness, honesty, strength and generosity. At one point, she turned toward Yep and said she was glad to have a philosopher at the table, because she had recently read about the concept of "nothingness," and found it a really rich concept for her own work as a psychiatrist.

She began explaining her understanding of it, and how it helps her think about things that are "not things" (like love and fear). I listened closely, because, as you know, this concept was and remained one of those concepts that fascinates me. The difference is that I would never have the guts to engage in a discussion on the concept of "nothingness" with a professional philosopher, armed only with the vocabulary of the laity, after two glasses of wine! She had no problem with it, however, and went on explaining why she found it such a great concept!

I was ashamed of your friend's attitude! He had that condescending smile, that barely concealed contempt, that medical doctors often use when patients attempt to use proper medical terms to discuss their diagnosis. Daddy used to call that "the smile of the political boss," elaborately friendly and warm when encountered at the charity fundraiser, civil on the street corner or at Sunday services, but someone who would not hesitate to destroy your reputation, bankrupt your business, burn your house, waste your car, if you ever reveal his *Mafioso* tactics.

Your friend's contempt was palpable under the politeness. His coldness seemed to suggest, "Hey little lady, you are in over your head. I'll be polite, but don't try to play on my turf." He mowed her down with heavy jargon. Her jaw dropped and she remained silent for the rest of the meal. I think she lost her interest in the concept of "nothingness," and I lost respect for Yep.

Why is it that everyone feels free to invent his or her own homemade brand of psychology, but not so with philosophy? It is quite acceptable to do dream interpretation over morning coffee, to discuss the "defensive reaction" of a colleague, or to explore the "unconscious dynamic" of a relationship. Everyone has her own ideas and theories about what is therapeutic and what is not. Being an amateur psychologist, a "bricoleur," a jack-of-all-trades fixing all kinds of psychological leaks, does not seem to pose a problem. The guy I consult when I have computer problems is the father of two little boys, identical twins. He has his own original psychological theory to explain why his toddlers are slow in developing language skills. He says, "Their psyches communicate like two computers working in parallel. Why would they be in any hurry to develop language skills?" His theory makes sense to him. His metaphor is, in fact, quite good, given what is known about the psychological development of identical twins. Why, then, are we so intimidated when we attempt to develop our own, homemade brand of philosophy?

Why should it be acceptable to interpret a dream but shameful to be an amateur philosopher, interested in the concept of "nothingness?" Faced with the experience of being human, aren't we all amateurs – the philosopher as much as any other? I am not suggesting that the ordinary person knows as much as the specialist educated in the history of philosophical concepts. It takes years of dedication to understand all the subtleties and nuances of concepts that have a long history. Rather, I am suggesting that we all share in the big philosophical questions. The difficult experience of having children and raising them with limited success was, for me, a reminder that we are born novices in all things. I knew nothing about parenting when I was required to begin it. I had no other choice than to start, even with my very limited skills. Despite the fact that parenting is one of the most important responsibilities of life, most of us are completely unprepared when we begin. We face birth, as well as death, as beginners, without benefit of rehearsal.

I heard a child trying to use the word "discombobulated." With great earnestness, it came out like this: "I feel dis-clum-blow-blu-tilated today." Those present smiled affectionately, but none were tempted to use the sharp knife of ridicule. Why, then, the facile contempt of so many philosophers for a mind that is just being introduced to a new concept? Isn't it normal that the first time one tries to understand "nothingness," one is a bit disclummed, blowblued and tilated by the novelty of it?

I thought philosophy was supposed to help us get wiser by discussing the biggies, the questions that come back every generation. Met with ridicule, the big questions recede in silence and it is a terrible loss for the soul. Most of us, when articulating our homegrown version of our philosophy of life, are doing a kind of intellectual bricolage that can be naively idealistic, somewhat incomplete and filled with contradictions. However, it allows for a vital exchange with others.

Truly, Claude, I cherish my half-baked philosophy, made up from all the leftovers of those *readings* and exchanges between us in our youthful days. Despite my lack of expertise, it still feels better than having no philosophy at all. Sometimes, nothing more than a wreck of a car, if it still works, can get one to a nice location. My philosophy is of that kind. It is all patched up, but it works. Having put it together myself, I know how to fix it when it breaks. I know it inside out, and I feel I could discuss "my philosophy of life" with anybody on this planet given a minimal shared vocabulary. Isn't that a step we all have to take for globalization to mean something grand? I wish you and your esteemed colleagues would cease judging "personal philosophies" by the same standards that scholars apply to their equals in the academy. Philosophy is so much more than a head-trip. Even a little bit of it can appease the heart's longings.

Your Sister

### Dear Sister: same to you

Dear Sister,

I am sorry to hear that Yep seems to have turned into a snob, betraying his ideal of Wise Old Man, but he is not dead yet, and maybe he'll come around when glory fails him. Sometimes, the past tense of the "has been" balances the future tense of the "wannabe" and, at last, one lives in the present. Time will tell.

I agree with your critique of "us" that is to say, the professionals of philosophy. I have the exact same problem with "you," the professionals of the psyche! Your field, as much as mine, has fallen prey to the esotericism of academic specialization. To appreciate a jargon, one needs, first, to want to "belong," and second, to know which intellectual clan one wants to belong to – both of which are contrary to globalization.

Allow me to consider, as an example, a concept dear to your clan: transference. There is an oppressive amount of theoretical elaboration about transfer and transference. Tell me if my basic understanding is still valid. I understood transference to mean childhood feelings that continue to be felt even after the disappearance of the person who incited them, even when faced with the evidence that the circumstances have completely changed. You were the one who pointed to the passage in Freud where he explains that transference is a "false relationship," since the patient is not talking to the person of the analyst, but to the person of his or her fantasy, a person who is no longer there, the ghost of parents.

The theme of false relationships happens to be a major philosophical theme because philosophical wisdom is expected to teach one to be fully present to the reality of the other person. The textbooks in psychology discuss this challenge as a problem of transference, but in a language that is not exportable, not globalizable because each clan develops its own coded jargon to defend its theoretical turf.

You analyzed your disappointment with the kind of philosophy that Yep represents for you. Let me tell you of my disappointment with the first psychoanalysis that I did, which lasted three years. The relationship to my analyst was so contaminated by the romantic infatuation with our transference that it took me a long time to become aware of my annoyance, because I was busy reading everything I could find about the phenomenon of "transference," as if it was some new discovery that would give me the key to my family drama. The relationship to mother had been, as you very well know, my main motivation to undertake analysis. The analyst's hypothesis was that the analysis of a transference would lead to my discovery of how I project mother's coldness on to others, beginning with him, the analyst. It took me three years to realize that the analysis of the transference was just as sterile and just as boring as when my first girlfriend insisted that we talk about you-and-me-and-our-relationship all the time. We – the analyst and I – were talking about "us" most of the time, all the while giving ourselves permission to disregard all those real women that I wanted to be able to make love to, had I been done with that damn transference!

Who's responsible for the failure? Certainly I am, but what if the analyst was also incompetent? Another possibility is that the concept of transference itself is a dangerous one, one that caused confusion for both of us. His insistence on transference gave me the illusion that he had a secret knowledge of the mysterious ways of the soul. How am I to know if he is competent, and not a self-centered person who uses transference to figure out who he is in the world?

So many in your profession seem to suggest that they know the map of the whole unconscious territory, it is seductive. After three years, I came to a point where I felt nauseated by the whole romance of transference and counter-transference and let the analyst figure it out for himself! I started over with another analyst, one who intuitively felt much more competent. He was not one to insinuate that he knew the cartography of the unconscious. He seemed to be "in service" to the psyche, like a faithful butler whose dignity is equal to that of the master. One cannot imagine the butler saying: "Sir, I have a transference problem with you," because the butler knows he is in service to something bigger than himself: not only a family and a house, but also a tradition, a culture. The master of the house, the house, and the butler are one and the same piece in a complex story. The new analyst was truly a servant of psyche, and so was I, and it was a much more interesting adventure. Very soon I was able to get closer to women I am attracted to. Fear of love receded. My heart expanded. Like yoga, whose benefit is to be had most of all in old age, analysis helped me put in place some interesting liberation strategies to avoid what happened to our mother as she aged. You remember how, toward the end of her life, she, who had been a sociable person, retreated into the insipid routine of her luxurious retirement home and did not perceive how the pampered artificial environment accentuated her natural tendency toward self-absorption. This growing egocentrism, and not her old age, was cutting her off from the world. She had always refused to be "psychological," always fearing to look inside, and now having emotions became increasingly unsettling to her. She did not care to put a name *to* her feelings, afraid of getting close to them. Even positive emotions, holidays, birthday parties or the celebration we organized in her honor all felt tiring to her, too much of a risk to feel something.

Maybe having been such a beautiful woman was a handicap. Her great physical beauty allowed her to remain unconscious. Our father was the one who worked at becoming conscious. When Dad died, she felt deprived of his devotion, and her heart did not have the strength to reach out to others. She resisted all our attempts to enrich her life. It was too late for psychological yoga. When I look at myself in the mirror, and see traces of that same stiffness in my facial expression, I am glad that I still trust the process of psychoanalysis; it is my psychological yoga. We all need a means of sustaining a supple psyche, one that remains capable of being interested in others.

I truly believe that we all have deep wounds that are deliverers of wisdom, if only we stop beating ourselves on our heads and instead try to find words, all kinds of words, from all kinds of disciplines and cultures. That is the gift of education: words. Like a teacher who initiates one into the beauty of language, the depth of psychological suffering can initiate one into the beauty of the psyche. Believe it or not, I am convinced that depth psychology can be as much a path to wisdom as philosophy. I am not suggesting that psychologists reject wisdom. I am sure you all worship it, but I am convinced that "wisdom" is not a word that you heard during your training, or that you use in the therapy room. There is no educational preparation for passing on to the next generation the hard-won collective experience formulated by wise human beings through the ages. The technical training of students in psychology has no room for a notion as impractical as "wisdom." It produces therapists who confront each new cultural issue as something novel, as if psychic suffering is a challenge now encountered by society for the first time. If only you could formulate for me, in a nutshell, what you think might constitute psychological wisdom, I would be grateful.

Your Brother

## Dear Brother: what is a good life?

Dear Brother,
Here it is in a nutshell: I think that psychological wisdom starts, just like philosophy, with asking questions. Psychologists have been in conversation for a hundred years now and you will find it interesting that the questions being asked are similar to the philosophical inquiry about what *constitutes* a "good life." We are asking: what does it mean to "grow up,"

to be a Mother, a Father, a Child, an Adult, a Man, a Woman? We don't agree on the answers, and that is where the conversation becomes interesting. Let me start with the conversation about the meaning of "mother."

Your Sister

# Chapter 9

# The archetype of Mother

A whole generation of therapists has favored the model of the developing child as the road map for the evolution of the personality. The language of "personal growth" belongs to this developmental model. The idea that we "grow," as a child grows (or as the economy grows), has come to replace what used to be imagined as the deepening of experience and the lifelong quest for wisdom. Approaches based on the monomyth of the inner child have let the wounds, the needs, the vulnerabilities of the inner child create a tyrannical divinity, the exact replica of a repressive monotheism. "God the Father," the jealous and omnipotent patriarchal deity, has been replaced by "God-the-Child," equally possessive and omnipotent. A whole generation of young adults won't grow up, caught betwixt and between the Child and the Adult, and the consequences of their failure is tragic for them as for the rest of society. This proliferation of infantile adults is unprecedented in history and typical of affluent societies. Good kids, intelligent, educated, competent in many areas, just won't leave adolescence. The problem has been analyzed from the perspective of sociology, anthropology, psychology, and economy, and the general conclusion seems to be that it is a byproduct of the unprecedented wealth of rich nations. Moreover, failure to mature is not limited to contemporary adolescents; it involves adults as well and is felt as a problem of civilization.

Developmental psychology, by placing the child at the center of our theories about the psyche, starts with a basic truth: our needy inner child needs our attention; otherwise, it won't grow up. Agreed! The archetypal Child personifies not only a fundamental vulnerability that remains in all of us, but also carries the principle of joy, of play, of spontaneity. However, it does not imply that we

should make of the Child the center of psychological consciousness. Self-proclaimed victims are invariably infantile adults not
wanting to take responsibility. Victimhood is a model for very real
infantile impotence and rage; in an adult, it is a waste, a dis-
empowering road map.

The generalized failure to grow up indicates a breakdown in our
mythology. Our myth of mom, dad and the kids seems to call for
more deconstruction before we can have reconstruction. Let's take
another look at the myth of mother, since it is the first one we
experience when growing up.

## The Great Mother: the cradle and the cage

Mothering offers an experience of pure power, a power women
often deny because they want to see only their love for the child.
Whether one describes this power positively – I give you life – or
negatively – without me you die – it remains power. In those first
months of life, the child's dependency gives to the mother the
ultimate power of life and death, a heady elixir for anybody. One
would expect that women who dedicate themselves exclusively to
their kids would be relieved when the kids grow up; but many
experience just the opposite. The end of mothering can also signal
the end of their power trip and they resent it.

As the child matures, he or she moves out of the Great Mother's
realm and the little mother is dismissed for a job well done. For
the super-mom, the end of the Great Mother's sovereignty elicits
such a deep identity crisis that she may misinterpret her resistance
to leave the throne as a proof of her unflinching devotion. For the
child, mom's tiresome maternal performance can turn into a
psychological tragedy as it does invariably when an archetypal
elixir has been drunk to the dregs and the partner forces more
down your throat. The gift of maternal love can turn into a curse
when her unconditional love becomes an albatross around the
neck of the child, preventing growth. The cradle becomes a cage.
We come into the world with our mother, but we die alone.
Between these two events, the infantile illusion of safety must thin
out until the child is strong enough to bear the responsibility of his
or her decisions.

The mother whose role is over has a similar learning to do, that
of empowering herself from a different source. It is also a service
to the cause of bringing forth a more egalitarian society. Although

patriarchy has been dominant throughout history, every man has had the early experience of being dominated by one woman: his mother. The more sexist the society, the more chances are that maternity is the only outlet for feminine power, thus underlying the mother's sentiments of maternal love with a huge power complex. The consequence is a vicious circle of reinforcement of male chauvinism, one which could explain why patriarchy has had such a long history. The grown-up sons, offered the reins of power, cannot resist the temptation to finally control women, to protect themselves from the original fear of mother, a fear that is generalized into a fear of the intensity of female emotions and power.

## Do I love you or do I need you?

The goal of self-sufficiency is an ideal and, as such, it remains unattainable. No mother can ever repudiate the sentiment of maternal love for her adult child; and no adult is ever over the need for mothering, as the mourning for our mothers shows, without regard to the age when it happens. The accumulated experience of mothers and fathers, educators, clergymen, rabbis and therapists confirms that nobody ever completely becomes an adult. The greatest spiritual leaders admit that the frightened needy child still lives in their psyche. Through our ordeals, it is human to yearn for some compassionate being to hold our hand, lend a hand, rally round and offer maternal affection and support. What defines an adult psyche is not the independence from a need for compassion and protection but a basic orientation toward achieving responsibility. In contrast, the psyche of unweaned adults is increasingly oriented toward manipulation to transform everyone around them into a Great Mother. The basic appeal is: "Please do it for me, it is too hard!"

Manipulative behaviors have at their source a perversion of the figure of the healthy child. A child is needy, vulnerable and dependent, but if the relationship with the adult is healthy, the child wants nothing more than to get stronger, let go of that helping hand, walk by herself, live his own life. The impulse to leave the cozy cradle to explore uncharted territory is the most fundamental expression of libido; it is a love of life, a love for the world that makes one want to reach out and experiment. Moments of regression, of wanting to touch home base and to reach for cover will happen each time we feel vulnerable, but the mature adult knows that permanent security is an illusion, and a trap.

Our myth of maternity suffers from a lack of differentiation between very different kinds of love. The child who says, "I love you, mommy," is expressing a feeling that has very little to do with love as we define it since the Greeks: a choice by two *free* individuals. The child – or any person – who cannot survive without the caregiver, cannot engage in what our tradition means by love. The toddler's hugs and kisses are, no doubt, totally endearing. One has to have a desiccated heart to remain cold at a child's eruptions of joy at being alive and loved. But deep down, we also know that the child is not really expressing love but need: "Please, mother, love me, feed me, protect me. Don't ever leave me and I'll be sweet and cuddly forever." As many an absentee parent has experienced, a baby will forget you much more quickly than your old dog, if the maternal substitute is good enough. The hugs and kisses will go to the new caregiver.

Unlike the ancients, we use only one word for all kinds of love. The Greeks had three:

1   Agape is love between brothers/sisters/friends; it can also be interpreted as a kind of devotion to the world, for humanity, or – as the Christians interpreted it – a command to love thy neighbor as thyself.
2   Eros is a passionate form of love that usually implies sexual attraction, attachment and a great intensity of feelings.
3   Philia means any kind of liking for something: I love music, birds, chocolate, books, cooking, hiking. Having only one word, we use "love" to say, "I love my dog and my dog loves me in return."

That the same word love is used for a spectrum of very different emotions creates a problem that is more than semantic because we spend the first part of our life differentiating all those extremely different emotions, all touched by the name of love. If one maintains that the feeling of the child for the mother is love, one is faced with a strange paradox. One would have to conclude that the teenager is incapable of love because of a furious need for independence and separation. The paradox here is that the teenager, in spite of obvious narcissism, is progressively getting closer to the philosophical ideal of freedom from need that is a prerequisite for love. Nobody ever reaches the philosophical ideal and, as a consequence, the "inner child" and "inner adolescent" in us continue to struggle with finding a balance between the need for independence and the need for connection.

## Avoiding neurotic contracts

The kind of autonomy that the average psyche can hope for can be described not only as a positive – an ideal of freedom – but as a negative – a capacity for avoidance of what is not love. It is another instance where the via negativa might be the only road. Just as it is impossible to define, in absolute terms, what a normal psyche looks like, we don't have a stable definition of love. We know with more certainty what it is not, which indicates a direction. It is not nowhere land; it is a way (via) where one knows only what to say no to (negativa). It is a path where you sense where the traps are, which is already a lot. Somebody on the via negativa is able to smell the destructiveness of worn-out psychological patterns. Avoidance can take many forms. Pitfalls, precipices, poisonous waters, and hidden traps are extremely useful indications on a map; they tell one where not to go. Feminism, for example, is such a map. The traditional patriarchal pact was originally – and still can be, under the right circumstances – a fair deal, based on a notion of love between man and woman that has a long history. One party takes care of the kids/the house/the familial and social circle, while the other earns the money. This deal may be as equitable as any other contract if both genders feel the freedom to engage in it as they wish. The inequality of power between partners is what spoils it. If the wife won't, or can't, grow up (because of restrictions imposed by law, tradition, or religion), the relationship turns into a parent/child one. In exchange for being taken care of, the woman is expected to submit to the authority of her husband (or brother, uncle, son, father-in-law). The husband is tied to his role as provider, not only for the children, but for the adult wife as well. His love feels like a responsibility, whereas the submissive wife's love feels like obedience. This we can recognize as not love.

Even in post-feminist cultures, there is no lack of candidates who will sign up for what they think is a good traditional deal between a man and a woman who believe they love each other.

The problem is not necessarily with the deal but with the wife's unconscious need for dependence (not love) when it finds its opposite in the husband's unconscious need to control (not love). A neurotic partnership may look like this: I'll be your daddy and pay the bills. In exchange, I'll maintain absolute control of the relationship. Romantic literature has consistently obscured the reality of neurotic choices with sweet lies. The handsome hero will convince the beautiful, fragile, childlike woman that she needs to let him take care of her financially, socially, psychologically, intellectually and spiritually. I'll take such good care of you that you won't need your own money. Man is the container and woman the contained. You'll do the feeling, I'll do the thinking; for example, I think one God is enough and he should be male.

Women and men who traveled the via negativa will smell the trap but younger couples may not. The post-feminist generation inherited a big capital of freedom from the feminist investments of their foremothers. What young woman needs an analysis of "patriarchal oppression" when she is traveling the via positiva of wanting it all: the security of a rich husband and the autonomy of a single girl with a profession? Most daughters of feminists (my darling adult daughter included) have very little historical sense of what the feminist war of liberation was all about. I have met high school girls who think it was about not wanting to wear girdles and bras. This ignorance keeps them in a naive positive dream of having simultaneously both the autonomy won by feminists and the security of the old patriarchal deal. In this girlish dream there is no contradiction between developing their own strong identity and, at the same time, keeping themselves safe and secure through a financially advantageous marriage. They have not yet traveled the via negativa. They believe they know what love is. The sweet illusion is as much a trap for young men, sons of feminists, who may long for the pre-feminist agreement. They romanticize the old contract and sign on cheerfully. I'll be your hero, provider, protector, and you'll be the Queen of the House, the Mother I can finally control. What neither of the partners are prepared for is the Hegelian power game of master/slave, whose complications sooner or later cause the deal to go sour. The education their generation has received is so unpsychological and so unphilosophical that few have any idea of the emotional cost of a love that hides a mutual agreement to remain unconscious. On the side of the woman, it implies that she remain a child. I belong to you as long as you provide for me, and my emancipation is out of the question. On the side of the man, it implies that he will have to sustain a heroic posture for a lifetime, often at the cost of his health.

Regression to dependency is a natural defense against the suffering that comes from discovering ourselves to be separate individuals. However, to develop psychological wisdom we must learn, early on, that even the most loving relationship cannot spare us the solitude of human destiny. There exists a psychological necessity to spread our wings, or, as Jean-Paul Sartre put it most succinctly for the benefit of my generation: we are condemned to freedom.

The idyllic illusion of an invincible parental fortress against all evil accompanies a good start in life. Mommy and Daddy provide a home where Baby is protected from dangers both within and without. The psychological gains are, however, positive only as long as the dependency is of an essential nature, due to the fragility of the human infant, or to sickness. But the romantic girl who dreams of rebuilding the fortress by marrying the hero, or her husband who believes he can buy himself a mother whom he can control, are victims of an unexamined myth that keeps them infantile. An adult who fails to mature is one whose energies are spent trying to re-create the situation where much is received and little is given in return. Chances are that such people will also raise children who grow up to be infantile adults.

The compassion with which a community deals with its sick and its disenfranchised has always been, and remains, an infallible criterion by which the level of civilization can be measured. All advanced cultures – some more than others – offer support systems for those really broken. Nevertheless, these same systems are susceptible to corruption and constantly need revision. In order to sustain a safety net (or safety nest) designed to provide compassionate recourse for the truly needy, it is crucial to stop the abuses by unweaned manipulative adults. The kind of developmental psychology that places our inner wounded child in the center of our consciousness has not helped them at all. Quite the opposite, it has given them words and means to pervert one of the most essential qualities for a community: the natural sense of compassion of most humans. The concept of "sustainable development" starts with the capacity to differentiate between the manipulations of infantile adults and the appeal for help, justice and fairness.

## "Soft" does not imply "infantile"

Roland Barthes, in his lectures at the College de France,[1] insisted that softness of manners, gentleness, lightness of touch were absolutely crucial to create community. Feminism also made him aware that valuing these qualities, which are considered maternal and feminine, would be turned against him, devaluing his intellect, through an indirect attack on his homosexuality. His prediction was correct. The problem is not so much with the dichotomy between soft and hard, as these two archetypal qualities both have their time and their space; soft belongs to the mother, hard belongs to the warrior. Yet, if one pole is systematically devalued, the collective psychic balance is lost, and that was Barthes's point. Vulnerability always accompanies an open heart, it is an essential companion of compassion. It is that vulnerability that one may come to reject, for fear of being perceived as feeble, frail, puny, indulgent, manipulable, penetrable: in other words, as showing a weakness typical of children, women, and – Barthes was right – of homosexuals. When hard means virile power and soft means feminine weakness, who would want to identify with the devalued pole? The essential yin/yang balance is then lost and the consequence for the psyche is catastrophic.

"Home" connotes a place that contains all that humans have invented to prevent the distress of the body. In our daily battle to survive, we humans need a base camp that provides protection, food, shelter, and warmth. Just as the body needs warmth, nourishment, and protection, the psyche needs an atmosphere where the heart finds its niche, its nest, its rest. This is usually called "tenderness." Without the capacity of humans to provide tender care to each other, the human race would have become extinct. Our culture has fewer and fewer psychic homes, places and moments, persons and situations where one can take off the armor, put down the defenses. A culture that separates people into "winners" and "losers" generates the kind of acute anxiety that is a rising phenomenon in all advanced cultures.

Psychology has often bought into the sexist bias that values the hard at the expense of the soft, a tragic confusion between "soft" and "infantile." For example, more value has been put on sexual potency (an expression of virility) while tenderness (a typically female form of connection) has been systematically undervalued or simply ignored. There are many experiments that demonstrate the crucial role of cuddles, hugs, smooches, affectionate nicknames, gentle manners, and playful affection for the development of language and intelligence, but, still, it is considered as part of a child's development. A popular stereotype is that tenderness is mostly something that a man (coming from Mars) doesn't really need but women do (because we come from Venus).

For sure, feminine personalities (which do not necessarily equate with women) give love, care, and tenderness because they crave it. It is a frequent psychological attitude to give what we most need ourselves, in hope of reciprocation. Unfortunately, because it has been for so long all that women had to offer, it has spoiled the value of the gift. Women opened their hearts because it was all they had to give: a gift of the powerless, a beggar's gift. It may be that it is only when a person experiences the effect of a radical disappearance of all sources of tenderness that the value of it is revealed. It took a near-death experience for me to realize that even if I am a woman and a feminist, I carried the unconscious sexist bias of my milieu and valued strength and intelligence over the capacity for compassion and gentleness. Not anymore. However, I still think that as long as women are deficient in the realm of power, tenderness and compassion will remain low on the scale of social values. In that context of devalued market, expression of gentleness and kindness is still risky. Whenever the balance of power is tipped, gestures of compassion can be misinterpreted as the animal gesture of submission – the offering of one's throat – and easily mistaken for a sign of weakness.

Only when I was a broken body, alone in an ER (Emergency Room) unit waiting for death and radically deprived of the honey of tenderness, did I begin to appreciate the extraordinary value of the song that the caretaker sang while I was letting go in her arms. Her voice, her gestures, her smell, her touch, her gentle soul expressed an invisible quality that was truly magical for me. As long as an unconscious attitude of sexism endures, her kindness is like a packet of sugar at the coffee shop: an inconsequential condiment, gratuitous and taken for granted. If we were to imagine a situation where sugar, honey and chocolate became a rarity, we would see the price of it going up. Considering that an ounce of pepper was once worth more than its weight in gold, one might imagine how quickly a cube of sugar, an ounce of chocolate, a drop of honey, could become a precious commodity, if all sweets became a rarity. As long as mothers are powerless, taken for granted, they are the packets of sugar offered at no extra cost. As both genders become increasingly free to develop both eros and power, the value of tenderness will inevitably go up in the libidinal economy of relationships.

If ever tenderness makes a comeback in psychological theories, it will certainly be given a jargon word, psychologists being fond of new terms they can commandeer; something along the line of the "immunological enhancement of positive relationships," or other variations on the "chicken soup effect." Neurobiologists may have to find a neurotransmitter that thrives on tenderness before psychological theories dare call it by its name and reconsider its value. Tenderness has at its root the maternal instinct of protection for life at its young, fragile, and needy stage. All humans, when wounded, depressed, lonely, fragmented, need that loving care. As sexism recedes, maternal qualities are considered "human" rather than only maternal, and the maternal archetype goes through a process of "degenderization," a true relief from the romanticizing of the mother role, so typical of a certain set of traditional family values.

## Get off the cross, we need the wood

If the first mistake of traditional psychology is an unnecessary genderization of the mother archetype, the second mistake is in defining the mother's role as sacrificial and servile. Behind that subtly slavish and sacrificial definition of the mother's role is what we might call a big lie: it is not the child who needs an enslaved mother, but an infantile or insecure husband. Culture has tolerated for so long that men who need to make sure their women are tied to the house 24 hours a day – if not barefoot and pregnant, at least busy and overwhelmed – that psychology has developed theories to accommodate their neurosis. Tolerance for such a paranoid attitude has been excused by theories about men's anxiety over paternity, or to their "natural" desire for sexual control and ownership of the offspring, or to womb envy, or to male genes, but rarely to backward traditions that allow objectification of the wife. Psychology is still contaminated by centuries of sexism that misappropriate maternity in favor of the insecure adult male and makes this a model of normality. Our traditional mommy myth is so powerful and ingrained that women themselves – as well as women psychologists – have bought into the myth of sacrificial motherhood and tie themselves up. The grim aspect of that mistake is that the child's needs are not met even by the sacrifice of the mother because it harms the identification process. What child would want to identify with a slave? It is no surprise that in very sexist cultures it is a curse to be born female. What these same sexist cultures still refuse to consider is the curse of being the son of a slave, the husband of a slave, and the father of worthless daughters. These men are crippled, deprived of the possibility of identifying with half their heredity.

With any kind of religious fundamentalism – Christian, Muslim, Jewish or otherwise – we have a good demonstration of what the rejection of feminism entails for the psychology of human relations. The status of the wife in some fundamentalist environments today is actually inferior to the status of a household slave in Rome at the time of Emperor Hadrian. Tradition, customs and laws gave more protection to domestic slaves in Ancient Greece than is given today to women in some very oppressive patriarchal systems. The Emperor Hadrian is said to have condemned a well-born lady to exile because she was mean to her slaves. When thinking about "slaves" in antiquity, we tend to confuse the status of slaves taken as prisoners of war, who were worked to death in the mines, with the domestic slave, a completely different reality. The domestic slave could set aside savings and buy back his or her freedom. The status of a domestic slave under Hadrian was in every way better than that of a wife in many fundamentalist sects today. The consequences of patriarchal regimes on women are obvious and have been abundantly documented, but less emphasis was put upon the weakening of the male psyche when men control women. A powerless queen suggests an impotent or feeble king; oppressed women produce immature sons; the weakness and unexamined fear of women deprives sexist men of experience of the deepest aspect of love. There can be no love between master and slave, as Hegel masterfully argued.

The self-effacing model of motherhood is still around in our supposedly post-feminist culture, because it has been internalized and made invisible. Schools of psychology are not exempt from the bias, and many fail to see that a mother can be too attentive, too giving, too self-sacrificing in an alienating way. I am not talking here about the kind of sacrifice that is a conscious choice, a decision to forgo or renounce something in order to serve a cause, raise a family, stay with the kids while they are young. A conscious choice is not the same thing as an unconscious alienation to a cultural model that costs a woman her identity, her libido, her sense of being fully alive.

Whereas previous generations of women felt and saw the limitations put upon their gender, young women of post-feminist cultures perceive their choice of motherhood as something that comes from their hearts, and, as such, as a personal rather than cultural choice. That is how a myth working in the background becomes invisible: one thinks it is a personal choice. Myth is always cultural, but always felt as personal, something that is felt in the heart. Many young women today can't see that feminism is far from passé, as some want them to believe. Such a profound change as equality of gender takes more than one generation, more than one culture, more than one appellation, more than one gender, more than one shot at it. It is an intergenerational, transgender, transcultural, global task that still needs to be carried on, by women as well as men, by psychologists as well as by politicians.

## Here is your mother: Thou Shall Not Devour Her

A decadent mother myth, where mother is servant to the child, derives its power from a basically sound psychological principle. At the beginning and end of life, humans are such a bundle of needs that of course they require service and devotion. In traditional sexist societies, the care of the young, the old, and the sick is considered a base position; unpaid, largely invisible, it is delegated to women. Gratitude not required. As a bonus, women are sometimes afforded Madonna status but most of the time they are demeaned. Traditional thinking also equates the biological mother and the archetypal Great Mother, which forces every woman who bears children into the archetypal role, whether or not she is gifted or motivated for motherhood. The first step in deconstructing a dysfunctional mother myth consists in degenderizing the maternal function.

I know a retired engineer who is infinitely better at mothering his three grandchildren than is his daughter. The kids are happier, more secure, better fed, better educated in their grandfather's large and comfortable house than in their mother's noisy, chaotic apartment. They spend weekdays under their grandfather's conscientious care and weekends with their mother. She is a very busy woman, productive, young, socially and sexually active. Her father is a gentle, homey man with a no-nonsense style of education. This child-rearing arrangement is entirely satisfactory. Yet the mother now feels guilty because she was told by her therapist and by the school counselor and by her women friends that her kids are probably – even if they don't express it – missing their mother. Wrong: her kids would get much less mothering if they were to stay with their biological mother rather than with their grandfather.

Confusing the archetype with the biological function can be very costly for a community, especially in a culture like ours, where the shortage of maternal competence is acute and the cost to provide it is steadily rising. Tying the archetypal role too closely to biology creates waste, lack, and unnecessary guilt. We easily forget that the archetype of mother (as with any archetype) is independent of gender. When, in a relationship, archetypes are confused with gender identities, it becomes difficult to even talk about the dynamic. How does one express: my mother is really a father, and my father more like a mother? The same is true with couples. The dynamic can be obscured when we take for granted that the archetype will follow the stereotype, as was the case in the following example.

## You don't really want a lover, you want a mother

My girlfriend is always asking for some sort of help: practical, financial, emotional, intellectual. She says she wants a man to be strong, because she herself wants to be feminine. The trouble with that story is that I don't feel she wants a strong male at all, I feel she wants me to be like a mommy, to cajole her and give her all she wants. At first I thought I had been trapped into a kind sugar daddy role. It's worse: she wants a sugar mommy! Our love-making does not feel like love-making. It is mommy/baby-cuddling.

The psychological deal between a sugar daddy and his girlfriend is based on money. It is an old contract in which both parties usually know exactly what is being bought and sold. The deal between a sugar mommy and her child-lover has received less attention because it is a psychological deal rather than a financial one: let me remain infantile, I'll give you control, and nobody has to know. It works as long as there are players for the game and as long as "Mother" is not recognized as an archetypal role, independent of gender.

At her first therapy session, I ask a young, exhausted and depressed mother of three the following question: Do you feel it is your family who insists on putting you in a servile role, or do you sense that you may be contributing to staging it so? I was surprised by the lucidity of her answer, which was: "My children seem to be aware of a weakness in me. They know I will take on the task. What is more, I think they feel – and I do too – that I need to take it on, to appear to have a purpose in life." She went on to say she had no idea where this weakness came from, that as a girl she had been autonomous and strong. She only knows when it began: with motherhood. She feels the love for her children and for her husband is now being eroded.

The next example is from the perspective of an adult son, one who wishes his mother had not been caught in such a servile model of mothering.

## Mother stole my libido

I am the son of a woman who is a living contradiction. On the one hand, she is an accomplished professional. She is an accountant and she does very well. Ideologically, she thinks of herself as a feminist. On the other hand, she is a sacrificial lamb on the altar of motherhood. One evening, we had a rather tough piece of meat. I saw her take my father's plate and cut his meat into small morsels, as one would do for a child. I could literally see my dad lose interest in his food, and detach from the scene of family dinner.

On another occasion, I heard my 20-year-old sister give my mother an order, "I am tired, draw me a bath." I did not understand why my mother – so professional at the office – behaves like a servant in her home. She assumes responsibility for every situation, shows no passion for anything other than family and home. She has done something to her kids that is difficult to put into words. It feels as if she has deprived us of our ability to feel desire. Our house was like the claim counter in a department store and mother was customer service. We were taught to bring every little frustration of the day to her, as if she could make everything right and compensate for life's difficulties.

After leaving home, I began to experience pleasures of which I had been unaware – creating a comfortable house, cooking a meal, receiving the care and affection of my wife. When these things were given to me by my overly generous mother, I did not experience them as pleasurable. Rather, they were like prerequisites before starting to enjoy life. We got all the prerequisites: comfort, security, good food, a good house, good clothes, plenty of stuff, but we never got to the part where you actually enjoy whatever is there to be enjoyed. To find the will to live, I had to learn to do things for myself, and to take pleasure in doing them. Until I left home, my personality was formed around the only experience my mother would allow us: needing her.

As kids, my two sisters and I were the first at school to own cell phones. They were to call mother in case we needed something. She would answer all our calls, exhausting herself in our service. Both my sisters are incapable of keeping a boyfriend for more than a month; both are friendless; both are depressed. My elder sister seems to think that love consists in imitating the slavishness of our mother. As soon as my sister is attracted to a man, she offers herself as his domestic slave. She can attract some really nice guys, but they are soon repulsed by her idea of love. She has followed the model my mother gave her.

My other sister, the youngest, went in the opposite direction, but it is just as bad. She is entirely driven by the desire not to become like Mom. The typical counter-dependent reaction. She thinks she can protect herself against slavishness by refusing to give anything to a man, except sex, which, for her, is mainly a bargaining power. She offers her body, but what she is really looking for in a man is not a lover, but somebody like mother, who will serve her. "Draw me a bath, buy me this, do this, do that, come here, go there, go away, come back." Love for her means a slave with a cell phone, someone she can call whenever she "needs" something.

As for myself, after two suicide attempts, I have been compelled to go into analysis. That's what gave me the courage to escape from the rotten paradise of our overly generous mother. I did not want to follow in the footsteps of my sisters, nor of my father. He lived his life as a prisoner, caught between two fears: that of losing my mother, on whom he was miserably dependent, and that of being married to her, because it confirmed his dependency.

Now that I have gained some measure of freedom, I see another trap: thinking that I can be the liberating hero of the family, that I might set free my mother, my father, my sisters. I know this is not something I can do. I am vigilant not to fall for a heroic myth, to replace the sacrificial myth of my mother. Wish me luck! Wish me strength!

Paradoxically, to avoid creating a "rotten paradise" of smothering maternal love, a mother needs a strong libido. She needs her own secret, or not-so-secret, garden. She needs another goal in life besides creating paradise on earth for her children; she needs plenty of moments when her children are not the priority, times when something in her life supersedes the demand for milk and cookies, attention and care. These instances communicate a rich message: there is not only a mother in my body, there is also a woman with a life of her own. I am a lover, a friend, a worker, an artist, a wife, a cook and a former girl who still enjoys dancing and swimming. Life is generous, it gives you one body but many selves.

The following woman had such a mother, and at 60, she tells how the non-sacrificial style of her mother remains the most crucial lesson her mother taught her.

## Go eat a strawberry

My mother had few choices. She worked her whole life because she was widowed with four daughters to care for. She brought us up on a single income, and one clear principle: you make your own choices. The summer of my eighth year, I skinned my knee. She dressed the wound, but I did not stop wailing and she gave me this advice: "Go pick a nice, ripe, red strawberry from the garden. Savor it for a long time, until it dissolves in your mouth, and think what a miracle of deliciousness a strawberry is. Then come back and tell me which of the two won, pain or pleasure." She called this her "tricks to shrink sorrows." It worked every time with me.

Given that I was a rather contemplative child, she would often send me to meditate on a cloud, to entrust my trouble to it and let the cloud carry my worry away. By insisting on self-reliance, my mother opened the vastness of the world: the flavor of strawberries, the flow of clouds, streams and rain, the purr of cats, the song of the wind, the lace of the ferns. She unglued us from herself, did not participate in our emotional dramas. In a house with four girls, there was always plenty of girlish whining, hormonal overflow, torrents of tears, and sentimental drama of every kind. Mom would give us a handkerchief and tell us in a very gentle voice, "Cry, cry, darling. You'll pee less!" I never felt she was being sarcastic or vulgar. To me, it meant that crying is simply to "pass water," a natural function which provides needed relief.

When we grew up and our heartaches were more serious, she offered a more complex ritual. She led us to the living room, a space that she had claimed as her study. She was a teacher, and her desk and her books were there. The disconsolate girl was invited to recline on our magnificent dark Victorian couch with a mahogany back, sculpted with roses, upholstered in burgundy velvet, stuffed like a big red whale –

the only good piece of furniture in the whole house. Draped across the couch was a woolen cashmere shawl, blue and ochre with silk fringe – a splendid gift she had received at her wedding. This shawl had a name: "the crying shawl." We had extraordinary permission to wrap ourselves in it when sorrow of the heart made us cold. She wrapped it around me for my first heartbreak. I was 14 and the boy I wanted to kiss refused. When I told my mom the story, she listened in silence, nodding. I reclined on the sofa, crying and crying for at least an hour. My mother read and sipped tea. I was "passing water."

When mother died, and the time came to distribute her things amongst her daughters, the most coveted item was the crying shawl. We threw the dice and it was I who got it. Two years ago, I gave it to my sister's daughter, who was going through a very difficult time. That shawl was like receiving comfort from her deceased grandmother. The crying shawl is still serving its role of practical poem, an object that carries the power of poetry, and the protection of a great ancestor.

## Crying is active

Crying is active. The body is in motion. The breathing accelerates. Emotions whirl. A movement stirs the heart and tears surge like water from a spring. The flow of tears cools the soul, water joining water. By contrast, in most forms of what the *DSM-IV* classifies as "Mood Disorders," "Anxiety Disorders" and "Somatoform Disorders."[2] the psyche is paralyzed by the stagnant mud of emotional chaos; there is no psychic movement; the cold molasses of thick sticky emotions doesn't flow. If and when there is movement (as in agitated states of depression) it is more likely to be manic agitation rather than efficient action. The one unfailing sign of a depressive state is an absence of progression in the narrative; the inner cinema plays the same basic plot over and over again, the story is stuck, the motion in the picture is gone. When a depression has at its root an unconscious choice not to grow up, to stay a needy child, usually there is someone in the environment who is willing – or forced – to play the role of Great Mother. This makes the slope of depression even more slippery because the patient can surrender, leaving all the action to the caretaker. The cost of such passivity is a life spent waiting: waiting for the depression to lift, waiting for whoever will volunteer to deal with the world. Having surrendered, there is no reason to move.

The Great Mother's role was, and still is, in many traditional cultures, the primary – often the only – role for women. Until recently, life was shorter, children more numerous, domestic tasks extremely demanding and choices limited. It made sense to spend one's entire life taking care of the young, the old, the sick, the house, the garden, and the chicken coop. Not anymore, and that is why the mother myth needs to be re-examined in depth, over and over again. Psychological theory is just now beginning the post-feminist revision of the mother myth, and in this task, I believe the Jungians and post-Jungians have a head start because of their archetypal perspective.

I know six men who brought up their children by themselves. Circumstances put them in the role of the Great Mother. All seemed to have a better sense of the balance between home and work, between their own needs, the needs of the culture, and those of their children; they were better at interpreting the role than any woman I know, including myself. All showed their kids at a very young age how to work the washing machine, cook spaghetti sauce and hamburger steak with onions, to make their lunch with the leftovers, and to be safe when alone by themselves in the house. All six of them limited TV time and imposed mandatory earphones. All resisted being indoctrinated into the maternal ideology of sacrifice. All had a good sense of humor and were angry at the failures of schools and communities in regard to children. None made their kids the absolute center of their life. None asked for canonization because they were acting as mother. These friends taught me a great deal about unnecessary sacrifices. They were Great Mother models.

## The maternal quality of a country, a house, a garden

Psychology's obsession with the biological mother, concomitant with the maternalization of therapy, has made us tolerant of the silliest of theories about mothering. A patient of mine had been told that the source of his neurosis lay in the fact that his mother had chapped nipples. When nursing he had felt rejected! Hard to believe but there is even a theory that claims that a mother's rectum, if too tight, can make a child neurotic. Do we need this kind of theoretical blah-blah to know that it is preferable to have a relaxed mom, ecstatic with her new baby, a content, sexually fulfilled woman, a generous breast giving unpolluted milk, a body emanating the sweet smell of motherly love rather than the sour perspiration of an exhausted, anxious, disappointed woman with a constricted life, a mean psyche and a tight rectum? Do we need a social science approach to test the hypothesis that some mothers are such that they repel the tiny mouth at their breast? Any farmer knows this much just by observing his livestock. One really wonders what sort of intellectual deficiency compels so many psychological researchers to spend their time – and our grant money – knocking down an open door.

Such a focus on the biological mother is a displacement of the cultural deficiency of our collective maternal complex. Developmental psychology has been so busy pointing an accusatory finger toward little mothers (stay-at-home moms, single moms, working moms) that it remains blind to the problem of the Collective Mother. Maternal qualities, or the lack of them, show up not only in mother–child interactions, but start with the decency or decadence of the mother archetype in the culture as a whole, in its organizations, architecture, laws, manners, styles of living. A maternal atmosphere manifests, or fails to manifest, in each of our cultural, political, educational choices; in each micro-decision that makes a country, city, school, family, or workplace, safe or threatening, supportive or punitive, easy on the body or assaultive to the senses and the soul. As a result of its obsession with the human mother, developmental psychology has diverted attention from our Grand Maternal Failure.

I would like to start with a very small, mundane and minuscule example, but one that reveals our blindness to the deterioration of the maternal archetype, a banalization of our maternal failure. Let's compare the atmosphere between two airports. I start most of my air travels departing from the tiny, pleasant, very maternal city of Santa Barbara, California, where the local airport has connections to some major cities. I park my car under a palm tree and walk into a terminal that looks like a Spanish villa. There are no blaring speakers, no interminable lines, no paranoid civil servants. I have never seen a passenger in a fit of frustration and rage, and all the agents show a gentleness and courtesy that does not seem faked. They don't seem to be overworked; most did not spend two hours in gridlock before arriving at their workplace; the doors and windows open to let air and sun in; the airport is small and most people working there know each other. The maternal quality of the atmosphere in this airport can be summarized in a few words: the senses are not under attack. At security check, I almost expect to be given a kiss on the cheek and handed my lunchbox. The ambiance at the airport reflects the ambiance of the city: tiny Santa Barbara has a sweet quality of life, and that is why those who have lived there have difficulty relocating.

By contrast, the next segment of my trip is usually the enormous hub of the Los Angeles airport, where one feels like a tin can being kicked down the sidewalk. The whole ritual has a paranoid quality. The boarding procedure adheres to a militaristic ritual – an absurdity considering the mounting evidence of its uselessness. Of course, it is not fair to compare a tiny domestic airport to a huge international hub. Nevertheless, those who make the decisions about air traffic regulations fail to consider the sensual experience of the body. It is the body that has to stand in one line after the other, endure the noise pollution of incessant, irrelevant messages from loudspeakers, wait for hours at the gate, occupy a noisy, aggressively lit room. One airport treats you with gentleness, while the other assails you with interminable inconveniences and a military scenario that is the result of a political strategy, not really a concern for the safety of passengers.

Psychologists will undoubtedly come up with new categories for the *DSM-IV*: airport rage, flight rage, queue rage. In the parable, one more straw is added to the burden and it breaks the camel's back. I am usually a nice, well-mannered camel myself. I don't bite or spew my coffee at airport agents; I am docile and diligent in demonstrating that I have no murderous intentions. Yet, I do feel something close to rage at the increasing burden of air travel. Do we really need a new theory about flight rage to understand the frustration of passengers who know they are being manipulated? For example, more and more passengers know that the fifth time the airline agent announces the plane will be delayed another hour, the cause may not be weather conditions, as the agent tells you, but airline profitability as well as political laziness at addressing the growing gridlock of air traffic. As an exhausted camel waiting at the boarding gate, I had better repress any expression of anger otherwise I become a camel with a "personality disorder." In other words, clinical psychology has inverted the meaning of the parable. The parable's wisdom points at the poor judgment of the camel driver who puts an excessive load on the camel's back. The clinical labeling doesn't examine the poor judgment of those who increase burdens; it puts a tag on the camel: camel with hostile tendencies. Not false, but not the whole story either.

The growing sense of harassment in air travel is only an example – as good as any – to reveal a blindness to the collapse of the maternal archetype. My hometown of Santa Barbara has one of the highest scores in the nation in evaluations of quality of living – which is the sociologist's way of saying a city with maternal qualities. The shadow of Santa Barbara is the mounting cost of such a sweet quality: houses are so expensive that many retired people have to sell their houses and leave. It is expensive in part because of the scarcity of towns that have such a sweet quality. The scarcity comes from the collective neurosis toward the maternal archetype, creating an unnecessary paucity, an artificial shortage, an ecological imbalance in archetypal energies.

Air travel stress I can tolerate, as millions do every year. I find it less tolerable to witness the collective maternal failure in education and health care. Who seems to notice that schools and colleges are built like barracks, furnished like prisons, with steel furniture screwed to cement floors, and dormitories like high-rise human file cabinets? Who examines the effect of enervating school schedules, never allowing for long periods of focused attention, no silence, no solitude, no beauty? Anybody spending a day in a public high school might think that the educators themselves suffer from Attention Deficit Disorder and wish to clone themselves. The style of communication between teachers and students is often shrill, tense, distrustful because both teachers and students are under increasing stress. Thousands of children, as well as teachers, are subjected to humiliation, rejection, ridicule, aggression, theft, and rape. Competitive sports are often brutal to the point of abuse. The noise, traffic, and atmosphere in public schools is harsh, tense, paranoid, socially competitive. In this toxic context, psychology's obsession with the biological parents seems like a scam to conceal the maternal neurosis of the collective.

Regarding the epidemic of child obesity, diabetes, Attention Deficit Hyperactivity Disorder (ADHD), and the increasing list of clinical disturbances in the adolescent population, a lot of good research has been available for more than a decade. It demonstrates the devastating impact of a diet saturated with the wrong kind of sugar and the wrong kinds of fat. One would think that the Food and Drug Administration (FDA) would have taken effective steps to avoid such situations. Feeding and protecting are the two basic principles at the very core of the mother archetype and feeding and protecting is supposed to be the mission of the FDA. All evolved nations have organizations whose mission relates to the maternal function of feeding and protecting the citizens. France has a law defining the contents of the baguette; Norway and Canada have outlawed transfat; and India has kept its traditional cuisine. In the US, the FDA has betrayed its maternal mission as has happened in no other evolved countries. Not only has there been no challenge of school authorities whose idea of "feeding the kids" is to invite fast food monsters to set up their stands in schools, it is now coming to the collective awareness that the FDA's allegiance is not to the citizens, but rather to the pharmaceutical companies and to the national economy. The federal law that prohibits the FDA from hiring experts with financial ties to pharmaceutical lobbies is one of those laws – like insider trading – that experts take pride in circumventing. It is so easy to hide the tracks and so much fun. The FDA serves, not the Mother Goddess, as it should, but the Money God.

Neither does the FDA seem to serve Apollo, the god of science. It is scary to read the details of some of the so-called scientific research undertaken to legitimize a new drug. The experimental schemes are so deficient, the number of subjects often ridiculously small, the duration inappropriately short, that one is not surprised when it is later revealed that, again, the scientists – as well as some FDA agents – were on the payroll of the pharmaceutical company owning the patent. It is as disturbing to read the legal arguments that the FDA uses against natural remedies that compete with prescription drugs. Why are they not as zealous when it comes to prosecuting doctors, nurses and schools who receive kickbacks for putting kids on Ritalin, Prozac, or sleeping pills? Why is the FDA so slow at reacting to the growing evidence that antidepressants may contribute to an increase of suicide among adolescents? Why did they not react 10 years ago to all the research showing the danger of a diet high in refined sugar and transfats? Why aren't they attentive to theories that show that ADHD might simply be the result of a multifactorial, psycho-ecological imbalance (the diet plus the frantic schedules plus the frenzied consumerism plus media overload plus a frenetic culture)? The FDA is comfortable with medicalizing ADHD and putting the children on a variety of drugs. Ritalin alone is a multibillion-dollar industry.

Our collective Mother markets junk food to her children and then puts them on drugs that harm them. When they get fat, have liver problems, attention deficit, panic attacks, social phobias, insomnia, suicidal impulses, early-onset diabetes, there are drugs for all of those "conditions." Could there be a more gruesome fairy tale than one where the mother invites the wolf into the nursery? My point here is not a political one but a psychological one. We suffer from a lack in our collective consciousness that makes us blind to all sorts of wolves in grandma's bonnet. Citizens need protection and nourishment, both of which are part of the archetype of Mother. A culture's failure in the maternal realm cannot be overcome if we don't first perceive it in all its fine ramifications. Psychological literature is flooded with theories linking almost all kinds of psychological disorders to parental failure. If a boy is having problems in school while both parents are at work to pay the rent, there are plenty of theories that might suggest it is the parents' absence from home that is the cause. It doesn't take into con- sideration that the boy's middle school is a terrible Mother, a place where the boy is regularly abused, ignored, ridiculed. A school should be both a good Mother and a strong Father. When the school system fails in both these archetypal qualities, it feels indecent to consider the child's failure as only mom and dad's failure.

When a first lady takes her role seriously, as Mother of the Nation, you will find an Eleanor Roosevelt in the coalmines of West Virginia; a Queen Mum surveying the streets of London after the war; a Princess Diana insisting on the removal of landmines; a Hillary Clinton passing laws to protect children and writing *It Takes a Village*. Nevertheless, a culture with a distorted maternal complex will attempt to put these women in their place by all means – like commenting obsessively on their outfits and hairdos but ignoring their ideas. They will be denied a role as mother of the nation, and we'll have a First Lady who concerns herself with the official china, lighting the Christmas tree, standing by her man in a designer dress, smiling at her own emptiness.

What would be sufficient for us to turn a critical eye toward the Collective Mother? Guns and knives are hidden in lockers; there is an unprecedented increase in adolescent suicides, psychotic break-downs, self-mutilations, depressions, and a host of ever-increasing psychological and psychosomatic symptoms. When did we start ignoring the collective maternal responsibility and begin blaming it all on the individual parents? Everything the Collective Mother does not provide, moms and dads are expected to compensate for. Public transportation is dangerous and inadequate, so parents become chauffeurs. Kids are addicted to fast food and reject the healthy meals cooked at home, and then the parents are expected to pay for medication and therapy. The greater the indolence of the Collective Mother, the heavier the burden on the individual parent and the greater the medicalization and infantilization of the population. Nobody would deny that incompetent parenting results in nasty psychological consequences, but what is the use of such drearily evident theories if we never consider the decadence of the Collective Mother? Atmosphere, décor, attitude, manners, style, architecture, sound, smell, taste, timing, pace, space, rhythm, textures, rituals: all have a direct consequence on the psyche. Who would Mozart have been without the beauty of Salzburg? Vivaldi without Venice? Da Vinci without Florence? Baudelaire or Gertrude Stein without Paris? Walt Whitman without New York and Chicago? Virginia Woolf without London? Poe without Boston and Thoreau without his Walden Pond?

Psychology has largely ignored the obvious fact that social and cultural factors can coalesce to support or hinder the psyche, putting an unfair burden on caregivers. Compassion fatigue of caregivers is inevitable when a culture is unwilling to develop maternal qualities. The excessive rate of burn-out and consequent demise of caretakers is the result of a vicious circle: the more a culture is a Bad Mother, the more it produces individuals who remain infantile, needing care and themselves producing another generation of violently frustrated infantile adults needing even more care. An environment that offers too little beauty, too little joy, pleasure, sensuality, wastes its little Mozarts and burns out its mothers. It is one of the surest signs of decadence because as much as a culture can show resilience when faced with economic setback, the very source of resilience is lost when the social fabric disintegrates.

One of depth psychology's tasks is to reverse the cultural trend that persists in defining the mother's breast in a literal and personalistic way and to start looking at the maternal function in a symbolic and collective way. "Mother" is an archetype and as such it is always present in one way or another in the life of individuals as well as in the life of nations. Thanks to George Orwell, our imagination about the possibility of a nasty tyrannical Father Figure – presenting himself as Big Brother – is quite sophisticated. I know of no such recent widely read work of fiction that would have sharpened our awareness that Mother can turn into Big Mother, her tits delivering plenty of the wrong kind of charity, the wrong kind of care, wrong kind of food, medicine, support, given in a way that invites her citizens to remain infantile and passive.[3] That collective Big Mother needs to get on the couch and receive psychoanalytic attention. Our actual welfare system hides a vicious refusal to let the children grow. It says: cash the check, shut up, don't ask for more, remain infantile, I don't care to educate you.

A revisioning of the maternal myth implies a revolution in values, manners, education, esthetic sensitivity, city planning, welfare programs. It asks for new ideas about human relations, communities, hard and soft, yin and yang. It asks for a parallel revalorization and redefinition of the myth of the Father. The symbols of Mother of the country and Father of the country are always linked. If one is neurotic, the other is too. Both archetypes are in need of a new deal.

Chapter 10

# The archetype of Father

The philosopher Blaise Pascal pointed out that "justice without force is powerless." Likewise, maternal compassion without paternal strength is powerless. Ecologists know the problem: the politician's tactic to neutralize them is to make sentimental speeches about Mother Nature and to pass generous laws for its protection, but laws with no teeth. No matter how devoted the activists in ecology, how ambitious their mission statements, if the laws for the protection of the environment are not enforced, it remains "justice without force." The mother who begs her husband to stop abusing the children but doesn't back it up with the threat of divorce, the good-hearted school teacher who meditates every day on peace in the world but can't control the class bully, the politician who is devoted to the good cause but has no power in the party – all are worthless good intentions. Again, Pascal: "Those who are unable to empower the just, end up justifying the powerful."

The previous chapter explored the need for compassion, gentleness and a healthy collective Mother archetype. The Father archetype, however, is just as crucial, as it personifies the will to win. The goal of attaining a better quality of living for all, a world with less stress and less violence, can only be reached if we collectively revisit both principles and their connection. A strong Father balanced by an affectionate Mother has been – and still is – interpreted literally by traditionalists; their discourses suggest that all would be well in the Kingdom of God if dads would only carry the patriarchal authority and moms do the nurturing. Traditionalists translate the archetypal necessity into socio-biological roles, a division of roles that may have worked in the past but obviously fails us now because the old myth of the family is going, going, gone. Nostalgia for what is gone is always a costly psychological mistake.

## Bad cop/good cop: not a literal reality

The most naive observer understands that the classic dynamic of good cop/bad cop is not to be interpreted literally. We all understand that the "good cop" is not necessarily, in reality, a guy with all the compassion (maternal archetype) while the other guy is powerful and merciless (paternal archetype). Why can't the traditionalists comprehend that the family dynamic is such a coupling? Good teams are all made by combining different archetypes. It is never required of the role players in the human drama to identify literally, biologically, with the archetypal role they are called to play.

Another example of that archetypal coupling was given to me by a student who was raised in an African-American community in Los Angeles. In her life, the biological fathers, in hers and most of her friends' homes, were absent. The grandmother would take on the maternal role, while the biological mother would take on the paternal role: it was she who earned the money, owned the car, dealt with grades, pocket money and school authorities. My student put it simply: "My mom is my dad, and grandma is my mom." She is expressing a simple psychological truth: as long as both archetypes are balanced, the psychological needs of the family are met, regardless of biological identities. Conversely, a family may have all the outside appearances of a balanced family, with a stay-at-home mom and a dad bringing home his salary, no abuse and no irregularities, yet there might be no deep mothering and no deep fathering taking place. Archetypal energies may be invisibly present or invisibly absent, and they are not necessarily defined by biological gender. Same-sex couples whose households provide all the complex mothering and fathering that kids need in order to grow up are a good demonstration of a non-literal interpretation of mom and dad. One does not need a degree in psychology to see that a lack of yang corrupts the yin; a lack of yin disempowers the yang. Psychology has "lacked the balls" to go after the obvious fallacies in the traditional family construct, where appearances hide all kinds of archetypal absences.

Knowing how to discriminate when a situation requires more yang and when it calls for more yin is one of the most important discriminatory functions that apply equally to individuals, families, institutions, and nations. Be it the fight of the serfs against feudalism, slaves against racism, or women against patriarchy, a lasting victory is always the result of a balance of yin and yang strategies. Yin strategies include educating, pleading, convincing, appealing to the highest values, and gaining the people's vote. Yang strategies are warlike: prepare the attack, fight the battle, win. Any imbalance and the yin finds itself powerless or the yang begins to self-destruct. If we look at our own life stories, even the most loving and positive relationships have periods that belong to a psychology of love and others that belong to a psychology of war and every psyche needs to be equipped for both. Couples fight about space, values, money, time, chores; they confront their versions of past events, their visions of the present and of the future. A maternal psychology teaches a rhetoric of love, understanding, communication, sharing, openness, compromise, and compassion. A paternal approach focuses on the balance of power in the relationship: one does what one has the power to do. Both approaches are necessary. The Greeks personified authority by the character of Zeus, their God the Father, holding thunderbolts in his raised fists. He was represented with authoritative furrowed brows and an eagle-like vision that could see everything happening on Earth. He was authority personified, a symbol of the power to establish the laws, implement them, and punish those who broke them. Zeus was the idea that power and responsibility are inseparable, as it should be in a father figure.

The Father archetype has many names: chief, king, leader, captain, general, president. All of them have in common the fatherly responsibility of those under his authority. That is why the captain goes down with his ship, why Truman said "the buck stops here" and why it is the president of the US, as father of the country, who has the red telephone and carries the moral responsibility of declaring war, sending sons and daughters to war.

This archetype is activated in all our relationships with figures of authority. We fear the Zeus figures or admire and trust them; we loathe them or we long for their protection; we are fiercely loyal or we want to dethrone them. Any person (man or woman) in a position of authority constellates the Father archetype for the others; not only kings, presidents and generals, but also the boss, the policeman, the teacher, and anyone who has power over us. When a woman finds herself in the position of the Father archetype, like the Egyptian queen wearing a fake beard to signify the authority of the Pharaoh, she sends signals that she is not to be mistaken for the Mother archetype. The power suit, the corner office, the expensive desk, the reserved parking place, they all will say that what lives here is yang. Conversely, a man in the role of Great Mother, who uses symbols similar to that of the ancient goddesses (the Pope's flowing white robe, his gesture of open arms that suggests "Come to me, little children") will say: what lives here is yin (or, as in the case of the Pope, wants you to believe so). In the psyche, an activation of the Father archetype signals an initiation into a warrior psychology. One develops a fascination for strategy and tactics, a willingness to face conflict, a love of victory, a budding of ambition, a desire for power, and a capacity to take risks.

## The Father principle in therapy

Frequently, at the start of family therapy, the stress can be so intense that the first task of the therapist is to work on the atmosphere, to make it more gentle, more supportive, safer, maternal. Nevertheless, if the goal is not later revisited, the therapist's unconscious preference for a maternal psychology may bring further imbalance because it suggests an impossible ideal for the family: that of a permanent nest, a haven from all external conflicts. The family cannot be only a haven because it is also the place where one learns life, and life is full of stress and distress. It is in the nature of human groups to generate tensions and conflicts; it is even one of the principal factors of evolution. A non-romantic, non-sentimental, non-Disneyfied psychological view of the family teaches us both the maternal capacity to protect what is fragile or broken (the newborn, the young, the sick, the old), and also the paternal wisdom to consider the family as the first battleground, training ground, our first psychic boot camp. The maternal utopia so prevalent today in some developmental approaches is dystopic when it prevents the paternal principle from reaching the children. Boys as well as girls absolutely need to learn the basics of war which are to remain cool, alert, focused in the face of threats. Forms of therapy that refuse the yang principle are sentimental lies. By offering only one end of the psychic spectrum, they perpetuate the model of the powerless Mother dealing with a violent Father: Please Society, don't beat the children; it hurts them. Please Society, invest in education, in health care. Please, absent fathers, come back and pay your due. It is a psychology of beggars that has little to offer to those who need a revolution.

The construction of identity is paradigmatic of the necessity of a psychic balance between yin and yang. Identity is built in part through what we love and identify with. It is as much built through what we exclude: I am not you, I refuse what you want for me, I resist your influence, I won't surrender. Civilizations, just like our individual psyches, define their identity mostly by rejecting what is happening on the other side of the border. Here, at home, we do not eat frogs, or dogs, or snakes; we do not drink that stuff or take that drug; we do not kill like that, we do not have this law, this belief, this God, this custom. Identities are built not only through shared values but also through common ideas about what is being rejected. An "enemy" can be anything or anyone that has the power to destroy what we are or hope to become. Teenagers are especially keen at defining themselves around common ideas of what they reject in adults. They need this oppositional attitude, which is one of the reasons why they absolutely need a strong, stable, father figure. To cut one's teeth, one has to bite into something that offers resistance. Too harsh or too soft an authority can equally damage the capacity of teenagers to do the necessary sorting, and create apathy, anomie, delinquency.

Feminist anger against patriarchy has been wrongly interpreted as anger at the paternal principle. No. It does not make sense to get angry at an archetype. It's like getting angry at the wind instead of adjusting one's sails, or like getting angry at the fact that we need red lights to regulate traffic, or that we might need a budget, a schedule, laws, rules and regulations for society to function. The feminist revolution was not a rejection of the paternal archetype, nor was it an empowerment of the maternal principle. It was, at least in my understanding, a revolt against a decadent monarchy: the ruling of one gender by another. No guillotine was required. It was not a case of "off with their heads" nor was it "off with their balls." What needed to be guillotined was an idea: the idea that "having balls" meant something literal, a biological apparatus, instead of an archetypal quality. The feminist revolt was followed by a feminist revolution and has been one of the richest examples of deconstruction in post-modern intellectual history. It deconstructed the patriarchal literalist definition of masculine power. It deconstructed literalism.

Zeus, as an archetypal principle, is eternal, but his name can mean man or woman, young or old. To call this archetype by the name of a Greek divinity is simply a cultural convention, a way of honoring our pre-Christian heritage and the wisdom it contains. One does not even need the fancy word of "archetype" although I find it simple and practical and it is now part of the common language. One could refer to it simply as the authority principle. Zeus is the basic emotion of: Oops! I'd better slow down or I'll get a speeding ticket.

The father archetype is corrupted whenever there is a dissociation between power and responsibility. Anybody who wants privileges without responsibilities always risks some form of the guillotine (off with the king, off with the lord, off with patriarchy). Feminists collectively declared that if women share the burden of responsibility, they should as well share the power and the glory. In that, feminists were revolutionaries and the impact of this revolution has only begun. Although psychologists have made crucial contributions to gender studies, their main impact seems to have been in thinking anew the male/female relationship. Yet, this rich area of studies has had less weight rethinking theories about the family, many of which seem immune to the insights of feminism, as if psychologists could pay lip service to feminism and then go on with the same old theories about family dynamics and child development.

I have supervised students in training, when they view taped sessions by experts on "family systems" to learn basic intervention techniques. The trainees also videotape their own beginnings as psychotherapists and receive feedback from their supervisors. These taped sessions are an interesting sample of current values being taught in courses on family therapy. I do not wish to name any particular school, as it is not always a problem with the theory, but rather a pervasive attitude that pre-exists in the mind of the student as well as in the mind of the expert who shares his or her practical experience through tapes and videos.

Here is a typical scene that I have seen repeated with minor variations. The video shows an aggressive teenager insulting his mother, talking as if she were not in the room. My mother is a whore! If she stays with my father, it is only for the money! The angry father springs up and imposes his authority: I forbid you to speak like that about your mother! The psychotherapist then turns to the father. Politely castrating, the psychotherapist invites him to cool down, to sit down, while "we" explore the emotion your son is expressing. The father frowns, sits down and broods. He has just received a humbling lesson in empathy from an expert. The psychotherapist has imposed his or her little theory: behind the hostility there is a wound. We are here to offer compassion and heal it. The theory is fine. Yes, there is a wound behind the hostility. Nevertheless the manner in which the session is conducted proposes a false egalitarianism by which the teenager's discourse is considered equal to that of the parent. It is a mistake, not because the teenager's opinion has less value than that of his father's, but because the father's authority is being transferred on to a psychotherapist who distorts it by acting like a compassionate, patient Great Mother.

The fallacy here is not the theory that behind an aggressive teenager is a hurt teenager, an idea that should not even need the support of a theory. The problem resides in the naivety of the psychotherapist who might not perceive that: (a) the therapist inflicts humiliation upon the father by giving him a lesson in parenting in front of his child; (b) the therapist is appropriating the paternal authority by posturing as the expert about the family; and (c) the therapist conceals this transfer of power by wearing the disguise of the supportive, gentle Great Mother. It is as if the psychotherapist were saying: "You are an incompetent father. Don't you see the wound behind the hostility? Now, watch how competent I am when talking to your son. How could a parent compete?"

The psychotherapist is invested with the authority of the specialist, bathed in the aura of the paid expert. Apparently, the aim of the intervention is to help the father communicate better and get closer to his son. In actuality there is another lesson that is communicated to the son, a lesson that is not as nice: You are excused for insulting your mother because you are expressing emotions (i.e., hostility) and Great Mother understands and supports the expression of emotions.

The paternal principle has a different agenda. Life in a group – and a family is a group – requires not only the expression but also the control of emotions. Families have to exercise the same self-control as do nations. Conflicts lead either to war or negotiations. A divorce, for example, is a war between two parties and if divorce is to remain civil and not destroy the children, it has to abide by certain rules, just as treaties are negotiated following a cease-fire.

We have often heard the oversimplification that Asians have difficulty expressing their emotions or that the English have a stiff upper lip that is the result of repression. There may be some truth in these ethnological observations, but it becomes a denial of some of their highest values when we confuse repression, which creates suffering, with self-control, which is the foundation for civilized behavior. A psychology that favors a maternal perspective, that makes the expression of one's emotions the primary value, is guilty of confusing repression with self-control. The adolescent who insults his mother needs to learn not one but two crucial lessons. The first is a lesson of consciousness – when he feels hurt, he needs to know that he tends to become hostile. The second is that there is no honor in insulting your mother, or anyone else. The adolescent needs to learn that to become a grown-up requires self-discipline, even when experiencing a legitimate emotion of anger. This self-restraint is a lesson that only an adult carrying the Father archetype can teach a child. The critique of the unfair, oppressive authoritarianism of the harsh severe patriarch – whose rule is to benefit himself – does not imply that the archetypal qualities of Father are less needed.

## There is no absolute adult

Nobody ever completely reaches the status of "adult." We all have our moments of regressive behavior. We yearn for the Great Mother each time we suffer and as we all suffer quite a lot, we all have a need for consolation from a little mother, a delegate of the Great Mother. Our narcissistic child never completely disappears as even the most individuated, illuminated beings have testified. Those who pretend to be "beyond" these regressive moments either lie, or they are unconscious. Nevertheless, it is within the means of the adult in us to educate that inner child, to control – yes, control – that potentially monstrous inner tyrant. The longer the inner child remains uneducated, the more severe the projections, the manipulations, the destruction, like a child breaking his toys. It makes one even more self-centered and thus feeds the vicious circle of abandonment.

### Confession of an immature adult

I am a 60-year-old woman and have been practicing law for 30 years. I lost my professional zeal a long time ago. At the start of my career, I wanted to champion teenagers and I specialized in defending troubled youths. This ideal was, in my case, the result of my refusal to grow up. Ironically, I did not serve my young clients' causes as much as I served my own neurosis. As an attorney, my style of defense never deviated and can be summarized in one sentence: basically, the delinquent is a good kid who has been abused by parents/society/the system and, consequently, the guilty party is that same collection of villains. This defense worked sometimes, but not all the time, as my strategy became increasingly predictable. What is worse is that the dogma of the innocence of the wounded failed me completely when it came to educating my own daughter. Her adolescent rebellion should have opened my eyes, but I did not want to see the flaw in my own logic. My only child, she had been at the center of my love and attention since her birth. I treated her as if she was a paragon of perfection. When she started resisting my affection, at 13, I was crushed. I could not hear what she meant when she said that I had turned her into a doll. I had certainly never insisted that she wear frilly dresses or any of that. She became insolent and accused me of having driven her father away. She even resented the fact that I never brought home a boyfriend, misinterpreting my restraint as evidence that I knew nothing of men or of love. She became manipulative, demanding, and spoiled. What is more, she scolded me for tolerating her lies and her schemes. We lived in a hell of our creation. Today she is 40, and we are only beginning to appreciate each other.

Last week, she reminded me of an episode that was a turning point for her. At 12, just before her rebellion began, she insisted on meeting her father. He was delighted. Up to that point I had rejected his involvement and I had paid for everything in order to bring up my daughter without his interference. She wanted to spend a summer with him, and they went to Spain. He was happy to find himself the father of such a beautiful, intelligent daughter. They had a great time. He is a photographer, and he taught her how to use his cameras and lenses. She came back with many photos of their trip. The first evening of her return, she wanted to show me her pictures and tell me about her extraordinary trip. I don't remember this episode, but it seems that I told her that it was too late in the evening and that the pictures could very well wait until another time. She felt as if I were telling her she had cheated on me by loving her father, that her good time with him was a betrayal of me. She felt a crushing sense of guilt and never showed me the pictures. It seems I never asked.

Now she is 40 and has had years of analysis. She is a much more conscious person, and we are able to talk about all this. As a teenager she had neither the words nor the lucidity to express what precipitated her hostility. After the trip to Spain, she felt as if it had to be either my love and not her father's love, or his love and not mine. When she became rebellious and began rejecting my affection, my biggest mistake was to conclude that her father was the cause of her adolescent hostility, that she was the victim of his manipulations to turn her against me. My preconceptions blinded me to reality. I attempted to protect my daughter from her father, certain that he was guilty of having wounded my angel of perfection. But what I did was to deprive her of a father. My daughter and I spent the next 20 years in a psychological mess. She suffered under the delusion that I was presenting her with an irreconcilable conflict. Either she could remain mine, my little doll, my only love, or choose to love her father and lose my affection entirely.

There was some truth to this. I wanted her all for myself. From the day of her birth, it would be her and me against the whole world, an unbreakable, symbiotic bond that no man could ever penetrate. She would be my great cause, my reason for living. I now know that my total devotion had very little to do with love. It was all about my own internal reality. I was the child; I was the wounded teenager needing

protection against an abusive and indifferent father; I was
the one with an unresolved father complex; I was the one
who needed a champion in a court of law; I was the one who
needed a symbiotic love with my daughter, excluding the
Father, because I had no inner image of what Father means. I
paid dearly for my immaturity, tears of loneliness and regret.

## The alchemy of psychic maturation

Ancient alchemists may have been lousy chemists, but they were
unequalled at suggesting metaphors for the invisible processes of
the psyche. For example, they saw that any maturation process
demands an impeccable sense of: (a) the right substance (for
example, the right ingredients for a particular recipe); (b) the right
timing (for example, the time when a fruit is ripe, or the order in
which the ingredients have to be poured in the recipe);[1] and (c) the
right intensity (for example, some ingredients cook at very low
heat while others call for the intense flame of a grill).

Becoming adult is one such process of maturation: (a) the basic
substances are mother-love and father-love, love being the very
essence in any recipe for the education of the young; (b) mother-
love comes first and father-love comes second, each having a
different timing; and (c) the intensity or heat of the mother
complex and the heat of the father complex have to be turned up
or down as the maturation process cooks up. The child feels the
heat at all times but sometimes it is a simmering and sometimes it
is a grilling. The combination of the variations in substance,
duration, and intensity is responsible for the infinite complexity of
the maturation process. Just like a sauce, the growing-up process
can cook well, the juices of childhood going through all sorts of
transformations (the alchemists used words like reduction,
evaporation, crystallization), ending up in a subtle distillation of
puer energy that will perdure in the adult psyche as a youthful
form of vitality and a capacity for joy.

When the maturation process goes wrong, one can use those
alchemical metaphors to imagine what ingredient is missing in the
mix (where is mommy? who is my daddy?), or what, in the timing,
was offered too soon or too late (where were you when I was a

kid?), or what went wrong with the intensity of heat that either burned the soul or didn't cook it at all. An aromatic sauce, carefully composed of all the right ingredients, will taste delicious. Cooked at too low a temperature, it doesn't take, doesn't thicken, doesn't coagulate to use the alchemical word, but cooked at too high a temperature, it turns to carbon, a complete failure of the whole process. Jungians are fond of using alchemical metaphors to describe the aspect of therapy that recapitulates (and corrects) the maturation process. They are strong images and can help us understand how a therapist's refusal to wean the patient is a recipe for a very sour brew.

## Therapy as alchemy

Compassion, gentleness, and caring are essential qualities in a therapeutic environment. No psychotherapist can manage without these maternal qualities – playing the role of Great Mother – for those patients whose "little mother" failed more or less tragically. The theory of transference is based on this capacity to push "replay" and "edit." Unfortunately, no one – no therapist, parent, spouse, or friend – can ever adequately fulfill the archetypal role of Mother or Father for the simple reason that, being archetypal, these roles are, as such, inhuman, bigger than the individual person, loaded with the millions of years of evolution of our mammalian species.

Perfection in parenting, in educating, in therapy, is impossible. We may do our very best, trying to give our patients – our children, our students – as much as we possibly can of the accumulated wisdom that defines each archetype. Nevertheless, being fallible persons, and not the divinities that we are expected to be, we also fail them, one way or the other. Either a parent is too good and impossible to emulate, or not good enough and deficient, or just good enough but somehow uninteresting and unimpressive. In cases of severe incompetence, the archetypal symbol of Mother or Father can be altogether missing in the psyche of the child. The body ages but the soul remains that of a child waiting for the Great Mother's embrace because the little mother never provided it.

Enter the therapist, good breast ready for transference of earlier unsatisfied primary needs for mothering. Young or untrained psychotherapists are especially eager to pour the honey of trans-ferential maternal love into the therapeutic elixir. They are also more likely to keep that one substance on the front burner for too long, never yielding to the Father Principle. The hyperglycemia of too much sweet attention and support brings on the equivalent of a hypoglycemic reaction – it breeds an intense neediness that is at the core of egotism and takes the patient even further from feeling the generosity of what is given with life itself. Because it is not reciprocal, the indulgence of a maternal therapist can delude patients into believing that the privileged attention of the therapist (for which they pay) is a model for relationships. It sets a patient up for rejection by others who are asked to do it for free. The demand – if you love me, you will listen with the same uncon-ditional attention as my therapist gives me – is eventually met with rejection: bye-bye, take care of yourself, baby!

The apprentice's mistake is not the nurturing per se. It is the most natural response to nurture people we love when they are in need. Rather than an error of substance, it is an error of duration (timing). Some patients are incredibly skillful and subtly mani-pulative at taking advantage of the maternal qualities of their therapist – and of every generous breast in their environment. They want to remain at the breast forever. What makes a therapist vulnerable to manipulation by these personalities can be a deficiency in the training, or an unconscious problem with the Mother archetype, which results in a failure to differentiate com-passion from weakness. Tolerance can hide passivity and failure of leadership in the Father's realm.

The mother who fears thorny topics around the dinner table, and, at all costs, forces everybody to fake a loving atmosphere in the family is not expressing sensitivity but her own fears. As a maternal ideal, peace around the table is part of good manners, something that everybody can appreciate, but when agreement is paramount and dissension intolerable, relationships are stripped of their complexity, conversations simplified to the extreme – like voting for good against evil. Everybody is nice, courteous, and respectful, politely wasting time. As productive dissension is eliminated, the family's ability to function synergistically evapor-ates. Something is missing in the mix: the paternal principle.

The realm of the Great Mother is one of tranquility – peaceful, profoundly restful. The good breast. The safe nest. The com-passionate listener. This serenity of the soul is one of the most beautiful gifts one can give or receive from relationships. It belongs to the Great Mother and it is an absolute rule around a baby's cradle. Babies who are treated harshly either die or become sick, or carry a psychic wound that will not heal until they get to taste what the old cliché calls "the milk of human kindness." A competent therapist provides a tranferential nurturing breast that helps compensate for the earlier deprivation. A suffering soul wants peace. The realm of the Great Mother offers that kind of peace each time we find refuge in the arms of loved ones. This transferential love – if we take the theory of transference seriously – also implies that there is a time for weaning. Some patients come in expecting – and often getting – a weekly dose of psychological cuddling. They gorge on the therapist's attentions, wallow in their psychological dramas, uninterrupted by a non-judgmental, sympathetic listener. Nevertheless, if this goes on too long, the therapeutic effect is nullified and there is a risk of carbonization of the sweet milk.

## Sorry, Oedipus

The tendency toward maternalization of therapy is a logical consequence of a psychological culture that is dominated by the mythology of the child. It is unfortunate that the best lesson from Freud – maybe the primary one, the one that has passed the test of time – does not receive more attention in psychology classes. Freud argues that the child has to be frustrated, that a child's victory over his rival for the mother's affection is dangerous, both for the child and for society. The critique of Freud often focuses on the fact that the desire of the child to possess the mother may not be as sexual as Freud imagined it. However, the basic postulate that a child needs to be "frustrated of a victory" in order to face the reality principle is still valid. Developmental psychology's propagation of the myth of the child as victim has resulted in a hesitancy by parents to set limits. It has also contributed to the proliferation of maternal therapists who are sweet and supportive but fail to help their patient overcome the natural narcissism of childhood.

The contractor who is putting a new roof on my house is a kind and sensible man. Knowing that I am a psychologist, he asks me how he should behave with his 14-year-old son. He wants to tell the boy that respect is a two-way gift, that it is too easy to be, at the same time, comfortably dependent and excessively demanding; that love is not a license to abuse; that the noise from his audio system, his belongings scattered all over the house, his exorbitant telephone bills, all of that is just too much. The father does not want to appear rigid and authoritarian as his own father had been, and consequently he is not sure if it is acceptable to express his frustration to his son. Why such doubt about his own need for respect? It points to a cultural failure, not only his personal failure. His instincts are good, but he cannot find the right attitude in the collective repertoire because children have been allowed to ascend to the family throne.

If not overcome in childhood, the rage of losing the status of little monarch only amplifies; it produces frustrated and mean individuals because they resent the loss of a power they used to have. Their psychological intelligence is spent mostly on manipulations to get that power back. They are always trying to receive the maximum, contribute the minimum, never realizing that this is a game that sooner or later ends with the feeling of being a deposed potentate. They want the privileges of childhood (security, support, innocence, angelic irresponsibility), but also – why not? – those of adulthood (money, sex, power, and nobody to tell them what to do). Their neurosis is fed by a consumerist culture that advertises self-indulgence as a virtue, to anybody with money: Indulge! You are worth it. It is a fact that adolescents in rich countries do have a frightening amount of economic power that contributes to the illusion of their independence. The tragedy of the unweaned adult is that no amount of success (or money) will ever compensate for the first loss, because a doubt remains as to the necessity of that loss. As the years go by and the fantasy of the restoration to the throne dims, the dominant feeling becomes the despair and the narcissistic rage that is characteristic of infantile adults. Those who love them feel sorrow for what might have been.

## A balanced approach to therapy

Rather than approaches specializing in the maternal attitude (the nurturing breast) and others in the paternal one (tough love), the training of therapists should encourage an alchemical finesse, and develop in them an awareness of what substance is needed, when (timing) and with what force (intensity). The psyche has periods when it needs a cradle in which to experience rebirth; it also has periods when it needs warrior training. One needs courage and ferocity to combat the monsters inhabiting the psyche. The art of psychological warfare calls for the Father archetype. Buddhism and Hinduism are good examples of spiritual disciplines of peace and love, but with a martial component in the mix. The novice is taught to battle with negative thinking, to wage war against the agitated ego, a monkey that should be controlled. In the same fashion, a competent therapist knows when to leave the Great Mother and migrate to the Father, with his warlike psychology.

The famous analyst Marie-Louise von Franz was well known for her confrontational, fatherly style. She lacked patience for clients in love with their wounds. She would simply dismiss a patient if she perceived a lack of courage. She seemed to be saying: Come back when you are battle-ready. I won't waste my time with crybabies. Her therapeutic manners aroused criticism – likewise her rigid and somewhat odd personality. Perhaps her intuition was correct, however. There are times when the therapist should follow in the footsteps of the martial arts teacher. The soft inner child needs a teacher who will turn him into the karate kid. If therapy offers primarily emotional support and comfort, it can add to the experience of neediness. To end the infantile illusion, the patient must want something beyond the loving, tender gaze of the mother.

The regularity with which I have seen apprentice therapists incapable of weaning their patients indicates a collective problem with both the Mother and the Father archetype. It is accompanied by the illusion that if only a psyche could be "cured" of its neurosis, it would bring about a kind of maternal paradise of harmonious relationships, functional families, good communications, emotional comfort. In this fantasy of maternal bliss, what is missing is the awareness of the necessity of being removed from maternal affection. The compulsory maternalism that acts as a dogma oversees the fact that the child needs not only a competent caretaker, but also needs for that person to walk away as soon as the child can accept the world as Cosmic Mother and start walking on his own.

Psychological maternalism has perverse consequences similar to those of political correctness – increased hypocrisy and accentuation of the shadow. Who has not heard of a therapist who acts nice and unconditionally supportive, not because the patient is in the process of repairing the maternal image, and not because that therapist is a great compassionate being, but because the unweaned client subtly lets the therapist know that this is what is being paid for. The patient ends up more desperate than before, but the therapist ends up with more "clients." An authentic calling to become a psychotherapist, like any vocational choice, implies a willingness to take risks. All matters of love also entail risk taking; therapy as well as education are harmed if concerns about money or reputation take precedence. The task requires sincere devotion. Otherwise, it is only a job and not a calling.

## A little mother's resignation

My son is 35 years old, a talented artist. He works hard and so do I. My life is as full as his, even though he doesn't think so. Because I live alone and I have always welcomed his visits, I think he believes I have nothing better to do! The truth is that I cherish the time we spend together. This last year, every time we scheduled a dinner he ended up canceling it. Last week he sent me an email, "Hi, Mom. I'll come by this Wednesday. Can we have dinner at your place? I could be there around six. I'll bring wine." That day, I left my office early and bought what I needed to cook the dish he likes best. l was really looking forward to this, and I poured myself a glass of wine while cooking and waiting for him. He cancelled!

Once again, he had a perfect excuse. Until now, I have reacted like an understanding mother: "Don't worry, honey. We'll have another shot at it." In that moment, I became a woman who is finished with child-rearing. I felt a completely different personality rising to the surface – not the mother, but the woman! I said to him, "From now on, if you want to come for dinner, you know my address. If I am home, we'll order a pizza. No more appointments." I said it without harshness but with finality.

The following Friday evening, he dropped by my office unannounced. We went out to dinner and had a great time. I feel that my resigning as a mother is beneficial not only to me but to him as well. A son who expects women to be eternally patient needs to be enlightened by his own mother. The rules of relationship between a man and a woman are not at all the same as the one between a mother and son.

## You love me at last? Too late!

One of life's paradoxes is that love is often offered precisely at the moment when one finally gives up because the price of love seems too high. I'm through begging for tenderness, for sexual pleasure, for respect, for help, for support. No more humiliation in exchange for devotion. No more psychological hemorrhaging. It is also a frequent side effect of therapy that, at the moment when the patient begins to feel detachment, the partner opens up and starts giving what had been withheld. It is no coincidence. As long as the patient sings the tune of "Don't leave me or I'll die," the partner cannot but resent the emotional blackmail, and reciprocity is impossible. When a sense of self-worth and independence is re-established, it brings either the possibility of mutuality or the end of the relationship based on a neurotic symbiosis.

A symbiotic state can be quite comfortable because it is a radical shortcut: to alleviate the existential anguish of freedom, it abolishes freedom altogether. As Jung remarked, a therapist can seldom help a patient who has just fallen in love and is in a state of sexual bliss. The honeymoon is maybe the only time when symbiosis is positive, because sexuality is symbiotic in nature. The honeymoon is a time when it feels as if love is the solution to all of life's problems. We and us are the most used pronouns during a honeymoon. We are going to solve everything. We are one. United, we are strong. Our love is invincible. The world revolves around us. A honeymoon that does not fuse, bond, mix the juices and melt the lovers into a common orgasmic explosion of joy is simply a failure. Unfortunately, the sexual embrace is ephemeral and each partner has to get back into his or her own skin, until the next embrace. For love to endure, the illusion of oneness must end and the paternal principle be honored. If the maternal dream of symbiosis persists, the individuals begin to disintegrate psychologically. Couples choose each other according to an unconscious plan that makes allowances not only for the development of their full potential of strength but also for the full potential of their neuroses. In the attraction that the other exerts upon us, there is sometimes a desire to match our weaknesses in such a way that we shall, sooner or later, be forced to evolve beyond them.

## I married a bomb detonator

I chose a wife whose personality pushed all my buttons, all the time. We were perpetually angry about something. My unresolved Mother complex was brought to the forefront, as if I married her so that she could put her finger in my wound; she did in a rather harsh way, repeatedly. I did the same to her. I think I married her because I needed to get away, once and for all, from the devouring mother. Our union was such hell that either we died of it or we learned from it. I learned. I stopped expecting to be taken care of and began breathing on my own. I don't know about her.

His unconscious strategy had been in choosing a partner who was even more unconscious than himself, a woman who absolutely refused to leave the neurotic pact. She would not budge from the contention that if only he. . . . Their relationship felt reassuring at first, because it allowed for mutual passivity. As soon as he began the work of self-analysis, he couldn't bear the relationship any more and broke it off. His partner's refusal to evolve provided him with two crucial lessons: (1) how not to be like the partner; and: (2) the insight that psychological stagnation was not a viable option for him.

In the next example, the wife's refusal of the paternal principle first appeared as an attractive aspect of her femininity, the kind of attraction that a very feminine and unconscious woman can exert on a man whose own anima is undeveloped.

## My pretty woman is only a mirror

My wife is like a package wrapped in very pretty paper, tied with a lovely, elaborate, fancy bow and nothing inside.

"Nothing?" one asks. And the pretty box would answer, "No! I don't have an inside. I am all wrapping. I am empty; that is why you fell in love with me. You can project what you wish; you can decide what goes inside the pretty box. Deposit your talent and I will give it an aura of glory. Put in your chaos, your weaknesses, your secrets, and I, the pretty box, will conceal your mess even from your own eyes. I can be either your hiding place or a showcase. Hear me well; that is all I intend to give you. Anything more is too hard."

She caught me in her mirroring game until I started feeling that I was utterly alone. She was a slave to appearances, a slave to a cultural definition of femininity, only a mirror. I remember a dreadful week that she spent shopping for the right kind of shoes to go with a green outfit she had bought the week before. After searching five days in a row for just the right color shoes to go with the color of the outfit, she finally found the right hue of green and asked me if I thought it matched. I was indifferent to her concern and answered absent-mindedly. She concluded from my lack of enthusiasm that her shoes did not really match. She searched for another dress that would perhaps fit with the shoes! That's when I started to cheat on her with a woman at the office. The other woman is a sensual, funny, easy-going woman whose clothes are totally lacking in style. Although I don't think my wife knows about my affair, or is pretending not to know, she has recently started drinking in the afternoon. I have given up trying to fill her soul, it is so empty, a cold abyss; I want out. What I see in the mirror is me: my fear, my cowardice, the emptiness in me that attracted me to the emptiness in her.

## Talking to children as a philosopher would

I believe it is possible to talk to children as a philosopher would and by this I mean to radically relate to the child as an agent instead of a subject. It is the surest way out of the maternal cocoon, and the strategy is valid for anyone afraid of spreading his or her wings. Provided one does not confuse this philosophical attitude with telling the child he is free to do as he pleases – a failure in parenting – one can go far with this philosophical mode. An agent, by definition, is somebody who wants to assume responsibility, whereas a subject is under the authority of someone else, a parent, a monarch, an indulgent therapist.

From the start, every child, by the very fact of coming into this world, can be considered a participant in the as yet unconscious decision to live or to die. The process of teaching a child to assume responsibility need not be presented in an overpowering way; it is simply a way of talking that allows for choices to be made. One of my patients, who was rearing her son by herself, wanted to work on just that kind of a formulation. We worked together on her little speech. The following summarizes the tone of the conversation she finally had with her five-year-old son about the psychological choices available to him.

## You have choices

Your biological father did not want to be a father. He said he knew deep down that he would not be a very good one and so he disappeared before you were born, never to be seen again. It seems that you really wanted to be born anyway, so here you are. At five, you have already learned how to be a strong and healthy kid. Now you can learn something else: that a child can be fathered by many different people. It doesn't need to be the person who contributed the tiny sperm. Many kids are born without ever knowing where that little starting cell came from. In some cases a doctor gives it to the mother in a little bottle, to fertilize the egg. The person who contributes the sperm is only a part of what a father is, and that part you received.

Grandpa, when he teaches you to use the electric drill, is giving you something a father might have given you. In some ways, it is even better, because you know that Grandpa knows a lot more about tools then anybody I know. Your swimming teacher, whom you like very much, teaches you to swim, just like a dad might teach you. My brother, who invites you every summer to his cabin on the lake, loves you as much as any father could. You can appreciate that. My sister, who is a real tomboy, teaches you how to tie a rope in fancy knots. She shows you how to kick up your legs, kung-fu fashion. Even though she is a girl, she can give you the kinds of things a dad might give his son. If you decide to, you can learn from each of them all the tricks a father might have taught you. Later, you may discover that having received all that good fathering prepared you better than most to become a great dad yourself.

This mother is only minimally speaking in the voice of a mother to a child, using instead the rhetoric of a companion on the road. She is not insisting on the fact that he is her responsibility; instead she points at possibilities that are there for him, if he decides to take what is offered. Whenever somebody expresses a need, a lack, a wound, it is tempting to cast ourselves in the role of Great Mother and give the support that seems to be lacking. The maternal reflex is a natural one with loved ones. Nevertheless, a competent psychotherapist also sees the shadow side of it and can sense that the timing for the Mother is over. The come to me poor little thing also communicates: I have a power that you don't have; I take care of you, but watch out, I am the one with the remote control of happiness. By contrast, talking to children in a philosophical mode is a training in becoming responsible for oneself, an initiation into the paternal principle.

# Chapter 11

# The invisibility of the psyche

Who do you want to be in this game? Many video games begin by giving the player a choice of identities. A depth-psychological analysis begins with similar questions. To feel like a player in the game of life, one asks, what is the name of the game? What is the nature of the obstacles? Who threatens whom? Who are my enemies, my allies? What are my tools, my means, my possibilities? What defines winning, and when is the game really over? For the greater part of human history, the game was one of physical survival, but nowadays the hordes of afflicted people are more likely to be suffering from depression, anxiety, suicidal feelings, and psychosomatic illnesses. Still, the heroic game is one where finding and fighting the enemy is crucial.

As long as misery was defined as hunger, cold, cruelty, and an abbreviated life expectancy, there was little attention paid to psychosomatic illnesses. In Europe during the Middle Ages, one child out of three was expected to die. An epidemic could suddenly kill two-thirds of a village. Infected wounds regularly turned gangrenous, rotting one alive. It was common to lose all one's teeth, to die of puerperal fever or to be crippled by rheumatism, all before the age of 30. These afflictions were as normal as lice in the beard, vermin in the bed, and carrion for dinner. Physical and biological calamities, as well as widespread poverty, were facts of life, seldom discussed. It is difficult to understand what historians mean when they point out that in pre-modern societies, poverty, famine, and epidemics were not considered social or collective problems. It was not widely believed that these problems could or should be addressed – an attitude unthinkable today in any advanced society. In fact, even the poor did not seem to make a big deal of their poverty. Certainly they felt hunger, bodily suffering, and the pains of injustice and cruelty, but they were part of a culture that did not see "poverty" as a social problem. Physical misery was not discussed, just as sexuality was not discussed in Victorian parlors. Hunger and cold remained private experiences of the body, often accompanied by shame. The body always knows what threatens it, yet, all through the Middle Ages, the culture remained blind to the physical hardship of the poor and destitute because it seemed "normal" for those bodies to suffer.

The one ritual that was provided by the culture was a place of worship to offer one's laments to God. Miserere, Miserere – God have pity.[1] Misery was not a subject for art, not a platform for politicians, not a good cause for heroes to show their capacity for rescue. Life was expected to be a vale of tears. The good life was something that the poor hoped for in the hereafter, in paradise. This attitude persisted as late as the nineteenth century and still does in certain places.

When Victor Hugo and Charles Dickens wrote their novels, they were both doing something revolutionary. They did not start out by preaching for compassion and reform because as artists they knew that didactic and moralistic tales do not sell, and these two authors were tremendously popular with all social classes. It was through artistic genius, not moral sermons, that they were able to bring poverty out into the collective consciousness. Their revolutionary act was to render images of poverty, to imagine it. Their fiction gave poverty new images and new stories, different from those the Church had imposed upon them. They created a mythology that shone a spotlight upon the tragedy of exploitation. Everyone began to see what was happening, not only to the poor and destitute, but also to the very fabric of their culture. Crowds were incredibly moved by the novels of Hugo and Dickens. Individuals were touched, transformed, and converted to a new idea of what poverty is. Poverty was finally imaged – put into images – made visible, given life through stories that then started to appear in songs, plays, paintings, jokes about the rich and greedy, and speeches to advance political agendas.

The function of literature, art, and also, to speak for my profession, depth psychology, is to search for the images that open the heart and make us see what is right there in our psychological reality. Dickens with his poor Oliver Twist, Hugo with darling little Cossette and his admirable Jean Valjean, condemned to prison for life for the theft of a loaf of bread, opened all hearts.

Their suffering, as it became literature, made visible the archetypal reality that had not been seen, named, or addressed. Their misery, and that of all who suffered from poverty, incarceration, abandonment, was elevated from shame. Their pain took on the nobility of human tragedy. The task of depth psychology is to do something similar for the imprisoned, oppressed, hungry, cold and lonely psyches. Without artistic transmutation, it is impossible to have a change of myth.

The psychological distress of a heartbreak may be the one exception that has always received the attention of artists. Lovesickness is a sentiment that has inspired more songs than humankind's preoccupation with God. Humanity enjoys a long and beautiful history in the art of expressing the sorrows of a broken heart in poetry, painting, sculpture, dance, and music in minor and major keys and on all possible instruments. The beautiful song of lament that is the fado, still sung in some villages in Portugal, is one among many lay traditions, as is the American tradition of the blues and country music, which both express the universal grief of a heavy aching heart. The words change, the feeling remains the same: I'm lonely. I miss you. Won't you come back? I yearn, I cry, I hurt. You're breaking my heart. Without you, life has no meaning.

Just as poverty was obvious yet remained psychologically invisible, we now have a culture that is going through an obvious outbreak of depression, addiction, and psychosomatic ailments. There is, right under our noses, a generalized bankruptcy of the libidinal economy, touching millions of individuals. The statistics are easy to gather for anyone interested, as they follow the rapid rise of income of pharmaceutical companies, showing an unprecedented situation of generalized psychological distress. Yet the epidemic nature of psychological distress remains mostly unseen, as if it is normal for those psyches to suffer. How many of those who regularly feel too exhausted to make love are aware of their psychological castration? How many of those who work too many hours, eat too fast, sleep too little, are caught in too many traffic jams, deal with unbearable bosses and impossible kids, are aware that the stress is killing them? How many violent children, going to impossible schools, living with stressed out parents, are conscious that they are "adapting" by getting used to feelings of loneliness, worthlessness and dispensability?

Depression is the form misery – to use an old word instead of a psychological concept – takes in affluent societies. Our psychic pain is solitary, mostly unconscious, psychologically invisible, and cannot be expressed as poignantly as the physical distress of past generations. Even when the apartment is safe, there is no risk of famine, the retirement plan is generous, the income covers the basics and more, still, the pain is felt, and what makes it worse is that the dramas are not of the kind that inspired beautiful hymns of Miserere. Rather, the nature of contemporary psychological misery sneaks in like the cold, keeping whole populations wrapped up in front of the TV,[2] immobilized while the heart freezes.[3] The popularity of songs of lament seems to have disappeared at the same period as the lullaby.

Today's unhappy souls suffer from what one could call emotional hypothermia as psychic death is in fact a process very similar to a deadly hypothermia with the same tranquil surrender to a fatal sleepiness, no energy left to fight. Cold penetrates the soul as it does the body – the deadly process is slow, sneaky, progressive and silent. It is the form that misery takes in our affluent milieus, its images the opposite of the fiery inferno. Hell is now a psychological place, a frozen state of the psyche, not the roaring furnace imagined by medieval Christianity. One is alone and lost in this icy hell; there is not even a community of sinners. The prevalent feeling is not a longing for God, but that of having been abandoned by all, God included, and nobody caring. Emotional hypothermia does not lend itself to song; there are no laments and no poignant lyrics. Gone are the Miserere sung in cathedrals with vaulted ceilings, clouds of incense, great organs, church choirs – all of which rituals used to heighten the experience and the expression of one's personal misery. To be honest, I don't miss any of these traditional religious rituals because the peripheral belief system attached to them is more than I am willing to accept. Nevertheless, equivalent, alternative rituals have not been invented.

What are our rituals for suffering in style and in good company? Today's iced-up souls are asked to suffer without passion – silently and politely. The pathos in their pathology is sedated. Gone are the words, the songs, the falling on one's knees with imploring hands raised up. The Victor Hugo and Charles Dickens of psychological misery are novelists, film-makers, theater directors, poets, songwriters. Yet, something is missing: an alliance between two worlds kept separate, because artists and clinicians snub each other.

It is not for a lack of clinical evidence that we remain blind to emotional hypothermia. The research is abundant, but it appears that we are not moved by the data, or at least not motivated to take action. For example, the famous Spitz[4] study on war orphans concluded that children will die if deprived of cuddling and love. That an experimental demonstration is needed to remind us of such common sense is in itself an indication of a loss of instinct. A century before Spitz, Jane Addams, who included maternal care and education as part of the mission of Chicago's Hull House (which she opened in 1889), knew what every parent should know when she wrote: "We are told that the 'will to live' is aroused in each baby by his mother's irresistible love for him, the physiological value of joy that a child is born, and that the high death rate in institutions is increased by the 'discontented babies' whom no one 'persuades into living.'"[5]

This failure to thrive was tragically demonstrated again with the children in Ceausescu's orphanages.[6] None of these children's physiological needs went unmet, but they were deprived of the intangible necessities of kisses, hugs, caresses and the essential frivolity of peek-a-boo, tickling games, laughter, and the daily drama of complex interactions. Their surroundings were clinically competent but emotionally cold, without passion, without suspense, without even tears. These infants seldom cried, but died nonetheless, from what was then termed "hospitalism," Spitz's term for what I call emotional hypothermia and others calls emotional deprivation, lack of social stimulation, lack of mirroring, low self-esteem, absence of self-image – and what poets call sadness, blues, broken heart, loneliness.

Half a century after Spitz's research we are barely beginning to question if perhaps all lonely, abandoned persons – not just babies – might not also suffer from a similar vulnerability. One epidemiological study after the other shows that, of course, they do, and that a broken heart can cause the immune system to break down too. Thirty years of research in sociology, psychology, psychosomatic medicine, show, without the shadow of a doubt, that the elderly and adolescents are the most vulnerable to emotional deprivation. Still our culture remains in denial like medieval kings witnessing a famine in their kingdom, or a Marie Antoinette and her feeble-minded king entertaining themselves to death while the country starved.

It took two years of analysis for one of my patients, an educated, well-adapted person, to "see" how dramatically his parents' divorce had affected him, 20 years after the fact.

## My psyche was their battlefield

I was a 12-year-old adolescent when I became the spoils of an undeclared war between my mom and dad. My body, and the legal custody of it, became quite literally a battlefield. I lacked the awareness, and certainly the capacity to express the violence that I was experiencing. There were no physical blows. In fact, I was a pretty spoiled kid, with all the pocket money anyone can ask for. The tragedy for me was that the raging war was invisible even to my own eyes. It happened inwardly, psychologically. I had no way of seeing it or expressing anything. I was in an emotional prison, with invisible bars, invisible beatings, invisible enemies.

A blind spot in a culture is like the blind spot in a driver's vision: dangerous. One of the primary tasks of psychotherapy is to help the patient find the words to make visible the invisible suffering of the soul. The warmth of a dialogue with another human being is often all that separates one from psychic death. As kids, we all learn from our parents to look both ways before crossing a street, not to run with scissors, to avoid poison ivy, snakes, scorpions, rabid dogs, and speeding cars. Because the danger of physical death is omnipresent, every culture, since the beginning of time, inculcates survival techniques in its children. Nevertheless, psychic danger is something we are just beginning to name, and as a consequence, contemporary affluent societies still adhere to a survival myth that belongs to the Middle Ages while ignoring other invisible wounds equally fatal. We continue to consider the growing statistics on depression, suicide, burn-out, and psychosomatic illness as clinical problems, and therefore individual problems, as if these were viruses that attack this specific person but not the rest of us. They are rarely recognized for what they are: problems of epidemic proportions, a collective suffering, something the whole culture has to see and address. If we took the research in our field seriously, we would have to consider that a psychological malaise that reaches epidemic proportions needs a different kind of attention. We would have to ask ourselves what, in our culture, makes the human psyche so vulnerable?

I had a patient who came in for a consultation, straight from his office, who was the most extreme example of psychological blindness I had ever seen. I had never met him before and when he arrived, his breathing was shallow, his eyes were wild, pupils dilated in terror like someone emerging in shock from a car wreck.

## Wounded to the core, and nothing shows

I just learned, by email, that my wife does not love me anymore. She won't be home tonight; she packed and left for good. Last week, we were talking of buying a bigger house to start a family. There was never any domestic violence, never any real threat to our marriage. She simply loves another man. She broke up with me, just like that – twelve lines in an email. In conclusion, she wrote, "Have a good life." Period.

He does not see the violence in this break-up. He does not see the murderous sweetness in her final dismissal. He does not see the story he is in and the shock it is causing him. His body language screams of a terrible suffering but he is like a deaf person shouting. If he had come out of a wrecked car with broken bones and a bleeding wound, the ambulance would have been called. Everyone around would have been eager to assist him. This man read his wife's email at 9.30am but stayed in his office until 5 pm. Finally he confided in his secretary and it was she who convinced him to consult a "doctor of the soul." Because his suffering is psychological, and therefore not as "real" as a broken bone, he feels the need to start our session by apologizing because his voice is unsteady, his hands are trembling, and he has difficulty breathing. He finally weeps and it is a relief, but he is terribly ashamed of this show of "weakness."

His blindness is ordinary, widespread; it occurs all the time. To take another common example, we all know that there are millions of young girls obsessively browsing through fashion magazines, trying to model themselves on Adobe PhotoShop bodies that do not actually exist as such. These magazines and their impossible ideals keep these girls buying, dieting, obsessing, and buying some more. The mythology of their culture does not help them understand the effect of having a beauty standard for

girls that is basically the image of a prepubescent boy, the real
object of desire of many fashion designers. Media analysts understand this; feminists write about it; but who teaches the girls about
academic research? And when they do read about it, what in their
adolescent culture makes them impermeable to it? Even the most
beloved princesses are obsessed with fashion, looks, and their
figures, just as are the stars of the American movie industry. When
even royalty – supposedly not victims of the adolescent subculture
– buy into the emaciated style, how can we expect a 13-year-old
girl to deconstruct, on her own, an unattainable beauty myth?
Who will initiate her into a different reality? Who will educate the
little princesses of this world into a reality that the culture largely
ignores?

## Cynicism is not lucidity, criticism is not contempt

There is no shortage of anecdotes and gossip about the cynicism
that is the trademark of the milieu of the film industry in Hollywood. Rudeness, lies, disrespect, contempt, and abuse poison not
only the professional milieu but also the very capacity of people to
relate to one another in their private lives. Just to work there can
scar one for life, and I am not talking about drug use; rather, it is
the psychology of the milieu. All seems fine as long as one is a
winner, a rising star, a glamorous persona, an independently rich or
influential player in the power game. But one soon discovers how
losers (a fading star, a not-so-talented-but well-connected-aspiring-
star, a not-so-young-and-yet-to-be-discovered-talent, a young-
talented-yet-not-well-connected-artist) will be discarded like
human garbage. Hollywood is a big thermometer for our culture
because it presents a blown-up picture of how it feels when the cold
draft of cynicism blows on human relations. Wherever an abysmal
gap separates winners from losers, men from women, rich from
poor, young from old, or one subculture from another, the tension
of living in such a community increases for everybody.

A friend who works in Paris describes his milieu of an advertising agency, and it is not much different from the milieu of the
film industry in Hollywood, and not so different from some
academic milieus I have experienced, and not so different from
families who worship only success. I asked my friend to describe
his experience of what he calls "management by contempt."

## Management by contempt

Our management style is touted as being direct and virile, but is, in fact, abusive and decadent. There used to be a line between the expression of criticism and that of contempt. Not anymore! Last week, I presented a draft for an ad campaign, a project on which I had worked all week. I had been asked to "think young" for a perfume ad. At 55, I am not "young." I wonder why I was put on that project, and why it should be oriented toward youth, when women in my age category – 50 to 60 – primarily buy this perfume. My supervisor, whose name is François, but likes to be called Frankie, is 20 years younger than I. Frankie is the epitome of a BOBO.[7] He was hired when our organization bought into the youth culture, following everybody else. Of course, he thinks only "youth" has value. He thinks naming a perfume "Poison" was the most brilliant labeling in the history of advertisement. That is about all the history he knows. He wants to be called Frankie because what he appreciates about American culture is extreme sports (which to me seems like the opposite of the idea of sport), and free fights (a glorification of viciousness). The kind of things I appreciate about American culture are, for example, that the percentage given by individuals to charities and non-profit organizations is the highest on the planet. He cannot see the value of that. He thinks even the Red Cross is a gimmick. We were born in the same city, from a similar milieu, yet don't live in the same world. The age barrier is the new iron curtain.

Here are the words with which Frankie rejected my draft: "This is absolute shit! Tell me you have just been lazy. Don't tell me you believe this actually looks young?" I know he does not think he has bad manners, because in his mindset he thinks his rudeness translates as strength, the sharp bite of the young wolf. For me, it is something else: verbal abuse, an adolescent lack of manners and organizational stupidity. Each time I deal with him, my stomach knots up.

I am a well-paid employee. I have seniority. I have some financial security. I may even beat him at the BOBO game, because I can retire now if I want to, and be the bohemian he is just mimicking. I know my work is fine because my ads sell, but this kind of atmosphere makes me sick, physically sick – diarrhea, nausea, lack of appetite. I will have to take early retirement, to stay alive. At 55, I truly am a "has been" because this culture of cynicism is not something I can work with. Whereas, for the young generation, cynicism is a value. I think it is their defense mechanism. They have seen so much corruption and manipulation; they think of themselves as more lucid, and I can appreciate that; it is true that we were somehow naive. And perhaps they are the generation whose task is to reveal that ours is a culture of death. I am no innocent and I do know how much gimmickry there is in any organization, even the Red Cross. I know how a charity can be a front. Yet, I cannot live in Frankie's cynical world and I am glad I can afford to retire. If, as my life expectancy predicts, I'm going to die at 85, it means I'll be around another 30 years and I'm interested in watching how such a culture of cynicism will age. How can somebody such as Frankie survive with contempt for all that brings happiness? I'll be following his story.

In countries where violence is expressed through torture, hasty executions, punitive amputations, cliterectomies and infibulations, the abuse is evident. One does not need to invent a new concept to describe the suffering of the little girl who is tied down while an ignorant woman mutilates her sexual organs, calling this a "ritual of initiation into womanhood." There is no need for new words to describe the agony of a boy having his right foot amputated for having stolen a bicycle, in front of a barbaric audience who calls this justice. Their conditions don't need to be interpreted to signify torture and death. The cowards who hide behind political correctness to accept such practices have forgotten what the term "civilized" means.

However, it is easier for us to see the barbarian aspect of such customs than to look at the abusive nature of some of our own practices. A teacher repeatedly shows contempt for the ignorance of a student, and later that student commits suicide. There is a hostile and dangerous atmosphere in the school and the authorities say there is nothing they can do about it because they are themselves overwhelmed, understaffed and living in fear. An organization repeatedly burns out its employees and fires them when they can't cope anymore. An IRS agent conducts an audit sadistically and treats the recently widowed woman as if her late husband had been a crook because his papers were not in order when he died, adding to her despair. A frivolous but legal lawsuit entangles you for three full years and the stress breaks your relationships with your partner. One's pension fund is bankrupted through corporate greed and corruption and you are told that is the way it is, get over it. You teach in a school where swindling students who resent your rigorous grading slash your tires and attack your daughter in the park. Your spouse regularly demeans you in front of family and friends until you come to loathe yourself. Your kids steal from your wallet to buy drugs. Your grandchildren imply that it is time for you to die so they can inherit. Your adult children come to visit only when they need a fat check and they think you don't see through their slender ruse. Your daughter doesn't want to grow up, lives with you on your small pension, and complains every day that it is your fault she is such a failure because you did not give her enough love. It is your last day at work, after 30 years, and nobody seems to notice, the management is new and you are part of the leftovers from the old gang. The impact of such violence accumulates in the psyche and destroys possibilities of joy as surely as does the repressive dictatorship of a priest, pope, imam, or rabbi.

With half the population on some kind of medication for psychological or psychosomatic problems, the fact that most schools of clinical psychology translate all collective misery into a personal problem requiring personal treatment, contributes to the invisibility of the epidemic. The pre-modern attitude toward the poor suggested that poverty was God's will, or bad luck, or fate, or the lot of your caste. This same attitude seems to have been recast as the tough luck of bad parenting, poor genes, poor tolerance for stress, a weak ego, or a neurotic heritage from one's family. If you had been poor a few centuries ago, a rich person might have offered you a lump of bread to get you through the day, but the problem was still not addressed collectively. Today, psychiatry does the same when it reaches out with an open hand to give you enough tranquilizers to get you through the month. It sure may help and it is better than nothing, but the blindness is still there. The suffering of the psyche is an invisible one. To address it, we all need to develop a night vision.

# Chapter 12

# The ultimate virtual reality game

Imagine two cameras: one captures the reality that is going on around your head; the other captures the reality that is going on in your head. The two cameras produce two very different films, showing two realities, outer and inner, each with their own style of realism. The outer reality of facts, in itself, has no meaning whatsoever; no story is possible with only that film. For meaning to happen, the events have to be somehow connected to the second, inner reality. Only then do we have a story.

A depth-psychological analysis draws from both tapes, cutting, editing, and mixing all the sequences from both cameras to create a meaningful narration, a new myth. A good metaphor for the process of an analysis is to imagine the patient sitting in the chair of the director, calling the shots, while the analyst runs around busily, with the triple task of script girl (last year in your dream you had a different outfit), audience (I am listening, I get the picture, I am following you), assistant director (this tone of voice sounds like whining to me), and critique (yes, I hear you say you love that person, but I am not convinced; I also hear some anger about the event).

The story about my mother not being maternal enough for poor little, needy, infantile me is not based on any new facts. The images recorded on camera number one are still valid, objectively true to my mother's behaviors and attitudes. The things she did, she did. The things she did not do, she did not do. Nevertheless, the story combining both the objective and the subjective realities is a relatively new story to me because camera number two, following my regression to a child's perspective due to physical pain, came up with a surprising film, done from the angle of looking backwards at my life. The feeling of having had a rather cold-not-very-maternal-mother is a new inner reality for me, who, all my life, believed that a competent, no-nonsense mother was supposed to be cold, just like mine was, unconcerned with the wild weeds that kids are. This is news to me, because when I was eight years old, the attitudes of my mother – like those of the nuns, like the isolation of a boarding school – all felt completely natural. The psyche being an ecological system, it adapts to its milieu so that even what is painful feels as natural as the weather, sometimes sunny, sometimes cloudy, sometimes stormy, on a continuum from cold to hot.

The story I arrived with in boarding school was a story made by others, one in which the Ladies of the Sacred Heart, because of their rigorous style, were considered the best educators in town. The fact that, just like my mom, they also lacked what I now interpret as maternal qualities was not perceived on my radar. How can a child of eight translate their abrupt manners, their contempt for tears, their snobbism, as being "non-maternal?" I do now, decades later, and this is called an "interpretation," one which has meaning for me, at least for this decade of my life. As all interpretations are subjective, it also implies that this chapter in my story may change again. Maybe I'll come to think of the Ladies of the Sacred Heart as a most inspiring model of militaristic discipline and will be grateful for it. After all, Mother Superior may not have been motherly, but she was a formidable General-in-chief.

In most of the adult relationships I had, following these childhood experiences, I expected the same kind of rational, competent, non-abusive but rather cold atmosphere, and of course I got it, creating the emotional climate I was used to. As long as I remained as unconscious as I had been of my need as a child, I did not ask of my relationships a maternal quality of affect. I did not know the taste of what I yearned for. It wasn't in my psychic programming, as my computer guy would say. Consequently, I suffered the same lack four times: (1) with mother; (2) with the nuns; (3) with many of my intimate relationships; and (4) in the academic milieu that I chose, partly because its coldness felt natural. Even with four repetitions of the experience, it still took me half a lifetime to find the words to tell myself that story.

For sure, I am slow to edit my tapes, but there are aspects of our psyche that move at a turtle's pace and others that jump like gazelles. Turtle though I may have been in this instance, a knock on the head finally brought a new narrative that changed my whole psychic configuration. With this new edition of my life's story, I know what I am looking for in relationships. Knowing what I yearn for, I find it. I have discovered a world filled with kindness, compassionate beings, possibilities for friendship, gentleness, affection, and love (all kinds of love). Feeling my thirst after crossing a desert, I search for streams of affection and drink of them. I associate with persons whose strength does not exclude kindness and I go out of my way to avoid harshness, rudeness, snobbism, meanness. Having seen the importance of tenderness for survival, I find that the world can be Good Mother. And, to my surprise, I see that men are as talented as women in expressing gentleness; it was I who was blocking it. In my new myth, Nature really has become Mother. The roses that consent to grow in my garden, aren't they sweet to respond to my regular applications of fertilizer? I feel loved by their glorious blooming. I take it personally. When I think of my life's trajectory, there is now a whole new virtual panorama. I see the presence or absence of the Great Mother in all situations, in all relationships.

I am intellectually aware that hatred is as omnipresent as love. The possibilities of war exist in every community, in every heart, all the time, everywhere. Nevertheless, perception being a function of the myth that organizes the psyche, I want to see less of war, for the time being. Ten years ago, had I been asked "What is your life's story?" it never would have occurred to me to talk about my childhood as having been solitary, a winter of the heart. My new myth has a vernal quality: the thaw of my psyche. This is my excuse for focusing on honey rather than vinegar, for the time being. No version of one's story is ever final. The eternal themes of war, love, beginnings, and endings are forever revisited and the seasons of the heart follow their own rhythm.

## Fictionalizing is inevitable

A fact is a fact. Immutable. If someone says, "Due to a car accident ten years ago, I had a leg amputated" there are no two versions of the objective fact of amputation. There is no subsequent version in which the lost leg grows back or the collision is averted. Historically, the amputation is complete. Nevertheless, as a person starts telling not just the facts but a story of the accident, the incident becomes infused with emotions and interpretations. In the act of editing and mixing both fact and affect, our existential freedom as well as our identity is created. The greater the level of consciousness, the freer one is to choose one interpretation over another. Our psychic identity derives from a fictionalization of facts which complicates the events into a story. In other words, it forms a myth.

The process of fictionalization is similar to the work of an historian who, although he or she is aware that the facts won't change, is nonetheless still motivated to contribute yet another interpretation of history, to add one's personal riff on the same events. Every autobiography – like every history book – contains an objective basis (the facts) and a subjective interpretation (the story, myth.) History written by the winners of conflicts and wars, and whose ideas dominate a culture, never has the same flavor as history rendered by the defeated. That flavor can be called an archetypal perspective. Flavor is essential in the mixing of the plot of events into a coherent dish. To continue with the example of the car accident that caused the person to lose a limb, one can tell the story from the archetypal position of victim: See how unlucky I am? Somebody hit me and I lost a leg. Oh, pity me! The same person may, however, at a later time, move into the hero archetype and, in that stance, using the same facts, tell a story of courage and hope: Let me tell you how I surmounted my handicap; see how proud I am of my accomplishments; I have discovered strength in myself that I did not know I had. The archetypal lens of victim is passive (bad things just happen to me), whereas the heroic lens is active (let me tell you how I surmounted my handicap.) Both reside in a story, but with very different plot outcomes.

The archetype of hero is similar to Jean-Paul Sartre's idea of freedom. He begins with the question: "What do I do with what was done to me?" What he called one's situation is the sum of the objective facts (gender, class, amputation, or the bars in the window of the prison). Freedom begins with how one interprets the situation, creates a version of the story, shapes the plot with a certain archetypal inflection. From his prison cell, Sartre began his treatise about freedom. Being imprisoned by the Germans was his lived and inescapable situation and what he did with it (write philosophy) was the expression of his freedom, the mythical amplification that gave his life meaning. Rather than equating his life with his situation, he amplified it in the form of a treatise on what – from the outside viewer's viewpoint – he did not have: freedom.

A very old friend of mine had a stellar career very early in his youth. From age 20 to 50 his myth was that of the family prodigy. He was labeled as the one with the talent, the glory, the money, and the honey. When he turned 50, the myth that had supported him so well suddenly collapsed. He grew resentful of all members of his extended family, feeling certain they were exploiting him by burdening him with the financial responsibilities for the whole clan. He began perceiving himself as their "cash cow" instead of their hero. The myth of the star/prodigy/hero recoiled into its opposite: the gullible fool, the beast of burden that carries everybody's baggage. He began dreaming of empty wells, blood hemorrhage, exhausted workhorses, starving to death, losing all his medals, feeling the pangs of famine in a rich country, and falling from the roof.

Jung called this kind of reversal an *enantiodromia*, a reversal of the myth into its opposite. The story that had been felt as glorifying was now felt as humiliating. He had become, mythically, his inverted double. He stayed in the victim's story for five years. Now that he is 55, when he recounts his life, the myth in which he situates himself has the same sequence of events, but the role in which he casts himself is neither that of hero, nor that of victim, but of somebody older and wiser, somebody who feels pride at having seen through the myth of both hero and victim.

Even if we were to apply ourselves to write a poly-biography by adding as many perspectives as we can conjure into awareness (e.g., my life as victim, hero, orphan, anima, animus, puer, senex, angel, devil, saint, martyr, soldier, general, mother, workhorse, fool, clown, lazy turtle and speedy coyote), there would still exist enough room left over for interpretation and change. Interpretations never become hermetically sealed, airtight, unexposed to change. Our human condition, by its very nature, makes any definitive version impossible; revision is our constant companion. Fictionalization is unavoidable and constantly at work, working our life events into revised narratives. We inevitably fictionalize when we talk as well as when we write. In the writing of this book, I cannot help but fictionalize a conversation with students, former patients, colleagues, family, friends, and, that most elusive of all characters; the unknown reader.

The goal of a depth-psychological analysis, in a nutshell, is to become minimally aware of the reigning myth that shapes us, that expands or contorts our being. The post-Jungian approach that calls itself Archetypal Psychology is, more explicitly than others, an exercise in awareness of what is implied by a change of myth. The ideas of Archetypal Psychology[1] are rich and complex but the method is simple. It starts by replacing "why" with "who," "what," "when" and "how." Who (which archetype, which sub-personality, which cultural or personal myth) is organizing my perceptions? Who is this person in front of me? A little princess, lonely and loveless, expecting me to play the part of the generous heroic prince? Or a queen, suggesting an alliance? Is this guy a big bad wolf? Has he just lost a shoe or devoured a young girl? Is this Narcissus-in-me having a fit because I wasn't introduced with a fanfare? Who is this person offering me love: the Great Mother's breast or the hungry mouth of an unweaned baby? Who surfaced in my consciousness when I woke up this morning? How do I behave when I most feel that I am an American? A Californian? An immigrant? What makes me feel like a woman? What needs to happen for my professional persona to show up, on time, and properly dressed? Who am I as a lover? A friend? A parent? What in that movie made me feel uncomfortable? When am I most furious? What is it that most bothers me in this situation? What brings out the puppy-in-me, one that wants to play when I should be grading papers? – a puppy aeternus complex!

## The fabrication of a myth, the dismantling of a lie

A myth occurs when the objective reality merges with the sub-jective reality in a kind of montage, and montages can lie – but they can inspire as well. A myth can support either revolution or the status quo; it can provoke enthusiasm, energy, action, or repression, depression, oppression. To see how a myth is fabri-cated, one might look at how it is deconstructed, undone, deleted. To break free, one needs not only the construction of a new myth but the deconstruction of the old one. Otherwise, the worn-out myth remains active but hidden, and because hidden, destructive. For example, for us to even begin to see the ridiculousness of an identity defined by the color of one's skin, we must first become conscious of a lousy, narrow-minded and damaging cultural myth called racism. Something hurts, and it has a name: racism.

Every orthodoxy struggles to enclose individuals in the domin-ant myth, by limiting the possibilities of escaping traditional boundaries and by minimizing changes. Naming the oppressive myth allows the beginning of a dismantling, forces it into the open for scrutiny and disassembling. One of the many tricks orthodoxy implements to maintain the status quo is to minimize the task of dismantling the old myth (for example, thinking that a new law is enough to get rid of racism) and to declare – too soon – the old myth gone, obsolete, antiquated. Political correctness will hide the fact that the new myth has not quite settled into place. "Racism, sexism, ageism. Where? Who? Not us! Not here! We have zero tolerance for it. How dare you!"

Like bacteria that grows back because the antibiotics were not given enough time to penetrate deeply into the vermin, an old powerful myth does not die without a fight. A young black actor who carries the hope of a post-racist society one day smells the old wounding: you are offering me the role of Othello simply because my skin is black. The role I am interested in is King Lear. The deconstruction was not yet complete, and although that young actor may have felt fine with his white friends, suddenly the old myth begins hurting again because it is not quite dead. The insistent bacteria still alive begin to infect the entire organism, both individual and collective.

Another example is that of the feminist revolution; it has been declared finished, a relic now of the recent past. Many young female intellectuals will gladly take a stand to declare feminism a cause for frustrated angry old radicals. Then, one day, a young woman at the university is shocked to discover that the professor she so admires, although having made a pass at her, is not really pleased by her intellectual admiration for his work and she is hurt to discover that he is embarrassed by female disciples. The admired professor would rather have male followers because he believes male disciples carry more weight. She can almost hear the sexist professor's thought: if women begin liking my work, I must be doing something wrong.[2] The more the culture sees through the still active sexist myth, the more successfully the young woman will be able to track how it still permeates her own consciousness as well as that of her professor. Only through the grit of conscious suffering can one reveal a lousy and outmoded myth that affects language, thought and behavior.

Gender identities, racial identities, professional identities, body images, self-ideals, all are always, all the time, between an old and a new myth. Like a Dionysian mask, an identity can be worn with more or less cynicism or enthusiasm. Only when a given identity begins to pinch, however, is one provoked to peer more closely at what its foundation is. Only then begins the task of dismemberment, deconstruction, destruction, and murder of the old myth. All so-called "personality traits" (of Blacks, Jews, Latinos, men, and women), all of which are culturally based, are revealed as unsustainable beliefs; the myth fractures, the dramatic story collapses, the unbearable orthodoxies explode and new identities emerge.

We all play our role in the vast social drama: we strut and fret; perform with brilliance or shyness; dress a certain way; act in a particular style; adapt our persona to the current trends; memorize the right lines, and hopefully become competent in a particular role. Social psychologists specialize in looking at the various forms and variations in which role playing is essential to life in society. Nevertheless, by remaining aware that it is only a role, we keep in our awareness the fact that the script can be modified if it becomes a source of oppression. Oppression comes from the tendency of any ruling orthodoxy to interpret what is unchangeable (color of skin, gender, age, national identity) as having a predetermined meaning, one that supports the dominant myth to the exclusion of any other stories. That is why myth debunking is a perennial and ongoing task. So is myth making: unending creation and destruction, which is the way of the created order in its own cycles of birth and death. Such is the vitality of life's recurring cycles.

## The dramatic model of psychological life

The Jungian and Hillmanian models of psychological life invite us to think about the psyche as a stage where the different stories are enacted, in their grand archetypal dimension. It is a metaphor that suggests, as does social psychology, that role playing is just that: playing at a role, an identity game. We all have a measure of freedom in how we play our identity games, but the game has rules, the script has a text, and the stakes for playing well – or not playing well – are usually very high. A supple persona implies an equilibrium between two equally pathological postures. On one side there is the pathology of the social actor who believes he plays no role, and is always authentic, when in fact that person has only one role and adheres to it rigidly. It is a closed mythology, a monomyth, a kind of sociological fundamentalism that precludes change, play (and) movement.

At the other end of that same continuum is the pathology of the person who does not take roles seriously enough, who plays a role inconsistently, claiming it is all a game anyway. That person is simply exhibiting a carelessness that has its root in irresponsibility, cynicism, or a development of the personality that stopped in adolescence. The partners in the game (i.e., the other social actors) don't know how to relate to such a person because there is no consistency, no constancy, no reliability. Our unease when faced with that kind of pathology is similar to that of suffering through a bad performance by an actor. Our discomfort has nothing to do with the fact that the actor is playing a fictive role – we know that – and everything to do with the poor interpretation of it. We tolerate such wobbling in adolescents, because their identity is still an unstable gel; they don't yet know which role or which game they fit into. That kind of volatility in an adult persona is disturbing. A professor who consistently refuses the authority of his position and hides behind students' presentations (this seminar will be whatever you make of it); a chef who can't keep his toque on his head; a conductor who won't wear a jacket; a bride who wants to wear jeans and flip-flop shoes for her wedding[3] – all may be felt as disgraceful by those who follow the current script. An incapacity to remain in a position long enough for the others to find their lines in the script is as problematic as the incapacity to budge from an obsessively rigid persona.

## A script is made of words, gestures, costume, décor

Psychological wisdom involves a regular editing of our scripted roles. An analyst can offer assistance in the task of revising our roles, suggesting the right words and editing our lines in the collective drama so that our persona becomes more chiseled and adapted to our talents. That is why analysis appears to many as an adventure of a literary, poetic, philosophical, mythological nature – even an intense metamorphosis through words, by words, and with words. If Jacques Lacan had had the talent, or the generosity, to express himself with more simplicity, his suggestion that "the unconscious is structured like a language" might not have ended up as one more fading faddish cliché and a larger number of practitioners would have benefited from his insights. Instead of a clutter of Lacanian buzzwords, we would have been able to consider his idea that, although we need it to become a person, the language game is always a betrayer. Words serve more than one master. Words are not faithful; their betrayal is obvious in the roles we have to play as social actors. (Lacan himself was a major player at creating confusion with words, in service of building his own glorious persona.) It is mostly with language that one plays one's role, constructs one's myth and, by resting on language so heavily, such an enterprise is always a most unstable creation. Even when we are delighted at having found just the right words to express our persona and tell our story, there is no guarantee that a reality abides behind the fiction. Moreover, words reveal their treachery in the analytic situation because it is essentially a word game.

Jacques Derrida was another word twister. Because of his thick and often inaccessible jargon, he reached primarily an academic audience. Few practitioners effectively or competently answered his invitation to consider the unconscious as a text and analysis as a deconstruction of that same text. Text, in Derrida's personal dictionary, is everything and anything that can be interpreted or deconstructed. Patriarchy is a text; feminism is a deconstruction of it. Your mother is a text for you and in therapy you attempt, with able assistance if you are fortunate, to interpret that puzzling text. Your house, your décor, the meal that you are serving: all are texts that your guests, with assumed or authentic pleasantness, struggle to read. Serving them chestnut-fennel crème soup as an appetizer may lead to a few interpretations, both welcome and unpleasant. Culture is a text. You yourself are a text to be interpreted by yourself. The responsibility of the patient in analysis is to read the text first and then to deconstruct its fixed meaning. As meaning can escape even the author of the text, analysis is a lesson in humility and can never pretend to uncover all meaning. The best one can hope for is to raise one's awareness of what is being said by the text, the context, the subtext; to develop an ear for what is being communicated; to intuit what is not being said and can nonetheless be felt. The text remains, at least in part, silent, inscrutable, always deserving of another run at it. Telling one's story does not take one to Truth with a capital "T." Truth remains elusive because it is based on facts that, like a text, can be interpreted in multiple ways.

Instead of looking for Truth, depth psychology – post-modern in its own original way – invites us to pay attention to the distance or the proximity between the stories we tell ourselves about ourselves as well as the stories others relate about us or to us. There exists a significant distance between the old script that kept my friend going for years (I am the prodigy, the success story of the family) and the newer one in which he envisions himself as having been used (I was naive and did not see I was just a cash cow for the whole clan). It is primarily through words that this distance is felt, offering an interpretation that opens one to change by shifting the myths one lives within. In the case of my friend, it saved his life because he was exhausted to the core by his heroic posture. His new myth, even if more painful than previous instances (it is not so pleasant to be going from "genius" to "cash cow"), nonetheless revealed crucial insights.

This form of psychological creativity eventually leads to what the Ancients called *amor fati* (love of one's fate), a concept I find most beautiful. To love one's fate does not imply a fatalistic attitude, nor a passive compliance with one's circumstances. Rather, it means a love of one's story, a comprehensive understanding that whatever happens is happening to me, a participant in the creation of my drama. Even my messes are my own; they are the turns I took in my story, and because my story is mine, I embrace and love it. My friend did not go from hero to victim, but from less wisdom to more wisdom, able to feel: This is me. This is my life. *Amor fati*. Friedrich Nietzsche[4] used this same notion of *amor fati* to signify the acceptance of what is and the love of what is becoming. He saw this disposition as the crowning achievement of the Dionysian attitude, a desire to know the specific form in which one's destiny unfolds.

## A myth is a metaphorical story

Another way to explore how words betray is to examine the inherent vagueness of any metaphor, a characteristic that makes metaphors the enemy of precision and objectivity, so critical for scientific rationality. It is for this reason that scientists have to adhere to a technical non-metaphorical language – except maybe when looking for a catchy title for their books. However, since human emotions are not objective events, technical language –

such as the clinical nomenclature of the *DSM* – fails to communicate the subjective meaning, which is best expressed in a style with symbolic resonance. When I tell my story, my style is necessarily different from, say, that of a biologist reporting on the speed of multiplication of a bacteria observed through the microscope for a given time. Like the biologist, I may begin with the facts. However, as soon as I use adjectives and adverbs, make interpretations and connections, I reveal my imaginal inner world – my mythology, my psychology. Subjectivity cannot be expressed without resorting to metaphor. I'll say for example: this relationship is choking me (metaphor); she is a vampire (metaphor); my boss is a slave-driver (metaphor); teenagers are tyrannical (metaphor); politics are rotten (metaphor); the economy is paranoid (metaphor).

Psychological analysis gained many invaluable insights from the structuralist approach of Lévi-Strauss by discerning the hidden ideological strength and abuse that language inevitably carries. For example, structures of opposition (night/day,[5] sky/earth, male/female, raw/cooked,[6] sacred/profane[7]) reveal the whole system of values that gives metaphors their power. While Lacan applied structuralist ideas to expose the structure of the unconscious, other depth psychologists, especially C.G. Jung and some of the post-Jungians, chose a very different road by focusing on the content of metaphors and myths, instead of their structure. James Hillman is probably the most radically post of the post-Jungians. Therefore, instead of asking, for example: "Does the story present a structure of opposition between night and day, or earth and sky?" Jungians and post-Jungians ask: "What emotion, what archetypal quality is personified by these characters, what kind of symbolism are we presented with here, which archetypes are constellated?" Of course, one could – and many do – argue that archetypes are structures, although the word structure (like paradigm, grid, pattern, or code) has different meanings for different authors.[8] But depth psychology does not focus exclusively on the structures.

Jung never achieved the academic recognition that the structuralists commanded and that failure may be, in part, because an archetypal quality – as opposed to a structure – cannot be translated into neat, quasi-mathematical schema such as those the structuralists were so fond of. The analysis of archetypes is much like reviewing a film: it is always a battle of interpretations. There is no mathematical modeling, no putting in a formula one's archetypal perspective. It exists beyond quantification, but exists nonetheless.

Let's take the example of reporting on the quality of a wine. The grower, like the scientist, can objectively report the year, the location, and even the chemical composition. The oenophile can certainly use that information, but that is not the key to his reputation. Like an archetypalist, the lover of wine has a rich vocabulary of metaphors to communicate to others the aroma, the color, the texture, and the taste. He might say, for instance, "cherry with a touch of blueberry," a "pepper finish," "a hint of tobacco," "an amazing leg," none of which literally appear or exist in the bottle. There is no blueberry, tobacco, or pepper in wine, and wine certainly has no legs. The magic of metaphorical language is that others tasting the same wine understand perfectly and so feel the metaphorical ingredient. The vocabulary that comes with developing a taste for wine, although metaphorical, is precise, constant, and relatively reliable. Taste buds get it.

By contrast, a technical description of the chemical structure is much more stable, but if one day a law were passed prohibiting the use of metaphorical language to describe the qualities of wine, it would be like robbing Dionysus to pay Apollo – a big pagan sin. It would be like the imposition of a totalitarian dictatorship on words. Inner life is just like wine; we need a metaphorical vocabulary to communicate the quality of our emotions. Feelings, like aromas, are spontaneously expressed by using rich imaginal language. For this reason among others, depth psychology is definitely in the camp of the humanities because our inner cinema is not so concerned with objective reality and logical structures; it belongs to other terrains of experience. Inner life is a virtual production whose truth is of the kind we call "artistic truth." Just as someone who has a nose for wine, a good depth psychologist can "smell" the archetype lending flavor to the mix: a strong taste of whining baby mixed with a touch of sadism; a strong warrior color, with an undercurrent of love kitten; immediate sweetness followed by a sour aftertaste of resentful matron; an untamed shrew covering a lovely queen – Shakespeare got that one.

## Who is telling the story?

Given that identity is not only expressed but fabricated through a narrative, it is crucial to teach analysts in training how to remain centered on the imagination of the patient. The influence of the therapist on the creation of the new myth is inevitable to a certain point, but it should be like playing the piano with four hands, with the analyst remaining on the left side of the piano. If the analyst exerts too much of an influence, the patient ends up with a story that reflects someone else's imagination, or someone else's theoretical orientation. Repeated experiments have shown that the patients of a Freudian psychoanalyst will find themselves in a narrative with some measure of Oedipal struggling. The patients of a Jungian analyst will have mandalas and shadow figures appearing in their dreams. The patients of a specialist on co-dependency might all be convinced that not liking to travel alone is a sign of co-dependency. We have also heard one story or another of false recovered memories and deranged psychotherapists who convinced almost all their patients that they had been victims of sexual abuse. They are the modern equivalent of Procrustes, the mythological character who cuts off the head or feet of his guests to accommodate the size of the bed. Usually healthy common sense, combined with experience, convinces most psychotherapists that if the theory does not fit, discard it.

The art of therapy implies the capacity to put one's intellect at the service of the patient, not just one's own ears and heart. Unfortunately schooling in psychology – under the influence of professional corporations such as the American Psychological Association (APA), whose means of control are those of a mafia or a monopoly[9] – involves less and less training of a critical mind and more and more technical learning and theoretical indoctrination. Students tend to believe in the superiority of one school over the others, buying into whatever the current theory happens to be about any given pathology, but will rarely discuss the fact that none of these theories have been reliably predictive of who will heal and who won't. The capacity to predict is supposed to be the validating principle of a scientific approach; for example, there are sexually abused kids who become compassionate human beings while others repeat the horror they have experienced. Anaïs Nin experienced incestuous relations with her father and went on to become a great writer. Why? Others were crushed by one lightly incestuous conversation. Where does complexity fit in a simplistic theory? Nobody is suggesting that abusive relationships can have positive effects, but rather that some theories may not consider enough the basic existential freedom of the victim. Simplistic theories create simplistic equations and incompetent therapists. "You have been abused" has been heard by many patients as a curse: "You are wounded for life, a diminished person."

Many psychotherapists, whose minds were insufficiently trained, have been attracted to theories about sexual abuse mainly because it supported their fear of sexuality. Their theoretical premise is undeniable: incest between parents and children is the strongest taboo humans have and breaking this taboo invites tragedy. Nevertheless, the ideologically rigid therapist, who "believes" in his or her theory as one believes in God, will not hear the particular case of the patient with all its idiosyncratic qualities.

I have heard many stories of incest, from "light" cases to the most tragic. Most students, when they begin studying cases of incest, will automatically link the trauma to the abnormal sexualization of the relationship. When one listens to the narrative more closely, it often appears that the traumatic emotion is not necessarily of a sexual nature. For one particular woman, the trauma she wants to talk about is the betrayal of the mother who refused to hear her. You are such a slut, to invent such a lie. For another woman, the pain that lingers in her psyche is the loss of the grandmother's affection. While washing off the blood of the rape by the adolescent brother, the grandmother said, "He ruined you. There is no washing off that kind of filth." This little girl felt cursed. Another wants to speak about her fear; not her fear of the abnormal sexualization of the relationship, but her fear of the father's violence and death threats. If you ever dare reveal our little secret, I'll kill you.

The impact of religious values that have remained unconscious goes undiscussed in most therapeutic milieus. The separation of Church and State still has a lot of "separating" to do in training institutes. Unconscious Judaism and Christianity still shape our psychological theories. Each time psychology attempts to define what a healthy relationship should be, one should watch for the old religious code lingering in the background. The deconstruction – and reconstruction – of spiritual values is part of every analysis, but for it to happen the analyst has to have examined his or her own religious values. This entails much more than an examination of past religious beliefs or practices. It involves all the residual deposits of two thousand years of Christian mythology, with its deep hatred of the body and of sexuality, of all that belongs to "the carnal world."

The number of psychotherapists who are unaware of their residual Christianity seems to be growing, rather than declining, due to a resurgence of a largely undifferentiated spiritual need. Freud's argument was that religion is a tragic illusion that a collective neurosis forces us to endorse.[10] Given his historical influence, it is disappointing to see how easily psychotherapists in training will make moral judgments based on old religious values, thinking they reflect a "new" spirituality. Many don't even see how retrograde is the discourse of most of the media's pseudo-experts who inevitably find fault with all sorts of sexual affairs. The kind of psychology that one hears on the radio or reads in newspaper columns regularly distills the old religious code. For example, an unwillingness to get married will be interpreted as a sign of immature behavior – fear of commitment – when it could be an authentic rejection of the values behind the marriage con-tract. Adultery is often equated with abuse of the partner. A teacher's attraction to a student becomes "harassment." Such judgments, disguised as "clinical," are almost always based on Christian marriage as a standard of normality.

Psychological theories that ignore the history of mores generate dogmas that are as alienating as those of traditional religions. To take a particularly problematic example, how can somebody with a degree in psychology lack the knowledge that in Ancient Greece, pederasty was part of the education of young men? What kind of ignorance makes a psychologist theorize that the sexual attention of an adult for an adolescent is inevitably, irremediably, essentially and without exception, destructive of the fragile psyche of ado-lescents? The sexual initiation of a boy, around age 12, was overseen by a 30-something adult, who was, at the same time, his teacher (pedagogue). The fact of giving sexual gratifications to one's teacher did not seem to create any kind of trauma, because pederasty was, in that culture, considered "normal." It was accompanied by a complex and rigorous code of manners meant to minimize the potentially destructive effects on the younger partner, and to initiate the young into the sexual realm as well as sociopolitical finesse. One certainly cannot say as much of the Christian Church. There never was any kind of "code of manners" to prevent the rape, on their wedding night, of young virgin brides who were often given, at 15, to rich old men, the age of the girls' grandfathers. The Church was ready to turn a blind eye. The girls were not free to say "no" to such arrangements; the ritual of being asked to say "yes" was one more hypocritical gesture of a Church unconcerned by legal rape. The priests were not interested in providing a gentle initiation in the art of lovemaking, for girls or for boys.

One can ask: which is more traumatic – a milieu where it is "normal" that the person who teaches you grammar in the morning also initiates you sexually in the evening, or a religion which gives a husband exclusive and total control over his wife's body? A Christian wife could not refuse her husband sexual service. Even if the man was brutal, even if repeated pregnancies threatened her survival, she could not say no. The old virgin men who ruled the Vatican, with no experience of sexual love, child-bearing or family obligations, gave their blessings to arranged rapes for centuries. They might have learned a thing or two had they been schooled in Ancient Greece. They might have learned that a sexual relation should be based on free will. The pupil could refuse sexual contact with the pedagogue, a privilege the Church still does not grant women. Second, they might have learned that the "art of love" is an important art form, an aesthetic experience that has to be taught and learned, for sexuality to be a pleasure and not an act of violence. Uninitiated sexist priests generated immense sexual misery. Yet, with all this history in the background, many psychologists quickly judge all that seems to them like illicit sex – or sex with even a slightly incestuous tonality – as "dangerous."

A father tells his daughter, a gorgeous, sensuous 18-year-old, "If I were 18 years old today, I sure would find you sexually attractive." This necessary confirmation of a daughter's feminine power by a loving father was brought into one of my classes by a student who saw this as an example of "incestuous overtones in the father–daughter relationship." The father simply wasn't a castrated male and had eyes to see what everybody around him could see as well: that his daughter was feminine and sexy and he did not deny it. In a culture that was not afraid of sex, this interaction would be understood as validation, a gift from the father. But half the class were convinced that it "might" be of an incestuous nature and a victimizing of the daughter.

Incest has traditionally been defined as sex between the parent and the child, or between siblings. The taboo against parent–child incest is shared by all humans, though, as Lévi-Strauss showed, defined quite differently in different cultures. Everywhere, at all times, in all cultures, incest hints at tragedy and for good reasons. Nevertheless, there are myths that relativize the taboo. I won't take my examples from Greek mythology, where stories of incest (Myrrh, Biblis, Phaedra) are a kind of literary device to show imaginal filiations. I'll take instead a biblical example: the incest between Lot and his two daughters. Here are two young virgins who believe they are, along with their father, the sole survivors of humanity. The girls deliberate on their options: Should we remain pure and virginal, at the cost of the end of humanity, or should we get dad intoxicated and steal his sperm? The Bible suggests that, in this case, incest is the moral choice.

All human values contain their opposites. When psychologists too easily equate trauma with precocious or illicit sexuality, they ignore the relativity of human values. This posturing as moral experts has become the new expression of a puritanical obsession. In cases of sexual harassment, the point is forgotten again and again that sexual harassment is a problem of unequal power, not a problem with sexuality. The sexual encounter becomes abuse when one partner has power over the other. That power relationship is at the core of the feminist analysis of patriarchy. It reveals how patriarchal law requiring the wife's submission to her husband actually poisons love and destroys desire. In the same fashion, a psychotherapist who uses the authority of the profession to hide his or her fear of sexuality will project it on to patients and it is a form of abuse. The following story shows how this bigotry might appear.

## Bigotry offered as expertise

My first therapist tried to convince me that my frigidity was the result of sexual abuse in childhood. She questioned me about my first sexual arousal, and I told her about how my sisters and I used to tease an uncle who was a drunken, lewd, old reprobate. I was brought up in a huge, Irish-American clan with a great variety of crackpots and eccentric personalities, including myself. The inappropriateness of my uncle's sexual behavior was dealt with in a fashion that the therapist absolutely could not comprehend. His wife knew that every Christmas holiday her husband not only got really drunk, but also exhibited inappropriate behaviors. He did this with all "skirts" regardless of their age, as long as they had breasts. He himself did not have daughters, only three sons.

Our holiday celebrations lasted for two or three days at our grandparent's farmhouse. They were big gatherings with lots of food and drink, and high emotion – very Irish. My aunt once called a family meeting of all the women and their daughters. Grandma was presiding. My aunt said to us girls, "If he lets the birdie out of the cage in front of you girls, here is what you do. You come near it and you give it a slap. Nothing to harm the little beast, but enough to get it back in the cage. Never forget the rule: you don't go anywhere alone with him, and you stay together. Don't let this wolf or any other wolf get you girls. You're the one in charge of your cherry."

We were never scared, never disgusted, only curious about the "little beast." The truth about this episode – a truth that the therapist was not ready to hear – was that we actually loved to provoke him. These games were definitely not traumatic, just an expression of our puberty. The last time we saw him, I was 15 and I suggested to my sisters and cousins that we lift our skirts together, and pull down our panties to show him our butts. The plan was to take a close look at what an erection looked like. We did this, but he said, "Sorry girls, the birdie doesn't fly any more." He had tears. He died a few weeks later of liver failure. He may have been a pitiful, sad character, but he was not a sadist. The therapist's attempt to convince me that this uncle had been the cause of my trauma I consider intellectual abuse. My adult frigidity had nothing to do with that event.

The explanation was simpler than that: my husband was an incompetent, boring, crude lover. He comes like other men sneeze. Wham. Bam. Atchoo. Over. Now that I have divorced him, and know what a good lover is, I know that the therapist made two major mistakes. The first was to consider my past (the uncle) as overriding my present (my husband). The second was to consider my uncle as a kind of psychopath, a child abuser, when in fact, he was just a pitiful old satyr. For him, a girl of 15 with fully grown breasts was not a child anymore. His Catholic mother had given birth to him when she was 16, and then produced nine more kids, and died at 36 of too many pregnancies. My aunt later told me that my uncle believed himself to be respectful of us girls, as he would never have risked impregnating any of us.

Strangely enough, that first therapy with such an incompetent therapist helped me a lot. I so wanted to disprove her silly theory that I took a lover just to prove her wrong, as an experiment to see if I really was frigid. I discovered that I was not and filed for divorce. Too bad for the therapist. She had not sufficiently worked on her counter-transference, and it showed.

## How is psychology a mythology?

The biographical facts of our lives do not change. My patient's uncle and his exhibitionist behaviors, her aunt's intervention, her vocabulary, the presence of the matriarch, the size of the family farmhouse and the length of their holiday celebrations, all are in the records as facts. In principle, a fact is something objective and verifiable, as Holmes would point out to his anima, his dear faithful Watson. On the other hand, our interpretation of the facts is essentially subjective, an unstable process that changes all the time shaped by a personal and cultural imagination. The analysis of the content of the psyche is not so much an examination of facts (which usually don't take much time to establish), but of how one imagines their meaning to be shaped, distorted (and) reconfigured.

A patient appears at the first session and tells me his story. One can extract from it a collection of facts, the summary of which looks like this.

### Five facts

1  My wife and I have been married for 12 years.
2  We have three kids.
3  Our house is a new construction, with three bedrooms and two garages.
4  My wife and I both work full time.
5  I filed for divorce.

These are the five facts established at the first session. Although this man was one of the most rational and "factual" persons I had ever met, his "facts" were not related in a way that would satisfy a detective. Inevitably, a narrator adds adjectives and adverbs, judgments, feelings, analogies and metaphors to fill out the facts with a fiction. In other words, he had a perspective on, and an interpretation of, the facts. The full narrative from that first session, once the subjective perspective is added to the facts, looked more like this.

## Five facts + perspective

1 After 12 years of marriage, there is not much passion left, only a boring, domestic routine and an equally boring sexual routine.

2 My wife had wanted to have three kids and we did. I had wanted only two. Three young kids is a heavy responsibility and I resent it.

3 Our new house is badly designed: with two garages there is more space for our cars than for our kids.

4 We are both workaholics, working more and more hours every year.

5 When I asked for a divorce, I was expecting her to try to save our marriage, but she did not even argue. I want to fix the marriage. It feels like a failure. I want her back.

The narrative continued to evolve, even if the fact of the divorce happens just as announced at the first therapy session. A year into the therapy, the story has new layers of complexity and further plot twists.

## Facts + perspective + time

6 The most difficult thing for me now is to sleep by myself, and to be deprived of sex. I had no idea how much I would miss her body.

7 I have responsibility for the kids every other week and I feel totally exhausted and angry.

8 She opted out of the house. She took an apartment in town with the money from the settlement. I kept the house, but I regret it. I feel trapped in suburbia.

9 I feel I have been abandoned.

10 I still hope she'll rethink that divorce and come back home.

> With the work of time and therapy, the house that felt too small, ill-conceived, too suburban, slowly wears a different valence. I took over the space of the two-car garage, made it into my private space, and I love it. I retreat there, the kids respect my territorial boundaries and I respect theirs.

The new meanings that emerge change even his memories. At the beginning of his therapy, what seemed most difficult for him was to sleep by himself and be deprived of sexual pleasure. Two years into the therapy, he says: the most difficult challenge for me, since the beginning, has been to learn to be a good father to my kids. The perception he now has of his past emotions has shifted under the influence of the emotions of today. The present always colors the past. He now feels as a joy what was then an ordeal. Two years ago, the responsibility of fathering was a negative experience but today it is a positive one. Even the story of the divorce is no longer a story of failure. Divorce brought me much closer to my children; I am a better person today. The following years saw the complete disappearance of his wish for his ex-wife to return home; his notion of a happy ending ceased to involve the return of his wife. Instead, he created a different story of the past which significantly defined his future.

The facts of a life follow a trajectory similar to a binary program in which only two possibilities exist: either an event happened (value of 1) or it did not happen (value of 0). By contrast, a narrative involves infinite possibilities of interpretation and has the capacity to travel in any direction, more like a hypertext than a linear line on a page. The task of imagination, then, is to carry that hypertext, upgrade it daily to the links that constitute our identity. One can, and must, come up with fresh interpretations that feel right, new links that feel meaningful, a process going on all the time, which is why the development of imagination plays such a crucial role in the quality of inner life.

Sartre was radical in affirming this creative process as the basis of human freedom. At all times, we are free to interpret our situation, choosing to be either coward or hero. Others followed with different formulations. Sartre's schoolfriend, Paul Ricoeur,[11] examined with phenomenological precision and academic language the dimension of time in the structure of one's narrative. First I have a vague sense of who I want to be, anticipating my identity (Ricoeur's prefiguration), then I play the role according to the persona I've created (configuration). Then, each time I explain who I am, I interpret anew each of these temporal elements (refiguration). Marcel Proust, in his *Remembrance of Things Past*, expressed the same insights, adding to the dimension of time, the dimension of place. His characters (for example, Swann) do not appear to be the same in the little village of Combray as in Parisian society. Proust reveals how our persona varies according to the location. Changing place is not only a movement in space, it is as well a change in our being, as we are a different person according to the place we are in. Similarly, the dimension of time inevitably modifies our perception of stories gone by. Time does not therefore simply pass; it transforms what it passes.

Facts acquire meaning when they are made an essential part of a narrative, one which will keep evolving until our last breath. The shimmering effect of the multitude of meanings comprises the nature of psychological vitality. That same vitality is lost when the narrative is forced into a genre (like that of the clinical case history, or the judicial deposition, or the one-size-fits-all narrative of redemption in the afterlife). Such forcing of the narrative demeans its subtlety.

A richness of imagination is the best cure against despair. Perhaps the most important question for the survival of the psyche is: Who shall I be, until I die? I have to imagine something, an interesting myth of some sort.

# Chapter 13

# Joy
## The antidote to anxiety

One of the most frequent mistakes of trainees in psychotherapy is to presume that the life of the patient would finally become meaningful if only the neurosis received treatment, the psychic bugs extracted, like a rotten tooth. This kind of naivety, which, in theory, ought to abate as the young therapist accumulates experience, is unfortunately found in many an experienced therapist because of the habit of considering all "ordinary" neurosis – the kind we all suffer from – as a medical condition instead of an existential problem. Most neurotic behaviors are more like an unfortunate addiction to a joyless life than a rotten tooth. Being neurotic is like a bad habit that wastes what life has to offer – this instant, this body, this love, this destiny. The ordinary neurotic personality is like somebody who possesses a colossal fortune and worries every day when the Dow Jones index goes down a few points. Lives that externally appear rich and adapted in every aspect can hide a neurotic misery that turns out to be a poverty of the imagination. The atrophy of the capacity to "imagine" is the breeding ground for all self-inflicted misery. Inner work, as it reveals the interpreting program running in the background, can modify my life's trajectory. Even a slight variation in the interpretation brings about a psychic shift that can make life more interesting (or more distressing). For the process of interpreting my story, I need words (nouns, adjectives, adverbs, verbs); I need symbols and metaphors; in other words, I need the complete kit of what is usually referred to as literature or mythology.

  Depth psychology, especially the Freudian school, has favored the conceptual approach, inventing theory after theory, against the "imaginal" approach.[1] This choice of concept over image may explain the humbling failure of psychology in treating the two most widespread contemporary malaises: anxiety and depression. Both are characterized by a poverty of images, and the corresponding paralysis of the capacity to feel joy.

## Anxiety: the fear without image

The Latin term *angustia*, formed from *angustius*, means a tightness, a closing of the throat that accompanies the perception of a danger for which one feels powerless, because the danger is not identifiable. The child afraid of darkness suffers from anxiety, not fear. Lost in the forest at night, one suffers from anxiety: what if I step on a venomous snake; what if a lion appears; am I going to die of thirst or hunger? By contrast, fear is always fear of something precise – a bear appears in front of me and I know what I am afraid of: the bear. Fight or flight, the two basic instincts of survival, are triggered by fear, not by anxiety.

Called by many names (angst, free-floating anxiety, anxiety neurosis, panic attack, phobia, insecure personality, excessive nervousness, social incompetence, fear of intimacy), anxiety has been the object of many definitions, theories, explanations and medications. It has also been made into the symbol of modernity. The clinical symptoms of it are quite obvious, as are the physiological effects of panic attacks. Difficulty arises when one tries to discover what the person is panicking about. Anxiety does not allow one to name what is feared. Not knowing what one is afraid of, action is repressed. One of the earliest definitions of anxiety, at the beginning of the twentieth century, was that of Pierre Janet:

> Chronic anxiety is a characteristic feeling of melancholic states. It is experienced as a vague pain, or rather a vague fear, a feeling that used to be called "moral fear," to indicate that it is a fear without an object. In reality it is something precise: the subject is afraid of his own action and suffers at the idea of it. This fear stops the possibility of acting, not in a momentary way, as when stopping to take a respite, but in a permanent way. This blockage of action can show up as a phobia, or as anxiety. When it spreads to many areas of activity, the person begins to look like a cornered animal that tries all possibilities of evading and finds itself trapped. The person freezes; no form of action seems adequate. There is no wish, not even a

dream of any kind of action. Living is impossible; life is unbearable. Acute anxiety leads to suicidal thoughts and tendencies. The basic feeling is always the same: the urgency of action, combined with the sense of the inadequacy or atrocity of any form of action.[2]

Janet's concept of anxiety as a "fear without an object" has been considered from many angles. For example, Gregory Bateson's concept of "double bind" describes a situation where the feeling of being trapped is conscious, but combined with an unconscious injunction that forbids you to become aware of the trap. Bateson's analysis of neurotic relationships insisted on the fact that it is not the contradictions – I love you and also I hate you – that create the neurosis; contradictory feelings are inherent in all relationships and we all live with those tensions. What creates madness is the injunction against becoming aware of the contradictions. The person feels something oppressive is going on but also feels that it should not be named, should not be mentioned. I will abuse you, treat you as less than human, but don't you dare notice it or mention it. There is a bear in the path, but the milieu acts as if there is none. The emperor is naked, but one is asked to perceive him as having clothes on. The person is thus incapable of fighting or fleeing, a paralysis that is the basic experience of anxiety.

Generally speaking, words like fear, terror, horror, shock and panic, belong to the register of fear, whereas words like dread, dismay and apprehension are associated with the experience of anxiety. In the nineteenth century, the word "spleen" meant a dark mood with a hint of anxiety. Each generation has fresh appellations for its malaise. Having the "metaphysical blues" was how my existentialist friends and I would have expressed our intellectual angst, a malaise of the soul without any physiological cause – apart from the overconsumption of espresso coffee, Gitanes cigarettes and sleepless nights. The other day, I heard an adolescent express his discontent by saying that his hard disk was bugged down, by analogy with a computer bug and the paralysis it causes to the program running the computer (his whole psyche). His "bug" came from having heard his parents announce their divorce. He was distressed about it, not knowing what would come of this new, undefined situation. This is anxiety.

By contrast, fear is a fundamental impulse that moves one into action. The research on animal fear, begun by Konrad Lorenz, has repeatedly shown that fear is a constant of animal life, a wisdom of the body that warns us of immediate danger. Physiologically, fear provokes an intense excitation of the neurovegetative system, a discharge of neurohormones that boosts the capacity for fight or flight, whereas anxiety does not allow for the discharge of the excitation, and when prolonged, results in psychosomatic damage. The term "excitation" includes all forms of enthusiasm, any impulse to create, to try, to taste, to do, or to fight and flight.

Anxiety is a vicious circle: inhibition of action produces anxiety and anxiety inhibits action in a kind of retroactive loop. Dreams of walking, yet staying put, or shouting with no sound coming out, or hitting which feels like hitting water, are typical anxiety dreams. We share fear with animals, but anxiety is reserved for humans. For Kierkegaard (and Sartre) anxiety is the result of our freedom to create ourselves. We are anxious as the result of the awareness that every day we intervene in our own destiny, every day we choose one path over the other.

The word anxiety and the word modernism often appear in the same sentence, just as post-modernism seems to call for the word irony, revealing the historicity of emotions. The historian Jean Delumeau, writing a detailed history of fear in the western world, shows how fear used to be more prevalent than anxiety, confirming that anxiety is a modern malaise. For example, in Middle Age Europe, people experienced intense fear of ghosts and spirits, the devil and his hell, sorceresses as well as inquisitors, the tax collector and the king's prisons, the evil eye, and bats. They feared outbreaks of leprosy, typhus (and) cholera, and were also afraid of doctors. They seemed to die with less anxiety and less fuss than we do, but they were terribly afraid of dying a sudden death, or without the last rites of Christianity, or in a strange land, or alone with nobody to receive their last words.

Delumeau also examines how the emotion of loneliness, so common today, was something that Romans positively dreaded. The typical Roman was almost never alone: he worked, ate, slept and bathed with company. Even urinating and defecating – at least in the public toilets built by Emperor Vespasian, the best latrines in the history of the city of Rome – were not a cause for isolation. There were no walls between the toilet seats, and the latrines even had artwork on the walls. The kind of forced solitude that is today the lot of the kid with the key to the apartment around his neck, the widower with nobody to talk to, the immigrant alone in a city, would have been felt in that earlier age like a psychological torture similar to the solitary confinement of prisoners. One of the Romans' exemplary punishments was exile. Being banished to an uncivilized island, with nobody to sleep with, nobody to share dinner and conversation with, seems to have been almost equivalent to a death penalty.

The history of fear also shows moments of brusque reversal. Novelty and change, for example, were feared for generations, until the valence was suddenly reversed. Goethe and the German Romantics began the trend, and finally in the twentieth century change became something that was generally experienced as positive, a factor of progress, evolution, youth. By contrast, many people today fear stability because they interpret it as boredom and stagnation, just as our ancestors feared change because they interpreted it as disorder, destruction, and anomie. The intense resistance of oral cultures to the changes brought about by literacy expressed their fear of change. It takes a colossal research, like that of Delumeau, to fully describe and demonstrate how incredibly intense was the fear of literacy, the fear of women, the fear of Jews, and fear of the Infidel. What is even more surprising is the regularity with which all sorts of tensions (political or psychological) were – until the rise of modernism – translated into fear by imagining an object of fear that explained the tension. When the object is a person, it is called "scapegoating."

The fear may have been absurd, unreal, with no reasonable basis, unfounded, contrary to common sense; still, it seemed as if anything were better than the vagueness of anxiety. Nobody knew for sure the cause of the plague, for example. Rather than suffering the anxiety of an unknown causality, medieval doctors were eager to find the object to be feared. Some said the plague was caused by a negative conjunction of the planets, and others by putrid emanations coming from the depth of the earth. Priests also pointed their fingers at sinners, who had surely offended God. The intensity of suffering was for the Church a great occasion to convince their flock that they were now experiencing God's anger in the form of the plague.[3] The priests offered a very precise image to go with their threat: the putrid wounds in the flesh were God's arrows, sent from the sky to punish the immorality of humans. Even when their explanation for the plague was incorrect, they nevertheless had an object of fear: the planets, putrid fog, God's wrath, anything to remain in the register of fear, not that of anxiety. Accordingly, their behavior was not one of a population paralyzed by anxiety, but extraordinarily active, in fact frenetic, in its attempt to leave the putrid city, or feverishly flagellating themselves to appease the wrath of God.

By contrast, our reaction to threats such as heart attack, AIDS, cancer, automobile accidents, pollution, terrorism and political corruption, creates an emotional environment of "anxiety," not of fear. Car accidents have killed or maimed more people than all of history's murderous tyrants put together. On every long weekend, more people die in car accidents than in any kind of terrorist attacks anywhere on the planet. Car accidents are one of the leading causes of death among adolescents. Yet, we don't have a clear picture of that monstrous aspect of modern life. Not only does it rarely appear in statistics, there are no cartoons, no nicknames for the car as killer, no movies revealing this Minotaur living in our basement, feeding on youth. There are almost no stories about car-as-monster, but many about car-as-friend; no imagination of that costly aspect of our adherence to a myth of modernity and individuality. There has been no real discussion of alternatives to transportation partly because the car is still a symbol of the self and that symbolism is still mostly unconscious. The imagination of car as monster is blocked by the imagination of "I am my car." As long as the car remains a status symbol, and unconsciously so, there can be no fear of that destructive aspect of our culture.

There is anxiety about increasing traffic and noise, parents' insecurity, old people not wanting to go out, people worrying about not having medical coverage (what if I get in a car accident?). One may or may not ever be victim of a car accident, cancer, unemployment, poverty, homelessness, physical aggression, rape, or theft, yet there is an omnipresent background of anxiety in the modern psyche. We all know for sure that car accidents are a major cause of death, but until it happens to me or a loved one, it remains a statistical reality, an abstract concept, something like a hypothetical wolf or snake that inhabits the forest and can jump on me anytime. How can I defend myself against an aspect of civilization that can victimize me anytime? No more than the citizen of plague-ridden London in the Middle Ages can I know, for sure, and without ambiguity, the conjunction of factors that will put me at risk of dying of this or that disease, even with all the precision of research by scientific laboratories. There do not seem to be proper courses of action. But the difference from the medieval sense of danger is that I don't have an image either.

Information about pollution of air, water, and food does not provoke fear, but anxiety; the enemy is everywhere, and nowhere for sure. Who to believe? Who to trust? "It" is everywhere, yet nowhere obvious enough to take action. Where is there a body of water polluted to the point of mobilizing a population as against a terrorist attack? Worse, how does one fight the effect of constant alarm created by well-intentioned conservationists whose main strategy consists in creating anxiety without a clear course of action, thus adding to the general paralysis?

The success of the genre of horror movies stems from the fact that – there at last – the monster has an image, a face, even if only a greenish blob. The hero alternately fights and flees, always in action, never doubting. Popular horror movies are action movies. By contrast, Hitchcock and Polanski were masters of a genre that was new when they began exploiting it. By hiding the object of fear, by suggesting rather than showing, they created an atmosphere of intense anxiety. They built up anxiety until the very end, when we are finally allowed to see the object of the terror. The resolution is near. Anxiety is created by hiding the object, fear by showing it. The sequence is often: (1) Anxiety; (2) Fear; (3) Flight; (4) Fight; (5) Victory, the End, game over! As Deleuze[4] pointed out, to create an atmosphere of angst, the director relies on out-of-field camera shots, a technique that reproduces the psychological condition of anxiety – hiding the object of fear, while hinting at imminent danger.

The elaborate mythology of the Ancient Greeks, filled with rich imagery of monsters of all kinds, played a role similar to today's cinema. It fed the psyche with images of what was to be feared. The variety and subtleties of monstrous images in Greek mythology are quite fascinating. A crushing monster (like Charybdis) does not terrify in quite the same way as Scylla, a monster that will drown you in a deadly whirlpool. Toxic relationships are filled with those kinds of subtleties. A relationship that crushes my ego is not at all like a relationship that drags me into the vortex of a depression. Every god, every goddess, represents a strength, a perfection, and each one also offers images of the destructive side of that same figure. These dual-sided constructs are like the automobile which offers fantastic speed, superb autonomy – a liberating invention, and at the same time a killer, cause for devastation and mutilation.

Equally true, we need both images. Even the loveliest of all goddesses – beautiful Aphrodite – brings up the image of the arrow that pierces the heart, the thorn on the rosebush, the tortures of unrequited love, the tears of abandonment, and the curse of frigidity, all part of her myth. The god Pan, from whom is derived the word "panic," personifies the terror of nightmare. Artemis, an image of the beauty of Nature, also shows the equilibrium of terror in animal life – eat or be eaten. Dionysus, symbol of vitality (zoe) and intensity, offers images of addiction, dismemberment, and madness. Zeus, a principle of authority, justice, and order, translates at times as tyranny and oppression.

Some of the nuances in the vocabulary of fear and anxiety are nuances not of meaning but of degree. For example, fear and terror are in the same family of emotion, because the difference between fear and terror is mostly one of degree. There is the same kind of similarity between mourning and melancholia; both have a similar emotional quality. There is no such similitude between anxiety and fear; the difference between these two emotions is not one of degree but one of kind. Fear has an object; anxiety does not.

Kierkegaard interprets the historical increase of anxiety as a consequence of the progress of rationality and lucidity. It is as if the gain from debunking old irrational fears was lost to an increase of angst. This phenomenon may be, as Kierkegaard suggests, an unavoidable consequence of the necessity of getting rid of literal beliefs in fairies, devils, ghosts, hell, gods, and all other carriers of irrational fears. Depth psychology adds another explanation: anxiety comes with the loss of images. This idea does not contradict Kierkegaard; quite the opposite. Rather, it suggests a look at the psychological consequences of not having images for what we most fear, now, today, in a culture where images have been replaced by concepts and fear with anxiety. One way of getting rid of oppressive mythologies from traditional religions was to move to a rational, conceptual mode of thinking. Fine! Done! Nevertheless, we threw out the baby (imagination) with the bath water (oppressive myths). Instead of getting rid of oppressive mythologies, we got rid of the imagination that had created them. To get rid of fairies, we stopped imagining nature. To get rid of the devil, we stopped imagining evil. To get rid of God, we stopped imagining what is greater than ourselves.

When old mythologies are corrupt and dysfunctional, one solution is to replace the ideas they symbolized by demonstrating their falseness, using the rationality of science. Nevertheless, for the psyche, the weakening of imagination is a trauma, because what is lost in the imaginal realm can only be replaced by new images, not by abstract concepts. There is no need to regress to a superstitious, pre-Homeric, magical, irrational sense of self to revive the images in the psyche. The re-mythologization of the world can be done without the return to religion. What is most repressed in contemporary culture is not God, who is still very much all over the place, it is imagination.

By re-imagining the object of my fear, the bear appears on the footpath. I can then find the proper action: run from it, fight with it, take it to the zoo, tame it, or avoid the path that crosses its lair.

## My mother is a combination of two monsters

Thanks to analysis, I have learned to live with my extreme introversion. I am a land surveyor, and as such I don't have to spend too much energy dealing with people. People exhaust me, but I now have a good life because I love the neatness of my work. I love music. I love my cat. I love swimming. I love books, and I have a few friends who are very much like me. The only thing that I really dread is having to interact with hysterical types, like my mother. Before analysis, I kind of knew that she was a hysterical case and a typical narcissist, but could not avoid getting sucked into her hysterical emotional vortex, or crushed by her harsh, cold remarks about me and how much of a social failure I am. At the beginning of my analysis, I had the most powerful dream of my life: I am enjoying summer, rowing my little boat on a lake where there are two cliffs on each side of a narrow strait in the lake. The cliffs are so high their summit is invisible. In the middle of one of these cliffs is a cave. I understand, with terror, that this is where my mother dwells. I hear barking and know she is coming out. A horrible, bitchy creature appears with many heads poised upon a long neck. She thrusts her heads out of the cave and searches for me. Her many mouths are filled with rows and rows of sharp teeth. Not finding me in my rowboat, she retreats into her stony cave and morphs into the hard rock of the cliff. I row away from it, but I am caught in a whirlpool and my rowboat spins like a devil.

I wake up in a sweat. When I tell the dream to my analyst, she mentions the similarity of my dream to the mythological figures of Charybdis and Scylla, two female sea monsters that were said to infest the Straits of Messina. Scylla was represented with six heads, each with a mouth containing triple rows of teeth, and twelve feet. She made her lair in a cave opposite the other female monster, a whirlpool called Charybdis. When sailors (including Odysseus) ventured through the straits, they risked a double danger. Either they would be sucked into the whirlpool that was Charybdis and drown, or they might be crushed between two hard rocks that were the body of Scylla.

This myth is such a perfect description of my dream that it is strangely calming. My mother is sometimes Scylla, sometimes Charybdis. Now I really "see," imaginally "see," the danger I experience each time I interact with her. Having the image of these two mythological monsters changed my whole attitude. I know what I am afraid of – either being crushed or being sucked in! Of course I always knew I had a "mother complex." But somehow, the abstraction of "mother complex" did not bring home the actual scene played in my psyche; it stayed abstract as concepts are. By contrast, imagining myself in the presence of these two monsters suggested a mode of action. I am now an expert in avoidance strategies, just like the hero Odysseus, who was, by the way, following Circe's advice in the art of avoidance.

For this man, a psychic relief occurred when anxiety was retranslated back into fear, which created a new possibility of action.

## Depression: a flattened imagination

Freud wrote about the "death wish," but one could as easily view depression as a "sleep wish," a desire to stay numb, to feel little, to keep the inner monsters sedated, quiet, unseen, unheard as "good" women were once expected to be. The lethargy of the imagination often hides a frustrated desire for dependence, an envy of the fate of Sleeping Beauty, a longing for a childhood paradise in which the world takes care of me instead of me taking care of the world. Depression's opposite is not happiness; it is rather a state where imagination comes alive. Once activated, imagination stirs up all the psychic monsters who were put to sleep by depression. Anxiety retranslates back into fear, allowing action. When imagination wakes up, it pours the salt of tears on every wound and signals the return of fear and terror. It intensifies pathos and drama, introduces a whole cast of cinematic characters, every one of which asks for clarification about the part each plays in the psyche.

A citizen of Ancient Greece, when caught in a drama, might have asked: "Which divinity have I offended? How and to whom can I make amends?" In psychological language it is just like asking: "In what kind of drama am I ensnared? In what plot, what genre, what period, what cast, what set, and in what kind of production am I playing my part? Am I in a victim's poor little me story or rather in a heroic save-the-family-business-nation-planet episode? Do I feel like an exhausted hero, tired of fighting one ordeal after another, or do I feel like a desiccated old virgin whose whole life was spent waiting for perfect love and never finding it? Do I lean more on the side of the big baby refusing to grow up, or am I inclined to play the part of the ever-generous breast to be devoured by all oversized babies that populate every milieu? Or I am the prodigal son who comes back home and – surprise! – nobody's home; they are all out playing golf and don't care about me anymore. Perhaps I am the star of the family, a winner, a success story, a champion, and sick to death that everyone in my environment relates to the persona, and nobody, including myself, knows who I am anymore."

The repertoire of stories is potentially infinite. Mythology has contributed a very long and incredibly rich list of the recurring motifs in the lives of human beings. The number of variations on each motif is also infinite, like variations on a musical theme. Given all the possibilities, it takes a healthy imagination to work

out the best script for one's particular situation. Only the imagination can come up with an artistic compromise between the
fantasy world of inner life and the objective reality outside. This
adjustment is what Jung called the process of individuation. He
saw it as a progressive integration of the shadow (in other words,
making the acquaintance of my monsters) and a constant balancing of the requirements of the ego with the orientation of the Self,
establishing a friendship between the conscious and the unconscious. Individuation is another word for what the Greeks called
the lifelong quest for harmony, or what others called being at
peace with the divinities. A post-Jungian author, such as James
Hillman, goes back and forth between Jung and the Greeks,
showing the constant effort of humans to "get the picture" of
what is going on inside.

Most psychotherapists, but not all, agree that a patient who has
no more desire for life may find a welcome relief in a targeted
medication. Most clinicians, but not all, can hear the silent moan
expressed by the symptom. Thousands of medical prescriptions are
written every day to relieve depression, stress and anxiety. If a
medication can relieve psychological suffering, why not use it? But
the adventure of exploring the unconscious is not a trip to the
pharmacy, but a lifelong quest to augment consciousness, a desire
to add to our humanity. Many, but not all, of the symptoms
classified in the *DSM* can be considered as forms of communication, as signs, as the symbolic language of the suffering soul.
Refusing to eat because the nurturing person just died is a
symbolic behavior. Depth psychology points at the tremendous
risk of treating that kind of manifestation as only a symptom.
Imagine someone who would consider sleepiness, delicious sensation in itself, as only a symptom of tiredness that a night's rest can
cure. This person would then lose the ageless poetry of the night as
well as the profound meaning of rest. It would reduce the human
being to a machine that needs maintenance if it is not plugged into
the socket of sleep eight hours out of twenty-four. Night does not
care for the clinical model. For any culture to survive, it needs its
artists to do their kind of work and we, depth psychologists,
specialize in the art of hearing the whispered song of the soul, in
keeping alive the psychological meaning of such words as rest,
night, love, joy, death.

Symptoms are strikingly similar to an artistic production. Like
all forms of art, symptoms draw their meaning from the emotions

they evoke. One of the things that a symptom will do is to slow down our daily habits of perception, or rather, the symptom is the slowing down, just as night is a slowing down, winter is a slowing down. The psyche has a seasonal slowing down, a time to feel broken, the ego defeated and letting go. The artistry is to facilitate that slowing down in order to find the nugget of wisdom that lies there along a winding road that first feels like an impossible detour. What is analysis if not a series of deviations, diversions that lengthen the experience and add meaning to it? What makes a good lover, a gourmet, an aesthete, if not someone who takes his or her time in pleasure, who turns inward, to experience, in slow motion, the pleasure of being? Psychological art is in creating, transforming, enjoying inner imagery, an activity that enriches time and brings slowness. The alternative is going through life like a hurried tourist, visiting the Louvre on roller skates, to get it over with. As one stops racing forward, one sees that slowing down in pleasure makes it absolutely possible to renew one's sensitivity.

Aphrodite, the Greek goddess who personified beauty and sensuality, had the divine ability to re-virgin herself each spring by taking a ritual bath in a river. That is what a successful analysis does: it is a long, ritualistic, slow, relaxed, sensual bath in the deep waters of the unconscious, a bathing that has the power to re-virgin oneself. This re-virgining cannot occur if the psychological suffering is considered only as a symptom and not also as a symbol. When a cure is needed, it should happen as fast as possible: here is my broken bone, my clogged artery. Start treatment now, get it done, fix it quick, please. But the unconscious – call it imagination – is interested, challenged, awakened by problems, puzzles, complexities, ordeals, quests and questions. In matters of the heart, all symptoms are, at the same time, crucial symbolic messages, letters that want to be read. A cure that chemically eradicates a symptom may also eradicate the symbol, leaving one with a soul that has been "equalized" like equalized background music (musak).

## I lost my cherry

To explain the Jungian concept of Self, teachers often draw on the blackboard a sphere, on the surface of which there is a dot (the ego). In the center of the sphere, something like a core, a nucleus, which represents the Self, where conscious and unconscious meet.

In the illustration used by Marie-Louise von Franz in 1964 to explain the concept of the Self, the Self is at once the nucleus and also the whole sphere. She writes:

> The organizing center from which the regulatory effect stems seems to be a sort of "nuclear atom" in our psychic system. One could also call it the inventor, organizer, and source of dream images. Jung called this center the "Self" and described it as the totality of the whole psyche, in order to distinguish it from the "ego" which constitutes only a small part of the psyche.[5]

Von Franz's atomic metaphor never quite seduced me. Instead of the nucleus of an atom, her text and even more her illustration seemed to evoke a cherry rather than an atom. Around the pit, like the pulpy flesh of the cherry, is the conscious personality of the ego, contained in its skin but interacting with others. The pit, although it constitutes the core of the cherry, is of a radically different nature than the edible part of the fruit. The normal development for a cherry shows a process where pit, pulp and skin all collaborate naturally to produce the deliciousness of a cherry. This summarizes, for me, the process of individuation.

I appreciate Jung's magisterial description of the process of individuation. It is such good literature, it makes one want the parts of oneself to hold together like a rich, red, round, individuated cherry, with pit working in unity with pulp and skin elegantly holding all together. When I really feel good, I am that cherry. Jung's juicy writing creates the desire to believe in the mythology of self and individuation.[6] Nevertheless, it is a mythology. Jung wrote this to Miguel Serrano: "So far I have found no stable or definite center in the unconscious, and I don't believe such a center exists. I believe that the thing I call the self is an ideal center . . . a dream of totality."

When I cracked my head on the cement at the bottom of the pool in Santa Fe, the nucleus, the Self, completely lost its centripetal capacity. At the place where the core used to be, there was a cyclone that swallowed all consciousness, abandoning my psyche like a person rendered homeless. My Self was gone on a trip, the cherry evaporated into cherry molecules floating in the atmosphere around my hospital bed. Pitted, de-cherried, I was disoriented, dispossessed, yet there was an interesting aspect to that experience.

I was discovering that along with the loss of center, loss of a core, the depression that I had felt before the accident was also gone. I had no sense of Self, but no feelings of depression either.

The depression had been replaced, overnight, by an impersonal fascination with the strange psychic landscape, one where all the landmarks had disappeared. To survive such fluidity of being, my only option was to swim in the Styx. I stopped expecting to experience life from the center. I existed with no unity, no holding center. "I" was a bunch of algae floating in the vast, expansive, centrifugal reality of psychic waters. It was scary, but not depressing. In my previous depressed state, I had thought that I was empty, a void, a big nothing, while in fact I had been a solid block of congealed negativity. It was only after meeting my death that I really became "nothing," a frightening yet freeing Nothing. There is no room for depression when nothing plus nothing equals nothing.

Before meeting Madame Death, I experienced my ego as the landlord of my psychic estate. The "Other" was a visitor that I would occasionally admit. Hello and bye-bye. Please don't waste my time. I have lots to manage. My estate is so large. My ego image is now completely reversed. I am the visitor, a grateful, humble guest, and the world is the host. As a guest, I don't dare criticize the schedule of events; I don't get to make the agenda. No more the Princess and the pea. Being conscious of my transitional status keeps me polite and grateful toward the world. I am not to claim the place as mine. I am provoked by the host into efforts of comprehension and assistance with the task of living in community. Dreams remind me every night that a guest may be tempted to dictate to the house servants (other egos), but a guest has no power over them. As a result of that humbling demotion, I am more comfortable than ever with archetypal psychology's iconoclastic warning. The psychological life is always lived in a liminal space, always on edges, thresholds, crossings, always betwixt and between. Yes. Now I am content with this state of affairs. The loss of my "cherry" was the end of my virginal psyche. The multitude of identities left their mark: butterfly, bull, Little Match Girl, child of the Great Mother, failed student, organic garbage, creature of light saved by transcendent filial human love. Each of these identities, or subpersonalities, has remained as a mode of being, a form of consciousness that visits me from time to time.

As my brain healed, I felt the return of the capacity to organize words in sentences, paragraphs, chapters – an extraordinary gift. Literacy is one of the greatest gifts a culture can give its members; it is only in thinking I had lost it that I found its immense value. The words are back, but their meaning is not quite the same. They too seem to come from a place of liminality. There are more and more moments where I don't feel like a participant in life's drama, but an observer of life's chaotic and fascinating activity. I go, with delight instead of judgment, in that slow mode that is almost a pre-reflexive consciousness – a cat-like consciousness, really. Liminality is a vast country that I have come to enjoy – being on the borders; edging instead of centering.

I have learned how the possibility of joy scares the ego as much as the possibility of love. I have tried to show in this book how the medical approach, which pleases the ego and works so beautifully when the problem is medical, can deprive one of the joy of the inner voyage. The medical model is inadequate to make sense of the agony and the ecstasy of inner life because the tragic, comic, epic, and lyric genres are inherent in the human narrative. Artists, not doctors, give us the words and images to become conscious of where, and how we suffer, where and how we rejoice. Every generation, every city, every college, every family, every couple, every person needs to find the right words, the right music, the right images and the right ideas, to express what are the painful things and what are the good things in life.

Art's purpose is never to give a picture of reality. It is not a statistic in image. It is not a news bulletin. Its task is to present reality in such a way that consciousness will deign to consider it anew. Art propels us to enter another form of reality, an imagined reality, where we discover the scope of possibilities waiting to be experienced. Depth psychology is a way out of a kind of psychology that will only consider what is, what the feelings are, instead of looking at what they could be. The next forms of depth psychology will depart more and more from the medical model. I like to imagine the practice of it as a celebration of psychological life, even when the examination of the psyche's content is painful. The essential task of depth psychology is to find the images that reveal emotional truth. In doing so, the imagination is revived.

Freud's definition of depression has the immense advantage of being simple: depression is the loss of the capacity to love. If one considers the corollary, it means that the goal of therapy is to heighten the capacity to love. An analysis is indeed a long conversation about love. It starts with love of ourselves, which is essential to the love of others. It includes love of things, all those things that were neglected because we stopped loving them, and expands to the love of the world, often in the form of pleasure derived from meaningful work. The medical approach is rightly concerned with ways to alleviate the depression, on the model of a medication that lessens fever, nausea, pain. The future of depth psychology is concerned with something else: to raise the fever of imagination, to amplify the loving connection that binds us to the world.

The conclusion I draw from the practice of the art of depth psychotherapy is that the more one has a choice of images, myths, narratives, scenarios, stories, paradigms, virtual scripts – call them what you like – to live by, the richer the life. To get to that multiplicity of possibilities, one needs to murder our identification with a lot of old, tired myths. One of the most wearisome is our fantasy of romantic love, a script based on dependence: I need that person and that person needs me. This poverty of imagination generates much suffering. Revising this kind of script is a skill worth acquiring, and it is the kind of education that depth psychology offers. How we relate to others and to ourselves depends on how we perceive the world, on what we imagine as possible, on how we remember the past and construct our version of what happened that caused me to be who I am. Nothing determines our quality of life in the future more than the myths in which we place the events of our lives. The more we can appreciate how a myth is an imaginal construction, the less the difficulties and tragedies of our lives appear insurmountable.

Our days are filled with complexities that did not exist a few generations ago, especially the complexities of finding one's identity, but this need not be a problem. Greater complexity means that one has more choices of contexts in which to deconstruct old myths and reconstruct fresh ones. The opening of the imagination reveals gaps in the fences that the imprisoned soul had not spotted, clues that the heart had missed. The first time my friend said "no" to somebody whose demands on this friend's time had been abusive, it felt to her like a revolution. It was indeed a revolution, because saying no, I won't do that for you, had never been "imagined" by her before.

Getting rid of monarchy had never been imagined before the Revolution, either. Too limited an idea of the possibilities acts like bars on a window, creating an inner prison. Some of the world's psychological wisdom is stored in each of our psyches and it is also stored in theories of psychology. It was my intention in this book to contribute my little bit by translating that theoretical legacy into a language cleared of its jargon, my memo for the next generation, the basis of my thinking about the next incarnation of depth psychology. The psyche is cultural and cultures evolve, just like medicine and computers evolve. To track the changes and set priorities, psychology can offer new images of what is to come.

I do not pretend to know what the next psychologies will be. I just know that for myself what is dead are the approaches that ask for an intellectual, rigid belief in a given theory about the psyche – however interesting that theory may be, including the ones I prefer or profess. Religions all claim they help build strong communities around shared values; yet, religion has always separated humans more than it has united them. The intellectual witch hunts, moral inquisitions, and social condemnations also exist among theoreticians of psychology whenever a theory is presented as absolute. Depth psychology doesn't need all those certitudes,[7] because the most important values for our psychic survival don't ask for the certitudes of belief. Instead, it asks for an acceleration of consciousness. This form of hyperconsciousness is based on values that we easily share, because they define us as humans. The tragedy and comedy, failures and victories, are not about problem solving for the living; they are life. They are tales of existence, tales about finding joy in the midst of struggle. Joy is a better teacher than pain, always.

# Schools of thought are families, bibliographies their family tree

Each author writing in the field of depth psychology presents a different picture of inner life, sometimes concordant, sometimes discordant. Depth psychologists constitute an intellectual family, with a family tree starting with Freud and a few other revered ancestors. The many dissensions, divorces, and rebellions are part of the family saga, like structural tension on the frame of an old ancestral house, which requires our attention and repair. In most families, discord leads to tension, not murder; to divorce, not deadly shunning. At Christmas or Thanksgiving, a "good enough" family is still able to share a meal together, in spite of internal battles and tensions. Intellectual families have the same range of possibilities, and allow the young disciples to build their identities through two different processes.

The first is a polemical approach – the confrontation of ideas – which strengthens one's capacity to eventually fight with any idea. An oral defense, as the word "defense" suggests, is a testing of a newcomer's capacity to defend ideas and serve them as a good soldier defends the country. This mode exists because hatred and wars do happen in the world of ideas, as much as in the world of families and nations. Intellectual wars exist because of a basic philosophical dilemma that no finessing will dissolve: how tolerant can one be with intolerance? Theories in psychology are not immune to those tensions and territorial wars.

Tolerance is easy when the others' values don't threaten my sense of survival; it is not so easy for a girl discovering that her homosexuality is interpreted as being caused by sickness and sin. To survive psychically, the girl will have to fight the theory, engage in a war against family values. Many of the students studying at the institute where I teach needed to deconstruct oppressive myths like they needed air to breathe. The history of ideas is full of fascinating wars of ideas, where those who refused to go to war for their ideas ended victimized. My guns are always ready against the sexism and racism of the three great monotheisms and I try to be a brave little soldier when it is time to attack. Ideas are intellectual territories; left undefended, they will be colonized.

The second approach that is necessary to build an intellectual community is a Dionysian one. It involves regularly falling in love with ideas offered by other members of the clan. One then wants to incorporate these ideas, digest them, become a living symbol of them. It begins with an attraction, a desire to melt into that particular cultural pot, a hunger for the delicious new recipes for thinking. *I like the way this group thinks, I want to join them, study with them, become one of them.* I felt that kind of appetite when I first read Hillman's *Re-Visioning Psychology*. With this massive oeuvre to satisfy my need, I was busy feeding myself for quite a while. I felt like a cat let loose in a creamery, a Dionysian orgy of ideas that I craved.

The Dionysian mode also has its own way of becoming destructive, when the strongly held enthusiasms are short-lived, following one charismatic star after another, rendering any real training of the mind impossible. Instead of a group, there is a master and his groupies. The group may have fun, a great sense of belonging, but the thinking becomes shallower and shallower. *Everybody gets an A, let's hold hands in a circle and not discuss anything that may spoil the fun!*

The polemical, war-like mode becomes self-destructive when a school of thought rigidifies in its position, like a scorpion turning its poison against itself. The symptoms of that form of decadence are the same everywhere: a tendency to consolidate group identity through exclusion, shunning, condemnation, contempt, issuing one intellectual fatwa after another, against anyone who strays away from the orthodoxy or dares to contradict the Master. An intellectual fatwa happens each time a clique controls teaching positions and tenure, research grants, scholarships, media. An example of fatwa can be found in Professor Alan Dundes's public contempt for Joseph Campbell's work, especially around Campbell's broad definition of the word "myth." None of Dundes's students, if they wanted to survive academically, could admit to having been interested in or delighted by Campbell. Discovering at a conference that the bookstore had put all of folklore and mythology books under a sign that read "Joseph Campbell," Professor Dundes writes: "I remember being almost relieved that at least none of my books were to be found in that section" (*Folkloristics in the Twenty-First Century*. American Folklore Society Invited Presidential Plenary Address, 2004. Published in the *Journal of American Folklore*, 118 (470): 385–408, 2005). Dundes's critique of Campbell is informed, intelligent, and articulate, yet it is so contaminated with contempt and even rage that one feels there is some complex at work. That kind of intellectual milieu self-destructs because academics sooner or later will migrate elsewhere to avoid the intellectual dictatorship. Academic freedom is supposed to stage confrontation, not give a show of hysterical contempt and shunning.

In order to have a balance, one should feel the freedom to diverge, but with enough group libido that there is a certain pleasure in confronting ideas. Some milieus won't allow real conversation. Over the years, I had my share of having to learn empty technical terms, the meaning of which is, too often, to keep others at a distance and erect theoretical boundaries. I have to answer, every semester in my classes, what is archetypal psychology and how is it different from the other depth-psychological perspectives? How can one interested in the unconscious dimensions of the psyche answer those questions *simply*? Most of my kind (professors/practitioners) have professional identities that are like a minestrone, which is a soup made of whatever vegetables happen to be in season (or in the refrigerator). My vocation being to teach and not to preach, I have mostly refused to belong to "a" school, which does not mean that I refused to follow a disciplinary track, or a master, as far as I could go, because that is how one learns something. There is also such a thing as intellectual politeness: listening to one's teacher or master until the argument is fully expressed, trying to keep under control the tendency to interrupt with too many instances of "yes, but I myself think."

I will now show my ID papers. Here is my family tree, my list of the authors that have shaped my vision of inner life, beginning with Freud and the post-Freudians, Jung and the post-Jungians. In that latter category, I must single out the work of James Hillman, who offers a radical reinterpretation of the theories of Jung. His work offers a large panorama, with a view of the history of psychology, its philosophy, its roots in Ancient Greece, and its future as a renaissance of psychological imagination. His approach has for me the supplementary advantage of being acceptable in academic milieus that are still very critical of Jung. Jung via Hillman is a strategy that has worked with the most critical minds. Hillman's take on Jung (which takes some and leaves some) travels through the Jungian country and then continues the voyage beyond. Although Hillman's oeuvre is now mostly behind him, it belongs to the next incarnation of depth psychology. His approach is that of someone who has consistently called for a renaissance of psychology, a call that his own work is answering. He represents the part of depth psychology that is opening up to an ecological thinking, reaching for the future and establishing itself back in the humanities and into the flow of the rising eco-revolution. For his many deliciously dense books, I am a grateful cat.

Some of the authors in the following bibliography are friends, colleagues or allies. I came to know their work through personal interactions, discussions, emails, exchange of references, and sitting down in a café at a conference gathering. Others are cherished dead paper gurus of my youth, such as Nietzsche, Jung, Sartre, de Beauvoir. There are also some obligatory references in my field and some surprises due to serendipity. My hope is that this long list of ingredients in my minestrone will somehow reflect not only my personal garden but the variety of influences that have shaped the evolution of depth psychology.

# Bibliography

Adams, M. V. (1996). *The multicultural imagination: Race, color, and the unconscious*. New York: Routledge.

—— (1997a). Metaphors in psychoanalytic theory and therapy. *Clinical Social Work Journal*, 25(1), 27–39.

—— (1997b). Refathering psychoanalysis, deliteralizing Hillman: Imaginal therapy, individual and cultural. In P. Clarkson (Ed.), *On the sublime: In psychoanalysis, archetypal psychology and psychotherapy* (pp. 109–122). London: Whurr Publishers.

—— (2001). *The mythological unconscious*. New York: Karnac Books.

—— (2004). *The fantasy principle: Psychoanalysis of the imagination*. New York: Brunner-Routledge.

Aizenstat, S. (2002). *Dream tending* [6 audiocassettes in binder, 7.5 hours]. Boulder, CO: Sounds True.

Avens, R. (1980). *Imagination is reality: Western nirvana in Jung, Hillman, Barfield, and Cassirer*. Irving, TX: Spring Publications.

Avens, R. (1984). *The new gnosis: Heidegger, Hillman, and angels*. Dallas, TX: Spring Publications.

Bachelard, G. (1964). *The psychoanalysis of fire* (A. Ross, Trans.). Boston: Beacon Press.

—— (1969). *The poetics of reverie* (D. Russell, Trans.). New York: Orion Press.

—— (1988a). *Air and dreams: An essay on the imagination of movement*. Dallas, TX: Dallas Institute of Humanities and Culture.

—— (1988b). *The right to dream*. Dallas, TX: Dallas Institute of Humanities and Culture.

—— (2002). *Earth and reveries of will: An essay on the imagination of matter* (K. Haltman, Trans.). Dallas, TX: Dallas Institute of Humanities and Culture.

Bair, D. (2003). *Jung: A biography* (1st ed.). Boston: Little, Brown.

Barth, J. R. (2001). *The symbolic imagination: Coleridge and the romantic tradition* (2nd ed.). New York: Fordham University Press.

Barthes, R. (1972). *Mythologies* (A. Lavers, Trans.). New York: Hill and Wang.

—— (1975). *The pleasure of the text* (R. Miller, Trans.). New York: Hill and Wang.

—— (1977). *Image, music, text* (S. Heath, Ed. and Trans.). New York: Hill and Wang.

Bateson, G. (1971). *Steps to an ecology of mind: Collected essays in anthropology, psychiatry, evolution, and epistemology.* Chicago: University of Chicago Press

Baudrillard, J. (1994). *Simulacra and simulation* (S. F. Glaser, Trans.). Ann Arbor: University of Michigan Press.

Beauvoir, S. de (1953). *The second sex* (H. M. Parshley, Ed. and Trans.). New York: Knopf.

—— (1959). *Memoirs of a dutiful daughter.* Cleveland, OH: World Publishing.

Beebe, J., Cambray, J. and Kirsch, T. B. (2001). What Freudians can learn from Jung. *Psychoanalytic Psychology, 18*(2), 213–242.

Berry, P. (Ed.). (1990). *Fathers and mothers* (2nd rev. and enl. ed.). Dallas, TX: Spring Publications.

Bion, W. F. (1977). Elements of psychoanalysis. In W. F. Bion (Ed.), *Seven servants: Four works.* New York: Jason Aronson.

Birkhäuser-Oeri, S. (1988). *The mother: Archetypal image in fairy tales.* Toronto: Inner City Books.

Bleakley, A. (1989). *Earth's embrace: Archetypal psychology's challenge to the growth movement.* Bath: Gateway Books.

—— (2000). *The animalizing imagination: Totemism, textuality, and ecocriticism.* New York: St. Martin's Press.

Bly, R. (1988). *A little book on the human shadow* (W. C. Booth, Ed.). San Francisco: Harper & Row.

Boer, C. and Kugler. (1977). Archetypal psychology is mythical realism. *Spring,* 131–152.

Bonnefoy, Y. and Doniger, W. (Eds.). (1991). *Mythologies* (G. Honigsblum, Trans.). Chicago: University of Chicago Press.

Brunel, P. (Ed.). (1995). *Companion to literary myths, heroes and archetypes* (W. Allatson, J. Hayward and T. Selous, Trans.). New York: Routledge.

Campbell, J. (1964). *The masks of God: Vol. 3. Occidental Mythology.* New York: Viking.

—— (1968a). *The hero with a thousand faces* (2nd ed.). Princeton, NJ: Princeton University Press.

—— (1968b). *The masks of God: Vol. 4. Creative Mythology.* New York: Viking.

Camus, A. (1955). *The myth of Sisyphus and other essays* (1st English ed.). New York: Knopf.

Casey, E. S. (1974). *Toward an archetypal imagination. Spring*, 1–32.
—— (1976). *Imagining: A phenomenological study*. Bloomington: Indiana University Press.
—— (1991). *Spirit and soul: Essays in philosophical psychology*. Dallas, TX: Spring Publications.
Cazenave, M. (1983). *La science et l'âme du monde*. Paris: Imago.
—— (1984). *Science and consciousness* (A. Hall and E. Callander, Trans.) (1st English ed.). New York: Pergamon Press.
Cobb, N. (1992). *Archetypal imagination: Glimpses of the gods in life and art*. Hudson, NY: Lindisfarne Press.
Comte-Sponville, A. (2001). *A small treatise on the great virtues: The uses of philosophy in everyday life*. New York: Metropolitan Books.
Comte-Sponville, A. and Ferry, L. (1998) *La sagesse des modernes*. Paris: Laffont.
Corbett, L. (1996). *The religious function of the psyche*. New York: Routledge.
Corbett, L. and Stein, M. (Eds.). (1995). *Psyche's stories: Modern Jungian interpretations of fairy tales* (Vol. 3). Wilmette, IL: Chiron Publications.
Corbin, H. (1976). Mundus imaginalis or the imaginary and the imaginal. *Spring*, 1–18.
—— (1981). *Le paradoxe du monothéisme*. Paris: L'Herne.
Dalai Lama XIV (2002). *Essence of the heart sutra: The Dalai Lama's heart of wisdom teachings*. Boston: Wisdom Publications.
Delcourt, M. (1961). *Hermaphrodite: Myths and rites of the bisexual figure in classical antiquity* (J. Nicholson, Trans.). London: Studio Books.
Delumeau, J. (1990). *Sin and fear: The emergence of the western guilt culture, 13th–18th centuries*. London: Palgrave Macmillan. (First published in French 1978).
Dennett, D. C. (2006). *Breaking the spell*. New York: Viking.
Derrida, J. (1981). *Dissemination* (B. Johnson, Trans.). Chicago: University of Chicago Press.
Detienne, M. (1986). *The creation of mythology* (M. Cook, Trans.). Chicago: University of Chicago Press.
Detienne, M. and Vernant, J. P. (1978). *Cunning intelligence in Greek culture and society* (J. Lloyd, Trans.). Atlantic Highlands, NJ: Humanities Press.
Dodds, E. R. (1951). *The Greeks and the irrational*. Berkeley: University of California Press.
Doniger, W. (1998). *The implied spider: Politics and theology in myth*. New York: Columbia University Press.
—— (2005). *The woman who pretended to be who she was: Myths of self-imitation*. New York: Oxford University Press.
Doty, W. G. (1993). Connecting the active and the passive: Monster

slayer and child born of water. In W. G. Doty (Ed.), *Myths of masculinity* (pp. 155–171). New York: Crossroad.

—— (2000a). *Mythography: The study of myths and rituals* (2nd ed.). Tuscaloosa: University of Alabama Press.

—— (2000b). What mythopoetic means. *Mythosphere*, 2(2), 255–262.

Downing, C. (1991). *Mirrors of the self: Archetypal images that shape your life.* Los Angeles: J.P. Tarcher.

Edinger, E. F. (1984). *The creation of consciousness: Jung's myth for modern man.* Toronto: Inner City Books.

Eliade, M. (1960). *Myths, dreams, and mysteries: The encounter between contemporary faiths and archaic realities* (P. Mairet, Trans.). London: Harvill Press.

—— (1963). *Myth and reality* (W. R. Trask, Trans.) (1st American ed.). New York: Harper & Row.

—— (1996). *Patterns in comparative religion* (R. Sheed, Trans.). Lincoln: University of Nebraska Press. (Original work published 1958).

Ellenberger, H. F. (1970). *The discovery of the unconscious: The history and evolution of dynamic psychiatry.* New York: Basic Books.

Ferry, L. (1995). *The new ecological order* (C. Volk, Trans.). Chicago: University of Chicago Press.

—— (2002). *Man made God: The meaning of life.* Chicago: University of Chicago Press.

—— (2005). *What is the good life?* Chicago: University of Chicago Press.

Ferry, L. and Renaut, A. (1997). *Why we are not Nietzscheans* (R. de Loaiza, Trans.). Chicago: University of Chicago Press.

Firestone, D. (19 July 2001). Ailing statue: Symbol of industry or pork barrel? *New York Times*, p. A14.

Fordham, M. (1974). Technique and counter-transference. In M. Fordham, R. Gordon, J. Hubback and J. Redfearn (Eds.), *Technique in Jungian analysis.* London: Heinemann.

Foucault, M. (1965). *Madness and civilization: A history of insanity in the age of reason* (R. Howard, Trans.). New York: Pantheon Books.

—— (1972). *The archaeology of knowledge* (A. M. Sheridan Smith, Trans.). New York: Pantheon Books.

—— (1977). *Discipline and punish: The birth of the prison* (A. Sheridan, Trans.). New York: Pantheon Books.

Franz, M.-L., von. (1981). *Puer aeternus* (2nd ed.). Santa Monica, CA: Sigo Press. (Original work published 1970).

—— (1993). Profession and vocation. In M.-L. von Franz, *Psychotherapy* (pp. 267–282). Boston: Shambhala.

—— (1996). *The interpretation of fairy tales* (Rev. ed.). Boston: Shambhala. (Original work published 1970).

Franz, M.-L., von and Hillman, J. (1986). *Lectures on Jung's typology.* Dallas, TX: Spring Publications.

Freud, S. (1953–75). *Standard edition of the complete psychological works of Sigmund Freud* (J. Strachey, Ed. and Trans.) (Vol. 24). London: Hogarth Press.

Giegerich, W. (1999). *The soul's logical life: Towards a rigorous notion of psychology* (2nd rev. ed.). New York: P. Lang.

Goldenberg, N. (1975). Archetypal theory after Jung. *Spring*, 199–220.

Guggenbühl, A. (1996). *The incredible fascination of violence: Dealing with aggression and brutality among children* (J. Hillman, Trans.). Woodstock, CT: Spring Publications.

—— (1997). *Men, power, and myths: The quest for male identity* (G. V. Hartman, Trans.). New York: Continuum.

Guggenbühl-Craig, A. (1971). *Power in the helping professions*. Dallas, TX: Spring Publications.

—— (1979). The archetype of the invalid and the limits of healing. *Spring*, 29–41.

—— (1991). *The old fool and the corruption of myth* (D. Wilson, Trans.). Dallas, TX: Spring Publications.

Guggenbühl-Craig, A. and Handel, S. (1995). *From the wrong side: A paradoxical approach to psychology* (G. V. Hartman, Ed. and Trans.). Woodstock, CT: Spring Publications.

Harris, S. (2004). *The end of faith: Religion, terror and the future of reason*. New York: Norton.

Heilbrun, C. G. (1988). *Writing a woman's life* (1st ed.). New York: Norton.

Hillman, J. (1979a). *Puer papers*. Irving, TX: Spring Publications.

—— (1979b). *The dream and the underworld* (1st ed.). New York: Harper & Row.

—— (1980). *Facing the gods*. Irving, TX: Spring Publications.

—— (1992a). *Emotion: A comprehensive phenomenology of theories and their meaning for therapy* (4th ed.). Evanston, IL: Northwestern University Press. (Original work published 1960).

—— (1992b). *Re-Visioning psychology* (3rd rev. ed.). New York: Harper & Row. (Original work published 1975).

—— (1994). *Insearch: Psychology and religion* (2nd rev. ed.). Woodstock, CT: Spring Publications. (Original work published 1967).

—— (1997a). *The myth of analysis: Three essays in archetypal psychology*. Evanston, IL: Northwestern University Press. (Original work published 1972).

—— (1997b). *Suicide and the soul* (4th ed.). Woodstock, CT: Spring Publications. (Original work published 1964).

—— (2000). *The force of character and the lasting life*. New York: Ballantine.

—— (2004a). *Archetypal psychology* (Rev. 3rd ed.). Putnam, CT: Spring Publications. (Original work published 1981).

——— (2004b). *A terrible love of war*. New York: Penguin.

Hillman, J. and Ventura, M. (1992). *We've had a hundred years of psychotherapy – and the world's getting worse* (1st ed.). San Francisco: Spring Publications.

Irigaray, L. (1985). *Speculum of the other woman*. Ithaca, NY: Cornell University Press.

Jacobi, J. S. (1959). *Complex/archetype/symbol in the psychology of C. G. Jung*. Princeton, NJ: Princeton University Press.

Johnson, R. A. (1993). *The fisher king and the handless maiden: Understanding the wounded feeling function in masculine and feminine psychology* (1st ed.). San Francisco: Spring Publications.

Jones, E., Jung, C. G., Hillman, J. and Marlan, S. (1995). *Salt and the alchemical soul: Three essays*. Woodstock, CT: Spring Publications.

Jung, C. G. (1963). *Memories, dreams, reflections* (R. Winston and C. Winston, Trans.) (Rev. ed.). New York: Pantheon Books. (Original work published 1961).

——— (1966–). *Collected works of C. G. Jung* (H. Read, M. Fordham and G. Adler, Eds. R. F. C. Hull, Trans.) (2nd ed.) (Vols. 1–20). Princeton, NJ: Princeton University Press.

——— (1988). *Nietzsche's Zarathustra: Notes of the seminar given in 1934–1939* (J. L. Jarrett, Ed. Mary Foote, Ed. and Trans.). Princeton, NJ: Princeton University Press.

Kearney, R. (1988). *The wake of imagination: Toward a postmodern culture*. Minneapolis: University of Minnesota Press.

——— (2000). *A place of healing: Working with suffering in living and dying*. Oxford: Oxford University Press.

Kerényi, K. (1951). *The gods of the Greeks* (N. Cameron, Trans.). New York: Thames & Hudson.

——— (1974). *The heroes of the Greeks* (H. J. Rose, Trans.). London: Thames & Hudson.

Kerényi, K. and Hillman, J. (1991). *Oedipus variations: Studies in literature and psychoanalysis*. Dallas, TX: Spring Publications.

Klein, M. (1975a). *Envy and gratitude, and other works, 1946–1963*. London: Hogarth Press.

——— (1975b). *The psycho-analysis of children*. London: Hogarth Press.

Kohut, H. (1971). *The analysis of the self: A systematic approach to the psychoanalytic treatment of narcissistic personality disorders*. New York: International Universities Press.

——— (1977). *The restoration of the self*. New York: International Universities Press.

——— (1984). *How does analysis cure?* (A. Goldberg and P. E. Stepansky, Eds.). Chicago: University of Chicago Press.

Kristeva, J. (1980). *Desire in language: A semiotic approach to literature and art* (L. S. Roudiez, Ed. T. Gora, A. Jardine and L. S. Roudiez, Trans.). New York: Columbia University Press.

—— (1982). *Powers of horror: An essay on abjection* (L. S. Roudiez, Trans.). New York: Columbia University Press.

Kugler, P. (1978). Image and sound. *Spring*, 136–151.

—— (1987). Jacques Lacan: Postmodern depth psychology and the birth of the self-reflexive subject. In P. Young-Eisendrath and J. A. Hall (Eds.), *The book of the self: Person, pretext, and process* (pp. 173–184). New York: New York University Press.

—— (1990). The unconscious in a postmodern depth psychology. In K. Barnaby and P. D'Acierno (Eds.), *C.G. Jung and the humanities: Toward a hermeneutics of culture* (pp. 307–317). Princeton, NJ: Princeton University Press.

Lacan, J. (1978). *The four fundamental concepts of psycho-analysis* (J.-A. Miller, Ed. A. Sheridan, Trans.). New York: Norton.

—— (2005). *Écrits: The first complete edition in English* (B. Fink, Trans.). New York: Norton.

Laing, R. D. (1967). *The politics of experience.* New York: Pantheon Books.

—— (1999). *Self and others.* New York: Routledge.

Lopez-Pedraza, R. (1977). *Hermes and his children.* Zürich: Spring Publications.

Loraux, N. (1986). *The invention of Athens: The funeral oration in the classical city* (A. Sheridan, Trans.). Cambridge, MA: Harvard University Press.

—— (1995). *The experiences of Tiresias: The feminine and the Greek man* (P. Wissing, Trans.). Princeton, NJ: Princeton University Press.

—— (2000). *Born of the earth: Myth and politics in Athens* (S. Stewart, Trans.). Ithaca: Cornell University Press.

—— (2002a). *The divided city: On memory and forgetting in ancient Athens* (C. Pache and J. Fort, Trans.). New York: Zone Books.

—— (2002b). *The mourning voice: An essay on Greek tragedy* (E. T. Rawling, Trans.). Ithaca: Cornell University Press.

Marcel, G. and Ricoeur, P. (1973). *Tragic wisdom and beyond; including, conversations between Paul Ricoeur and Gabriel Marcel* (S. Jolin and P. McCormick, Trans.). Evanston, IL: Northwestern University Press.

Marlan, S. (1997). *Fire in the stone: The alchemy of desire.* Wilmette, IL: Chiron Publications.

Meade, M. (1993). *Men and the water of life: Initiation and the tempering of men* (1st ed.). San Francisco: HarperSanFrancisco.

Miller, D. L. (1981). *The new polytheism: Rebirth of the gods and goddesses.* Dallas, TX: Spring Publications.

—— (2004). *Hells & Holy Ghosts: A theopoetics of Christian belief.* New Orleans: Spring Journal Books. (Original work published 1989).

—— (2005a). *Christs: Meditations on archetypal images in Christian theology.* New Orleans: Spring Journal Books. (Original work published 1981).

—— (2005b). *Three faces of God: Traces of the trinity in literature and life.* New Orleans: Spring Journal Books. (Original work published 1986).

Moore, T. (1983). *Rituals of the imagination.* Dallas, TX: Pegasus Foundation.

Murdock, M. (2003). *Unreliable truth: On memoir and memory.* New York: Seal Press.

Neumann, E. (1970). *The origins and history of consciousness.* Princeton, NJ: Princeton University Press.

Nietzsche, F. W. (2000). The birth of tragedy (W. Kaufmann, Trans.), *Basic writings of Nietzsche* (pp. 1–144). New York: Random House.

Noel, D. C. (1990). *Paths to the power of myth: Joseph Campbell and the study of religion.* New York: Crossroad.

Onfray, M. (1993) *La sculpture de soi: La morale esthétique.* Paris: Grasset.

—— (1996) *Le désir d'être un volcan.* Paris: Grasset.

—— (2005) *Traité d'athéologie: Physique de la métaphysique.* Paris: Grasset.

Otto, W. F. (1954). *The Homeric gods: The spiritual significance of Greek religion* (M. Hadas, Trans.). New York: Pantheon.

—— (1981). *Dionysus, myth and cult* (R. B. Palmer, Trans.). Dallas, TX: Spring Publications.

Pardo, E. (1984). Dis-membering Dionysus: Image and theatre. *Spring,* 163–179.

Pfister, O. (1917). *The psychoanalytic method* (C. R. Payne, Trans.). New York: Moffat Yard.

Piaget, J. (1966). *The child's conception of physical causality* (M. Gabain, Trans.). London: Routledge & Kegan Paul.

Ricoeur, P. (1967). *The symbolism of evil* (E. Buchanan, Trans.). New York: Harper & Row.

—— (1970). *Freud and philosophy: An essay on interpretation* (D. Savage, Trans.). New Haven, CT: Yale University Press.

—— (1977). *The rule of metaphor: Multi-disciplinary studies of the creation of meaning in language* (R. Czerny, Trans.). Toronto: University of Toronto Press.

Ricoeur, P. and Wallace, M. I. (1995). *Figuring the sacred: Religion, narrative, and imagination* (M. I. Wallace, Ed. D. Pellauer, Trans.). Minneapolis, MN: Fortress Press.

Romanyshyn, R. (2001). *Mirror and metaphor: Images and stories of psychological life.* Pittsburgh, PA: Trivium. (Original work published 1982).

Roscher, W. H. and Hillman, J. (1972). *Pan and the nightmare*. New York: Spring Publications.

Roustang, F. (1986). *Dire mastery: Discipleship from Freud to Lacan* (N. Lukacher, Trans.). Washington, DC: American Psychiatric Press.

—— (1983). *Psychoanalysis never lets go* (N. Lukacher, Trans.). Baltimore: Johns Hopkins University Press.

—— (1990). *The Lacanian delusion* (G. Sims, Trans.). New York: Oxford University Press.

—— (2000a). *How to make a paranoid laugh, or, what is psychoanalysis?* (A. C. Vila, Trans.). Philadelphia: University of Pennsylvania Press.

—— (2000b). *La fin de la plainte*. Paris: Odile Jacob.

Rowland, S. (2002). *Jung: A feminist revision*. Malden, MA: Blackwell.

—— (2005). *Jung as a writer* (1st ed.). New York: Brunner-Routledge.

Samuels, A. (1985). *Jung and the post-Jungians*. Boston: Routledge & Kegan Paul.

—— (1989). *The plural psyche: Personality, morality and the father*. New York: Routledge.

—— (1993). *The political psyche*. New York: Routledge.

—— (2001). *Politics on the couch: Citizenship and the internal life*. New York: Profile Books.

Samuels, A., Shorter, B. and Plaut, F. (1986). *A critical dictionary of Jungian analysis*. New York: Routledge & Kegan Paul.

Sardello, R. J. (1995). *Love and the soul: Creating a future for earth* (1st ed.). New York: HarperCollins.

—— (2001). *Love and the world: A guide to conscious soul practice*. Great Barrington, MA: Lindisfarne Books.

Sartre, J.P. (1946) *L'existentialisme est un humanisme*. Paris: Nagel.

—— (1956). *Being and nothingness: An essay on phenomenological ontology*. New York: Philosophical Library.

—— (1964) *Les mots*. Paris: Gallimard.

—— (1972). *The transcendence of the ego: An existentialist theory of consciousness* (F. Williams and R. Kirkpatrick, Eds.). New York: Octagon Books.

Schama, S. (1995). *Landscape and memory*. New York: Knopf.

Seinfeld, J. (1993). *Interpreting and holding: The paternal and maternal functions of the psychotherapist*. Northvale, NJ: Jason Aronson.

Slattery, D. P. (2000). *The wounded body: Remembering the markings of flesh*. Albany, NY: SUNY Press.

Slattery, D. P. and Corbett, L. (2000). *Depth psychology: Meditations in the field*. Einsiedeln: Daimon-Verlag.

Solié, P. (1980). *Psychanalyse et imaginal*. Paris: Imago.

Spitz, R. A. and Cobliner, W. G. (1966) *First year of life: A psycho-analytic study of normal and deviant development of object relations*. New York: International Universities Press.

Stein, M. (1984). *Jungian analysis.* Boulder, CO: Shambhala.

—— (2006). *The principle of individuation: Toward the development of human consciousness.* Wilmette, IL: Chiron Publications.

Stern, D. N. (1985). *The interpersonal world of the infant: A view from psychoanalysis and developmental psychology.* New York: Basic Books.

Stroud, J. and Thomas, G. (1982). *Images of the untouched: Virginity in psyche, myth, and community.* Dallas, TX: Spring Publications.

—— (1995). *The Olympians.* Dallas, TX: Dallas Institute Publications.

Szasz, T. S. (1961). *The myth of mental illness: Foundations of a theory of personal conduct.* New York: Hoeber-Harper.

—— (1970a). *Ideology and insanity: Essays on the psychiatric dehumanization of man.* Garden City, NY: Anchor Books.

—— (1970b). *The manufacture of madness: A comparative study of the inquisition and the mental health movement.* New York: Harper & Row.

Tacey, D. (1998). Twisting and turning with James Hillman. In A. Casement (Ed.), *Post-Jungians today: Key papers in contemporary analytical psychology* (pp. 215–234). New York: Routledge.

—— (2001). *Jung and the new age.* Philadelphia, PA: Brunner-Routledge.

Vernant, J.-P. and Vidal-Naquet, P. (1990). *Myth and tragedy in Ancient Greece* (J. Lloyd, Trans.). New York: Zone Books.

Veyne, P. (1988). *Did the Greeks believe in their myths?: An essay on the constitutive imagination.* Chicago: University of Chicago Press.

Watkins, M. (2000). *Invisible guests: The development of imaginal dialogues.* Woodstock, CT: Spring Publications.

Winnicott, D. W. (1957). *The child and the outside world.* London: Tavistock Publications.

—— (1965). *The maturational processes and the facilitating environment: Studies in the theory of emotional development.* New York: International Universities Press.

—— (1971). *Playing and reality.* New York: Basic Books.

Zeldin, T. (1995). *An intimate history of humanity.* New York: HarperCollins.

Ziegler, A. J. (1983). *Archetypal medicine* (G. V. Hartman, Trans.). Dallas, TX: Spring Publications.

Zoja, L. (1995). *Growth and guilt: Psychology and the limits of development.* New York: Routledge.

—— (2001). *The father: Historical, psychological, and cultural perspectives.* Philadelphia: Brunner-Routledge.

# Notes

## Preface

1 The first edition of the *Diagnostic Statistical Manual of Mental Disorders* (*DSM*) was published in 1952 by the American Psychiatric Association. It is now at its fourth edition (*DSM IV*).

## 1 Denting my thick skull

1 I know a cat who might object to the comparison but she can't read, so I am safe.

## 3 Therapy as cure: the medical model

1 She was correct in her diagnosis: the *DSM-IV* defines a Transient Simple Motor Tic Disorder (code 307.21, pp. 108–116 of *DSM-IV*) as one that "occurs many times a day, nearly every day for at least 4 weeks, but for no longer than 12 consecutive months" (otherwise, it becomes a Chronic Tic Disorder).
2 *DSM-IV*, p. 108.
3 *DSM-IV*, p. xxx.
4 *Female Homosexuality*, New York: Evergreen Black, 1969.
5 *The Manufacture of Madness*, New York: Harper & Row, 1970.
6 The emphasis on homosexuality as a "sickness" was replaced by an elaborate and convoluted set of definitions of the problems that may arise when one experiences feelings of discomfort with one's assigned sex. Gender Identity Disorders are now defined as: "strong and persistent cross gender identification accompanied by persistent discomfort with one's assigned sex." In other words, if the person is comfortable with his or her homosexuality, the *DSM* won't categorize homosexuality per se as a pathology. *DSM-IV*, p. 535.

## 4 Therapy as investment: the economic model

1 Appendix I of the *DSM-IV* (p. 898) is an attempt to assess "culture-bound syndromes." The clinician is invited to take into account "how cultural considerations specifically influence comprehensive diagnosis and care," but the application of such concern in the coding system is another matter.

2 Luce Irigaray made a similar point when examining the theories about female hysteria, a crucial concept in the history of psychoanalysis. She argues that hysteria is mostly a failure to speak with words, so the body takes charge of communicating the emotions. The hysterical woman is caught in an impossible choice: either she remains silent or she uses the language of the father that can only further repress her because of its essentially patriarchal nature. The hysteric's body is all that is left for her as a means by which to communicate.

## 6 Therapy as redemption

1 Vaclav Havel, who went from being a political prisoner to the president of his country, had an acute sense of the necessity of a healthy sense of the absurd, especially in the political arena, to avoid totalitarian ideologies. Havel's *Theater of the Absurd* acts as an antidote to all forms of "isms." See David Barton, *Vaclav Havel*, unpublished dissertation. Pacifica Graduate Institute, 2006.

2 The one critique that I have most often heard about Sartre's existential psychology is that, by denying the unconscious, his psychology ends giving too much importance to the ego. Contrary to that cliché, my understanding of Sartre is that his notions of freedom, consciousness and lucidity all involve a readiness to look at what one would rather keep hidden. Although he does not favor the term "unconscious," his notion of "bad faith" is akin to a refusal to examine one's deeper motivations and cover the truth with rationalizations and defense mechanisms. Sartre does not give too much importance to the ego but rather insists on the importance of lucidity to keep the ego in check.

Rollo May's book *Man's Search for Himself* (New York: Norton, 1953), which was read by a whole generation of psychologists, also contained some of the usual clichés about Sartre's philosophy. Rollo May wrote: "One wonders what will happen to Sartre's existentialims at it gets farther away from the French resistance movement. Some astute critics have stated it may go authoritarian: Tillich believes it may go into Catholicism, and Marcel predict it will go Marxist." None of this happened, rather the opposite. Bernard Henry Lévy, revisiting the philosophical and literary legacy of Sartre considers it one of the major contributions in the twentieth century. Lévy's book is titled *Le siècle de Sartre: enquête philosphique* (Paris: Grasset, 2000). *Sartre: the philosopher of the twentieth century* (Malden, MA: Polity Press, 2004).

3 Sartre's idea that "hell is Others", which one could as well translate as

"bliss is Others", was suggesting a rapport with other humans and with the world that is very similar to the basic intuition of eco-psychology. It suggests that since there is no tight boundary between me and others, me and the world, we all suffer the destruction of the environment in a very personal manner.

4 Marguerite Yourcenar, the first woman ever to be admitted at the French Academy, seemed absolutely fine with the fact of having had no mother.

5 Such as Sam Harris, Luc Ferry, André Comte-Sponville, and Michel Onfray.

6 James Hillman, through his body of work, analyses in depth the problem of literal thinking in the field of psychology.

7 "Deux amours ont bâti deux cités. L'amour de soi, jusqu'au mépris de Dieu, la cité terrestre, l'amour de Dieu, jusqu'au mépris de soi, la cité céleste." Augustin, *La Cité de Dieu*, livre XIV.

8 Especially in his Heroe with a thousand faces.

9 The word "zoë" from which we derive zoology described that essential quality of Dionysus.

10 Another example of a huge shadow is with Muslim religion; it presents itself as egalitarian, yet it is one of the most sexist on earth and one in which the gap between the poor and the rich is an abyss.

# 7 Boundary issues: "You, science. Me, humanities."

1 *Encarta Encyclopedia.*

2 One fascinating demonstration of the power of myth is in Carolyn Heilbrun's *Writing a Woman's Life* (New York: Norton, 1988). This classic literary study from the famous Columbia professor has been a required reading for all students of psychology sitting in my classes. She shows, through her analysis of the literature of a period, how the legal rights (for example, the right for a woman to divorce) have little meaning unless the cultural myth also changes. She demonstrates how a women's psyche (her perception of herself, her psychology) is tied to the cultural myth about female identity.

3 Such as Adams, Samuels, Stein, Lopez-Pedraza, Guggenbühl-Craig, Guggenbühl, Hall, Watkins, Zoja, Cobb.

4 Such as Casey, Avens, Downing, Miller, Slattery.

5 See Bibliography for works by James Hillman.

6 Published in *Harvard Magazine*, January–February 1997.

7 One should also mention the proliferation of approaches that use the word "therapy" (such as: marriage and couples therapy, family therapy, sex therapy, art therapy, dance therapy, drama therapy, music therapy, play therapy, hypnotherapy, grief therapy); or the word "counseling" (such as: career and life-style counseling, pastoral counseling, schools and youth counseling, cross-cultural counseling).

## 8 Brother philosophy, sister psychology

1 *Diagnostic Statistical Manual of Mental Disorders*, Fourth Edition (*DSM IV*) (Washington, DC: American Psychiatric Association, 2000), p xxxi.
2 *DSM IV*, p. xxx.
3 The letter was to J.S. Beck, sent on October 1792 and is published in *Kant: Philosophical Correspondence, 1759–99*, A. Zweig, Trans. (Chicago: Chicago University Press, 1967).
4 James Hillman defines the capacity to "see through" as the basis of psychological intelligence, a capacity to read, to see through *to* the myth or archetype being enacted in any situation. Hillman does not borrow any of Sartre's heavy conceptual baggage, but ends up in a territory that feels familiar to existentialists.

## 9 The archetype of Mother

1 Roland Barthes, *Comment vivre ensemble: Cours et séminaires au Collège de France 1976–1977*, texte établi, annoté et présenté par Claude Costes. Et: 1977–1978. Texte établi, annoté et présenté par Thomas Clerc, Le Seuil/Imec.
2 The category of Mood Disorders in the *DSM-IV* includes most forms of depressive disorders as well as bipolar disorders. The category of Anxiety Disorders includes Panic Attack, Phobias, Obsessive-Compulsive Disorder, Post-Traumatic and Acute Stress Disorder, and the different forms of Anxiety Disorders. The category of Somatoform Disorders includes most of what is generally understood as psycho-somatic and is defined by "the presence of physical symptoms that suggest a general medical condition and are not explained by a general medical condition, by the direct effect of a substance, or by another mental disorder."
3 Philip Wylie's *Generation of Vipers*, a book that Jung admired, was a severe critique of the "Big Mothers" (New York: Farrar and Rinehart, 1942).

## 10 The archetype of Father

1 The Greeks had the word "kaîros," which meant anything that was done or said at just the right moment, not too soon, not too late, just precisely when it would have its full effect. (See Plato, *Ethics to Nicomaque*, II, 1104.1.9.)

## 11 The invisibility of the psyche

1 "And what is God's excuse for not responding?" (Woody Allen)
2 An average of three and a half hours a day (*Time Magazine*, November 2006).

3 On average, one minute a day of physical contact with another human being, which includes hugs, caresses, love-making. (*Time Magazine*, November 2006).
4 René Spitz did most of this research during and after World War II, but continued to study the effect of emotional deprivation on infants. A good summary can be found in: René Spitz and Godfrey Cobliner *First Year of Life: A Psychoanalytic Study of Normal and Deviant Development of Object Relations* (New York: International Universities Press, 1966).
5 Jane Bethke Elshtain, *Jane Adams and the Dream of American Democracy* (New York: Basic Books, 2002), p. 83.
6 See, for example, the report of Gail Kligman, *The Politics of Duplicity: Controlling Reproduction in Ceausescu's Romania* (Berkeley: University of California Press, 1998).
7 BOBO: Bohemian Bourgeois.

# 12 The ultimate virtual reality game

1 Especially the work of James Hillman.
2 It is an old story, and still happening! For example, Carl Jung could no more escape the sexism of his time than his contemporaries. He too would have preferred male followers and the appreciation of male colleagues. He candidly expressed his disappointment in attracting mostly women disciples, even when they devoted their whole intellect to helping him with his work. See D. Bair *Jung: A Biography* (1st ed.) (Boston: Little, Brown, 2003).
3 If the flip-flops are in themselves a fashion statement, or if the jeans are a way of saying "I don't believe in marriage," it becomes a line in the unfolding of a story of rebellion. It is when the refusal to dress up expresses a laziness, a carelessness, that it becomes a refusal to play in the social game.
4 Nietzsche used the notion of Amor Fati in his *Zarathustra*, and also in *Will to Power* (tome II, Intro., p. 14).
5 G. Durand, *The Anthropological Structures of the Imaginary* (M. Sankey and J. Hatten, Trans.). (Brisbane: Boombana Publications, 1999).
6 C. Lévi-Strauss, *The Raw and the Cooked* (J. and D. Weightman, Trans.). (New York: Harper and Row, 1969).
7 M. Eliade, *The Sacred and the Profane: The Nature of Religion* (New York: Harcourt, 1959).
8 The post-Jungian author, Michael Vannoy Adams, in his *The Fantasy Principle* (New York: Brunner-Routledge, 2004) argues that in classical, conventional Jungian analysis, archetypes are defined as structures, whereas he finds it more accurate, from a post-structuralist perspective, to consider archetypes like *constructs*.
9 To be "accredited" (licensed) as a clinician, one has to study in an "accredited" school, pass an exam on the "accredited" theories and behave within the "accredited" code of ethics.

10 The argument is similar to that of the philosopher Ludwig Feuerbach, the author of *The Essence of Christianism*. He considered religion to be an alienation which has at its core a reversal of values. The person alienates his or her desires, hopes, values in favor of a god symbol that then carries all the essential and best attributes of human values (compassion, justice, power). The role of the philosopher is then to liberate humanity from this theological oppression, through a systematic deconstruction of the mystification of religion. Feuerbach's analysis is a core influence in the work of Freud as much as that of Karl Marx.

11 P. Ricoeur, *Time and Narrative* (K. McLaughlin and D. Pellauer, Trans.). (Chicago: University of Chicago Press, 1984).

## 13 Joy: the antidote to anxiety

1 Michael Vannoy Adams writes a convincing demonstration of how psychology has consistently moved away from what he calls the *Fantasy Principle* and how this constitutes an impoverishment of culture.

2 Pierre Janet *De l'Angoisse à l'Extase* (1926). My translation: "L'angoisse chronique est un sentiment caractéristique des états mélancoliques; il se présente à la conscience comme une douleur et surtout comme une peur vague, que l'on a souvent appelées des douleurs et des peurs morales, pour indiquer qu'il s'agit d'une douleur mal précisée, et d'une peur sans objet. En réalité il s'agit d'une chose fort précise: le sujet a peur de sa propre action, et souffre à la pensée de l'exécuter. Cette peur arrête l'action d'une manière définitive, et non d'une manière momentanée, comme dans la halte, ou le sentiment de la fatigue. Cet arrêt de l'action et cette angoisse peuvent être localisés, dans les phobies; quand ils sont étendus à un grand nombre d'actions, l'homme ressemble à une bête traquée qui essaie successivement toutes les issues et n'en trouve aucune: il ne peut plus faire aucun acte, ni en désirer, ni en rêver aucun; il ne peut plus vivre, ni tolérer sa propre vie. L'angoisse aigue amène l'idée de la mort et les tentatives de suicide. Le sentiment, qui reste au fond toujours le même, est celui de l'urgence de l'action, et en même temps, du caractère défectueux et abominable de toute action.")

3 They are still trying the trick: hurricanes, earthquakes, (and) AIDS are often presented by fundamentalists of all creeds as divine retribution.

4 Gilles Deleuze, *Cinema: The Movement Image*, Vol. 1. (Minneapolis: University of Minnesota Press, 1986).

5 Carl Jung, *Man and His Symbols* (London: Aldus Books, 1964), p. 161.

6 Miguel Serrano, C.G. *Jung and Herman Hesse: A Record of Two Friendships* (New York: Schocken Books, 1966), p. 50. In David Miller (1995) "Nothing almost sees miracles!", *Journal of Psychology of Religion*, 4–5, 1–25.

7 "It is not incertitude that creates madness, it is certitude" (Nietzsche).

# Index

abuse: physical versus psychological 171–2
abused men and women 38
academia: as house of rationality 95
academic milieu: survival of women in 94–6, 100
Addams, J. 166
Adler, A. 86
adult psyche: as orientation towards achieving responsibility 116; as somebody capable of assuming responsibility 160
alchemy: images of psychic maturation 150–3
Allen, W. 26
American Academy of Psychoanalysis 86
American Psychiatric Association 85
American Psychological Association (APA) 26, 29, 91, 187
*amor fati*: as love of one's fate, of one's story 184
analysis: by acknowledging monsters 68–78;
as adventure 56; as conversation between friends 56; as heroic encounter with inner monsters 69; as metamorphosis through words 182–3; as raising capacity for love and imagination 213; as re-virgining of oneself 209; as singing or dancing with one's soul 43, 91, 208
anima: psychology belonging to 102
animus: philosophy belonging to 102
anti-psychiatry: English, 93
anxiety: defined as fear without an object 202–4; definition of fear 198–204; as incapacity to feel
joy 197–8, 204; as the "metaphysical blues" 199; and post-modern psyche

202; as symbol of post-modernity 198–202; vicious circle of 200; ways of naming fear 198–9
anxiety disorders 25, 131
Aphrodite 67, 70, 75, 204, 209
Apollo 70, 75, 136, 186
archetypal approach: as aesthetic experience 46; becoming aware of one's myth 178; developing psychological polytheism 70–1; editing of life's scripts 174–8, 181–2, 185, 213–14; as education in lucidity 46, 90; as existing beyond quantification 185–6; as inner voyage 42; as map through psychic devastation 64–6; as meaning given to events 177, 185–6; victim versus hero 177
archetypal father and mother: in African-American community 141; family's need of balance 141–3; good cop/bad cop 141; yin versus yang strategies 141–2, 144
archetypal reality: the invisible made visible 164–7
Archetype of Child 16–17; fed by consumerist society 154; God-the-Child as replacement for God-the-Father 114; infantile adult 15; infantile citizens and cultural values 138; inner child 14–15; the inner child monomyth approach 114, 153; and manipulation to transform everyone into a Great Mother 116, 147; Puer Aeternus (Eternal Child) as 16; as self-proclaimed victim 115
Archetype of Father: 17–18, 152; as balance between power and responsibility 142, 145; God the